BEYOND RACE, SEX, AND SEXUAL ORIENTATION

The conventional interpretation of legal equality or equality under the law singles out certain groups or classes for constitutional protection: women, racial minorities, and gays and lesbians. The United States Supreme Court calls these groups "suspect classes." Laws that discriminate against them are generally unconstitutional. Although this is a familiar account of equal protection jurisprudence, this book argues that this approach suffers from hitherto unnoticed normative and political problems. The book elucidates a competing, extant interpretation of equal protection jurisprudence that avoids these problems. The interpretation is not concerned with suspect classes but rather with the kinds of reasons that are already inadmissible as a matter of constitutional law. This alternative approach treats the equal protection clause like any other limit on governmental power, thus allowing the Court to invalidate equality-infringing laws and policies by focusing on their justification rather than the identity group they discriminate against.

Sonu Bedi is an Associate Professor of Government at Dartmouth College. He is the author of *Rejecting Rights* (2009) and coeditor of *Political Contingency* (2007).

Beyond Race, Sex, and Sexual Orientation

LEGAL EQUALITY WITHOUT IDENTITY

Sonu Bedi

Dartmouth College

CAMBRIDGE
UNIVERSITY PRESS

32 Avenue of the Americas, New York, NY 10013-2473, USA

Cambridge University Press is part of the University of Cambridge.

It furthers the University's mission by disseminating knowledge in the pursuit of
education, learning, and research at the highest international levels of excellence.

www.cambridge.org
Information on this title: www.cambridge.org/9781107018358

© Sonu Bedi 2013

First published 2013
Reprinted 2014

A catalog record for this publication is available from the British Library.

Library of Congress Cataloging in Publication data
Bedi, Sonu.
Beyond race, sex, and sexual orientation : legal equality without identity / Sonu Bedi,
Dartmouth College.
     pages   cm
Includes bibliographical references and index.
ISBN 978-1-107-01835-8 (hardback)
1. Equality before the law – United States.   2. Discrimination – Law and legislation – United
States.   I. Title.
KF4764.B43   2013
342.7308'5–dc23   2013002794

ISBN 978-1-107-01835-8 Hardback

To my friends

CONTENTS

ACKNOWLEDGMENTS

I presented earlier versions and parts of this book at the American Political Science Association Conference, the Association for Political Theory Conference, the Dartmouth Legal Studies Workshop, the Law and Society Conference, the Loyola Law School Constitutional Law Colloquium, the Northeastern Political Science Conference, the University of Chicago Public Law and Legal Theory Workshop, the University of Wisconsin at Madison, Vanderbilt Law School, Wesleyan University, and the Yale University Political Theory Workshop. These provided productive and stimulating environments to vet various arguments of the book. I thank the participants at these venues for challenging my overall thesis suggesting ways to sharpen and strengthen it.

I also had the good fortune of receiving feedback and encouragement from Bruce Ackerman, William Araiza, Albena Azmanova, Monu Bedi, Caitlin Borgmann, Brian Fitzpatrick, Deborah Gershenowitz, Michael Goodhart, Bernard Harcourt, Randall Kennedy, Victoria Kennedy, Andrew Koppelman, Claudia Leeb, Elvin Lim, Stephen Macedo, Andrew March, John Nowak, Terri Peretti, Stephen Siegel, Craig Sutton, and Laurence Tribe. A Law and Society 2011 author-meets-critics panel on my first single-authored book organized by Ronald Den Otter proved helpful in writing this one. I thank Randy Barnett, Joel Grossman, and Lawrence Solum, who participated on the panel, for their invaluable comments. In particular, I thank John Graebe, Ronald Den Otter, Gerald Rosenberg, and Howard Schweber for reading large portions of the manuscript and providing extensive comments I could not have done without. I thank the reviewers for providing constructive criticisms. My colleagues at Dartmouth have been extremely supportive throughout all the stages of this project.

I benefited from a junior faculty sabbatical fellowship in writing the book. Students in my spring 2012 seminar titled "Race, Law, and Identity" read portions of the manuscript and provided fruitful comments. I thank John Berger, my editor at Cambridge University Press, for his unwavering support. He saw the potential of this project early on. It was a real pleasure working with him. Finally, I also thank the Cambridge University Press production and editorial team including Anuj Antony, Elizabeth Budd, Alison Daltroy, and Paul Smolenski for their invaluable assistance. They made the process effortless.

Earlier versions of Chapters 2 and 3 were published in *Studies in Law, Politics, and Society*, vol. 58 (2012) ("Judging without Rights: Public Reason and the Counter-Majoritarian Difficulty") and *Polity*, vol. 42, no. 4 (2010) ("How Constitutional Law Rationalizes Racism") respectively.

I dedicate this book to my friends, my life partners. Their love and support have always sustained me. I could not imagine a world without them.

INTRODUCTION

The Equal Protection Clause of the Fourteenth Amendment, one of the most significant clauses of modern constitutional jurisprudence reads: no state shall "deny to any person within its jurisdiction the equal protection of the laws."[1] Under the conventional interpretation of this clause, the United States Supreme Court (hereafter "the Court") scrutinizes more carefully those laws that invoke or discriminate against a particular group, or what the Court calls a "suspect class." Those groups that constitute suspect classes inform the list of prohibited classifications. Under current constitutional doctrine, laws discriminating on the basis of race,[2] alienage,[3] and national origin[4] get strict scrutiny: where the Court asks whether the law is narrowly tailored to serve a compelling state purpose. Laws discriminating against sex get intermediate scrutiny:[5] where the Court asks whether the law is substantially related to serving an important governmental purpose. Those laws that do not invoke a suspect classification merely receive rational review, the most deferential standard of review. Under rational review, the legislation must only have a legitimate purpose, and the means must be rationally related to that purpose. The more the Court strictly scrutinizes a law, the more likely it will be struck down. According to Adam Winkler, between 1990 and 2003, 73 percent of all race-conscious laws subjected to strict scrutiny in federal courts were struck down.[6] Ultimately, the scrutiny framework turns out to be

---

[1] Sec. 1, Amendment XIV, Constitution of the United States
[2] *See, e.g., Bolling v. Sharpe* (1954); *Loving v. Virginia* (1967); *Grutter v. Bollinger* (2003)
[3] *See Graham v. Richardson* (1971)
[4] *See, e.g., Oyama v. California* (1948); *Korematsu v. United States* (1944)
[5] *See, e.g., Craig v. Boren* (1976)
[6] Winkler 2006: 839

doctrinal shorthand for whether a law will be upheld or struck down. This means that whether a group counts as a suspect class makes all the constitutional difference.

The suspect class framework and the tiers-of-scrutiny approach (strict, intermediate, and rational) that accompanies it are a familiar feature of modern equal protection jurisprudence. Central to this framework is determining which groups count as suspect classes. After all, there are many groups in society: racial groups, the local Parent Teacher Association (PTA), gays and lesbians, women, a simple book club, blondes, or those with a particular eye color. Most are not suspect classes. Cass Sunstein argues that the core purpose of the Equal Protection Clause is "an attempt to protect *disadvantaged* groups from discriminatory practices, however deeply engrained and longstanding."[7] Currently, racial minorities and women are "in" – they count as protected disadvantaged groups, making race and sex a suspect classification; gays and lesbians are "out" – they do not count as a suspect class. Scholarly work has argued that they ought to count as one, thereby rendering sexual orientation a suspect classification under the Equal Protection Clause.[8] If the Court affirms gays and lesbians as a suspect class, prohibitions on same-sex marriage would receive higher scrutiny. This, in turn, would no doubt doom such prohibitions.

This book challenges this identity or class approach. It draws from political theory both to criticize current constitutional doctrine and to elaborate on a more salutary one. Although the problems of identity are well established, scholars have largely ignored their relationship to the suspect class framework. Constitutional legal scholars focus on the doctrine with little to no attention to its political weaknesses, and political theorists focus on the difficulties with the language of identity with no attention to constitutional doctrine or, in particular, the suspect class analysis. I argue that there is a deep dilemma with the suspect class framework, with *how* the Court strikes down equality-infringing laws and policies. On one hand, it is clear that racial minorities, women, and gays and lesbians require constitutional protection given the kind of discrimination each has faced. On the other hand, by elevating these

---

[7] Sunstein 1988: 1163 (emphasis added)
[8] *See, e.g.*, Ackerman 1985, Ely 1980, Feldblum 1996, Steiker 1985, Sunstein 1988, Yoshino 1996

groups but not others to suspect status – treating them as constitutionally "special" – the Court turns out to stigmatize them. It forces individuals who belong to these groups to highlight the way they are different from everyone else.

This book argues that in doing so, the suspect class framework suffers from at least four problems. First, the Court's need to demarcate certain groups but not others as suspect classes undermines a robust notion of individuality. It perversely requires that the Court define what it means to be a member of a particular identity group, a group that must be conceptually prior to the individual. The suspect class must be "out there" to be defined. After all, there has to be some permanent, biological, or fixed nature to the trait, a trait that defines the class. This is why the Court generally requires that this trait be immutable. But this requirement of immutability points to the way in which identity reifies the relevant group, denying the experiences of individuals.

Second, by invoking identity to invalidate laws and policies under the Equal Protection Clause, the Court exacerbates the sting of the counter-majoritarian difficulty. Alexander Bickel defines this difficulty as one in which the Court "thwarts the will of representatives of the actual people of the here and now; it exercises control, not in behalf of the prevailing majority, but against it."[9] It is a difficulty precisely because the Court *thwarts* rather than affirms majority sentiment. But the suspect class framework makes this difficulty worse, because the Court is not taking into account the interests of all, only those of the relevant identity group or class, in striking down legislation. In *Brown v. Board of Education* (1954), the Court reasoned that "separate but equal" is unconstitutional because it harms black children. Segregation "generates a feeling of inferiority as to their status in the community that may affect their hearts and minds in a way unlikely ever to be undone."[10] The unconstitutionality of segregation arises from its effect on a particular group – here, a racial minority. Similarly, to contend that a prohibition on same-sex marriage is invalid because it harms gays and lesbians makes the discourse about a particular group. This straightforwardly characterizes the constitutional objection as entailing

[9] Bickel 1962: 17
[10] *Brown* at 494

the interests of some individuals – those who are members of the suspect class – rather than the interests of everyone.

Third, the Court's use of strict scrutiny perversely affirms the very racist beliefs it seeks to counter. If I choose a sledgehammer to crack a nut, I assume that the nut may be difficult to crack. I err on the side that it may be quite strong. Similarly, by scrutinizing such laws more carefully, the Court perversely gives credence to the bogus claims of racism. It suggests that racist laws and policies are based on something other than mere hostility. Otherwise, why does the Court need to impose strict scrutiny to realize that a law is based on racial animus? Simultaneously, strict scrutiny dooms remedial legislation – legislation that seeks to ameliorate the status of racial minorities. It needlessly makes it more difficult for a legislature to gain constitutional approval of affirmative action policies.

Fourth, the tiers-of-scrutiny framework turns out to be too subjective, allowing individual justices to decide cases on ideological rather than constitutional grounds. Although it may have comparative value in deciding cases (a law struck down under intermediate scrutiny ought to be struck down under its strict scrutiny counterpart), this framework has little actual content. For instance, the Court has defined the meaning of "compelling" in radically different ways. In *Korematsu v. United States* (1944), the Court upheld Japanese interment, reasoning that national security constitutes a compelling purpose under strict scrutiny. In *Grutter v. Bollinger* (2003), it upheld Michigan's race-based affirmative action policy, reasoning that racial diversity in higher education constitutes a compelling purpose under a similar level of scrutiny. Is achieving racial diversity in higher education as compelling as national security? There is no principled answer to this question because what counts as compelling and what is merely, under a lower standard of review, legitimate are empty placeholders that permit individual justices to fill in as they see fit. Defining what is an important versus a compelling purpose is a policy question that ought to be left to the relevant democratic legislature. It will not suffice merely to say that higher scrutiny is a tool of judicial review that seeks to smoke out illicit or invidious rationales. The suspect class framework does not clearly explain what, as a constitutional matter, "illicit" or "invidious" means. For if it did, there might not be need for higher scrutiny.

This book elucidates an alternative, extant interpretation of equal protection jurisprudence, an interpretation that avoids these problems. This interpretation is not concerned with suspect classes and tiers of scrutiny but rather with the kinds of reasons that are inadmissible as a matter of constitutional law. I argue that the Court already deems constitutionally inadmissible justifications for laws and policies that are based on animus or on the idea that a particular way of life is intrinsically better than another. In fact, whereas the tiers-of-scrutiny approach traces its roots to the mid-twentieth century,[11] this alternative approach has constitutional roots that may go farther back.

This book looks to cases such as *Yick Wo v. Hopkins* (1886) and *Romer v. Evans* (1996) to flesh out the principle that laws and policies based on animus are unconstitutional under the Equal Protection Clause. In both cases, the Court struck down racist and homophobic policies, respectively, without imposing any kind of higher scrutiny or deeming racial minorities or gays and lesbians a suspect class. *Romer* struck down a Colorado state amendment that discriminated against gays and lesbians on grounds that the Equal Protection Clause invalidates laws and policies based on a "bare . . . desire to harm" a group.[12] In *Yick Wo*, decided more than a hundred years before, a unanimous Court held that San Francisco authorities did not have the power under the Equal Protection Clause to grant laundromat licenses to whites but deny such licenses to those of Chinese descent. The Court reasoned that executing a law in this manner was an instance of "arbitrary power."[13] The Court made clear that "no reason for [such discrimination] exists except hostility to the race and nationality to which the petitioners belong, and which, in the eye of the law, is not justified."[14] The Court did not impose any kind of higher scrutiny in arriving at this conclusion.

Constitutional law also deems inadmissible laws and policies that rest on the idea that a particular orthodoxy or way of life is simply better than another. In *Cleburne v. Cleburne Living Center* (1985), the

---

[11] *See, e.g.*, Robinson 2005, Siegel 2006, Simon 1978
[12] *Romer* at 634
[13] *Yick Wo* at 370
[14] *Yick Wo* at 374

Court invalidated a city ordinance that required a permit to establish a home for the mentally challenged. The city did not require a permit for homes used for other purposes including "apartment houses, multiple dwellings, boarding and lodging houses, fraternity or sorority houses, dormitories, apartment hotels, hospitals, sanitariums, nursing homes for convalescents or the aged."[15] The Court refused to deem the mentally challenged a suspect class. Without imposing any kind of higher scrutiny, the Court held that under the Equal Protection Clause, there were no "legitimate interests" that justified treating a certain living arrangement – in this case, a home for the mentally challenged – differently from others.[16] That is, the Court reasoned that city violated equality under the law or legal equality by favoring or privileging homes that were used for certain purposes rather than others. The Court concluded "that requiring the permit in this case appears . . . to rest on an irrational prejudice against the mentally retarded."[17]

This kind of unconstitutional favoring is also evident in *West Virginia v. Barnette* (1943), where the Court held that a law forcing students to recite the Pledge of Allegiance was unconstitutional. Although the case arose under the First Amendment, the Court articulates a more general proposition about our Constitution:

> If there is any fixed star in our constitutional constellation, it is that no official, high or petty, can prescribe what shall be orthodox in politics, nationalism, religion, or other matters of opinion or force citizens to confess by word or act their faith therein. If there are any circumstances which permit an exception, they do not now occur to us.[18]

This language suggests that the state may not compel its citizens to follow certain kinds of orthodoxies or ways of living. *Lawrence v. Texas* (2003), invalidating a law criminalizing gay sex, informs this kind of argument. Although *Lawrence* invoked the constitutional right to privacy to strike down a sodomy law, it also reasoned that mere moral considerations are constitutionally insufficient for lawmaking under a

---

[15] *Cleburne* at 447
[16] *Cleburne* at 442–8
[17] *Cleburne* at 448
[18] *Barnette* at 642

standard of rational review. The Court held that "the fact that the governing majority in a State has traditionally viewed a particular practice as immoral is not a sufficient reason for upholding a law prohibiting the practice."[19] The state may not impose a way of life on its citizens simply because it finds such a life intrinsically worthwhile. In the same way, the Establishment Clause ("Congress shall make no law respecting an establishment of religion"[20]) prohibits government from favoring a certain religion over another or favoring religion over non-religion. The clause deems unconstitutional laws and policies based on the idea that a Christian way of life is better or superior to a Buddhist one or that a religious way of life is better or superior to a nonreligious one. I argue that constitutional law already dictates that the state may not "prescribe what shall be" good or acceptable for its own sake.

So, rather than making the constitutional objection to laws such as Jim Crow or prohibitions on same-sex marriage about the language of identity or suspect class and the scrutiny that accompanies it, the Court can make the objection about the reasons that underlie such laws and policies. Jim Crow was based on racial animus just as the Colorado state amendment was based on animus against gays and lesbians. Prohibitions on same-sex marriage are similarly problematic, because they rest on what a majority views as a religiously improper meaning of marriage. This makes the constitutional objection not about groups or identity but simply about the reason underlying the law.

In *Village of Willowbrook, et al. v. Olech* (2000), an often neglected case in scholarly work, the Court held that a town had violated the Equal Protection Clause even though there was no discrimination on the basis of race, sex, sexual orientation, or any other identity classification. Grace Olech asked the village of Willowbrook to connect her to the local municipal water supply. The village conditioned the connection on Olech granting the municipality a thirty-three-foot easement, instead of the standard fifteen-foot easement required of other residents. Olech contended that the village treated her differently, because she had filed an unrelated lawsuit against the city. She sued claiming that the village violated the Equal Protection Clause in asking for

[19] *Lawrence* at 577
[20] Amendment I, Constitution of the United States

an additional eighteen feet. The Court unanimously agreed reasoning that the village's decision to ask for fifteen more feet was "irrational and wholly arbitrary," thereby violating the Equal Protection Clause.[21] There was no language of higher scrutiny that informed the opinion. This points to an understanding of equality under the law that is not about suspect classes or classifications. After all, *Olech* had nothing to do with subordinated groups or identity. It had only to do with those *reasons* that are constitutionally inadmissible, reasons such as animus that can take aim at any group or anyone.

I draw from contemporary political theory's commitment to public justification to expound on and clarify this underlying logic of equal protection. The principle of public reason or justification is a familiar one.[22] John Rawls famously suggests that "the limits imposed by public reason" apply to "constitutional essentials and questions of basic justice."[23] The Supreme Court, according to Rawls, is an "exemplar" of public reason.[24] As Rawls puts it: "our exercise of political power is fully proper only when it is exercised in accordance with a constitution the essentials of which all citizens as free and equal may reasonably be expected to endorse in the light of principles and ideas acceptable to them as reasonable and rational."[25] This is not about some actual consensus but what reasonable individuals would accept. This commitment to public reason excludes those justifications that cannot in principle be accepted by all.

One variant of this principle of public justification is a commitment to antiperfectionism or liberal neutrality, a commitment that holds the state ought to remain neutral among competing conceptions of the good life. Howard Schweber provides a powerful defense of this kind of public reason or what he calls "public justification."[26] Such a theory of justification requires that democratic citizens proffer reasons that one's fellow listener could accept. This kind of justificatory constraint

[21] *Olech* at 565
[22] *See, e.g.*, Ackerman 1980, Forst 2002, Gaus 1996, Greenawalt 1995, Habermas 1990, 2001, Larmore 1987, Rawls 1996 [1993]
[23] Rawls 1996 [1993]: 214
[24] Rawls 1996 [1993]: 216
[25] Rawls 1993: 217
[26] Schweber 2012

rules out those reasons from the realm of law making that do not meet this principle.[27] For instance, this kind of public reason contends that conceptions of the good life are illegitimate justificatory grounds for state legislation. That is, the state may not pass laws and policies grounded in the belief that a particular way of life is intrinsically better than another. These beliefs are perfectionist ones, because they point to what counts as a decent or virtuous existence. They seek to articulate how we as individuals can live more perfect lives. Precisely because individuals may disagree over the inherent worthiness of certain ways of living over others, such beliefs are not in principle shareable by all. Liberal neutrality eschews them. It is about what is right, not what is good.

This book does not seek to articulate a new theory of jurisprudence. It does *not* aim to argue that constitutional law fully accepts liberal neutrality. My argument is not that radical. I realize that the Court does not even the use the words "antiperfectionism" or "liberal neutrality." My argument treats this theory as a lens through which we can tease out an interpretation of the Equal Protection Clause that does not look to identity or suspect class. This book fleshes out the underlying logic of this interpretation by drawing on some of its similarities to liberal neutrality. In doing so, I apply this framework to various cases that are often framed under a suspect class analysis. This methodological approach is similar to the "law and economics" model of adjudication. This model suggests that, properly understood, the law operates on economic principles such as self-interest and the reduction of transaction costs, even though courts do not explicitly invoke such principles.[28] This book suggests that at its best, equality under the law is about ruling out laws and policies that are based on constitutionally inadmissible reasons or rationales, rationales that liberal neutrality may also consider illegitimate.

Now, I realize that this conception of public reason is controversial, challenged by liberals and nonliberals alike.[29] For instance, Christopher

---

[27] *See generally* Solum 1993; *see also* Den Otter 2009

[28] *See generally* Epstein 2009, Posner 2010

[29] *See, e.g.,* Galston 1991, George 1993, 1999, MacIntyre 1988, Raz 1986, Sher 1997, Sandel 1982

Eberle makes the strongest case for concluding that a religious rationale ought indeed to suffice as a morally legitimate basis for lawmaking.[30] Others seek to defend liberal neutrality from these and other criticisms.[31] Lucas Swaine makes a powerful argument that even theocrats – those who favor a strong role for religion in politics – should opt for a conception of public justification that largely avoids appealing to religious rationales.[32] So, if the most hard-core of religious observers should prefer a kind of commitment to liberal neutrality from their own moral position, it ought to be the choice of those who hold a more watered down version of the role of religion in politics.

A more fundamental criticism of liberal neutrality is that it is self-defeating. The idea that the state ought to remain neutral among competing moral values in justifying laws and policies is itself a moral value. So how can liberal neutrality ever be truly impartial?[33] One way to mitigate and maybe even avoid this objection is to realize that this kind of antiperfectionism does not require that the state be neutral to all moral values in justifying laws and policies. Rather, it requires that the state only be neutral to conceptions of the good. This means that the state may not deem a particular way of life worthwhile or valuable *for its own sake*. Liberal neutrality may base laws and policies on the idea that a particular way of life has benefits for others. For instance, passing a law that prohibits assault on the idea that doing so benefits others does not violate antiperfectionism. Liberal neutrality only rules out those laws and policies based on the idea that a particular orthodoxy is inherently good. Or consider that laws relating to drug abuse or environmental protection do not seem to rest on the idea that certain ways of living are intrinsically better for the individual who undertakes them. Rather, these laws are about benefitting or protecting *others*: Environmental protections ensure that future generations are not saddled with a less habitable world. Drug abuse laws may seek to protect others from anti-social behavior. The point is that these laws are qualitatively different from a law that prohibits a kind of consensual sexual activity on the

---

[30] Eberle 2002. *See also* Perry 2003
[31] *See* Clayton 2006, Lecce 2008, Quong 2011, Schweber 2012
[32] Swaine 2008
[33] *See, e.g.*, Galston 1991, George 1999

idea that such activity is inherently better than another or that a certain way of life is sinful or contrary to some religious doctrine. Such laws violate antiperfectionism. I realize that even highlighting this feature of neutrality may not satisfy its critics.[34] This book does not seek to defend the soundness of liberal neutrality as a philosophical matter. As Andrew Koppelman thoughtfully suggests:

> Neutrality is unsustainable when it is formulated this abstractly, but it is nonetheless a valuable political ideal. One of the many ways that government can go wrong is to take a position on some question that it would, all things considered, be better for it to abstain from deciding.[35]

So I leave to one side the question of how to formulate the doctrine "abstractly." This book elaborates an understanding of legal equality by drawing from the idea that neutrality is, at the very least, a "valuable political" ideal. In doing so, I seek to discern an underlying system that already motivates constitutional law. Michael Perry recognizes the difference between the following two questions: "is religion a morally legitimate basis of law-making in a liberal democracy?" and "is religion a constitutionally legitimate basis of law-making in the United States?"[36] This book is about the second question, not the first. As Perry goes on to argue, the Establishment Clause, makes clear that religious rationales are inadmissible in justifying laws and policies.[37] Even if scholars may disagree about the moral legitimacy of deploying religious beliefs in lawmaking, such beliefs are constitutionally illegitimate.

In fact, the Court has interpreted nonestablishment as an endorsement of religious neutrality.[38] In *Epperson v. Arkansas* (1968) (invalidating an Arkansas law that forbade the teaching of evolution in public schools), the Court holds that the "First Amendment mandates governmental neutrality between religion and religion, and between

---

[34] *See* Sher 1997; *but see* Quong 2011: 12–13
[35] Koppelman 2004: 633
[36] Perry 2009: 105
[37] Perry 2009: 112–14
[38] *See generally* Foley 1992

religion and nonreligion."[39] Government may "not aid, foster, or promote one religion or religious theory against another or even against
the militant opposite."[40] This means that the state cannot favor Chris-
tianity over Islam, nor can it favor religion in general over atheism or
vice versa. To take sides in how we understand the relevance of faith
in our lives (whether it be that faith is very important or not important
at all) is to adopt a conception of the good life that the Establishment
Clause prohibits. This is why Justice Sandra Day O'Connor famously
suggests that by favoring a religious way of life, the state sends a message to "nonadherents" that they are "outsiders, not full members of
the political community, and an accompanying message to adherents
that they are insiders, favored members."[41] Rather than finding reasons
that all – adherents and nonadherents – can share, the state endorses a
particular religious conception of the good. In fact, Perry says that this
conclusion has implications for a ban on same-sex marriage: "[I]f the
only rationale that accounts for the [ban] depends on the premise that
same-sex sexual conduct is contrary to the will of God," such a ban is
unconstitutional.[42]

This book argues that *Lawrence v. Texas* (2003) informs this logic by
declaring morals legislation unconstitutional. Such legislation is nothing other than legislation based on a conception of the good life – in
this case, the belief that gay sex is morally wrong or intrinsically inferior to its heterosexual counterpart. *Lawrence* makes clear that "[t]hese
matters, involving the most intimate and personal choices a person
may make in a lifetime ... are central to the liberty protected by the
Fourteenth Amendment."[43] This liberty entails the freedom "to define
one's own concept of existence, of meaning, of the universe, and of
the mystery of human life."[44] This "concept of existence" looks an
awful like a conception of the good. The language of "mystery" and
"meaning" point to the idea that these beliefs are not about what kinds

[39] *Epperson* at 104
[40] *Epperson* at 104
[41] *Lynch v. Donnelly* (1984) at 688, concurring (upheld city's display of nativity scene under
the Establishment Clause). *See also Lee v. Weisman* (1992) at 601, concurring (held that
school prayer delivered by religious figure violated the Establishment Clause)
[42] Perry 2009: 114
[43] *Lawrence* at 574
[44] *Lawrence* at 574

of lives have extrinsic or public benefits – hence, the Court's concession in an earlier case that homosexuality counts as a "victimless" crime.[45] Rather, these beliefs are about what lives have *intrinsic* moral value, beliefs about various kinds of orthodoxies that the state may not impose on its members. Just as the state may not compel students to recite the Pledge of Allegiance, it may not privilege for its own sake one kind of sexual or intimate orthodoxy over another.

In *Lawrence*, the Court makes clear that its "obligation is to define the liberty of all, not to mandate [its own] own moral code."[46] The state may not base laws and policies on the idea that one way of living is intrinsically better or more worthwhile than another. The law struck down in *Lawrence* was not based on reasons that "all" can in principle accept. Justice O'Connor's concurrence in *Lawrence* specifically appeals to the Equal Protection Clause as prohibiting legislation that is based on mere "moral disapproval."[47] There is an underlying logic that connects cases like *Lawrence* to the cases decided under the Establishment Clause. Laws that privilege a certain religious practice or a certain consenting sexual practice are based on perfectionist reasons, reasons that constitutional law often deem unconstitutional. Just as individuals disagree about what kind of sexual or intimate life is worthwhile for its own sake, so too do individuals disagree about the importance and relevance of faith in their lives. Religious neutrality constitutes a specific commitment to the more general principle of liberal neutrality. Taken together, the Establishment Clause and cases like *Lawrence* mean that laws and policies may not be based simply or only on religious or moral beliefs about what counts as the good or worthwhile life.

Tellingly, *Perry v. Schwarzenegger* (N.D. Cal. 2010) looks to both *Lawrence* and the Establishment Clause in striking down Proposition 8, California's prohibition on same-sex marriage, under the Equal Protection Clause. *Schwarzenegger* makes explicit the constitutional logic I defend in this book. As the first federal court to invalidate a prohibition on same-sex marriage, *Schwarzenegger* does not deem gays and

---

[45] *Bowers v. Hardwick* (1986) at 195
[46] *Lawrence* at 571
[47] *Lawrence* at 582, concurring

lesbians a suspect class. Rather, the court holds that a "state's interest in an enactment must of course be secular in nature. The state does not have an interest in enforcing private moral or religious beliefs."[48] The court then concludes that limiting marriage just to opposite-sex couples fails this standard. Such limitations are not based on a "secular purpose."[49] Rather, they privilege a certain kind of intimate or romantic life over another, in this case, improperly valuing heterosexuality over homosexuality on moral or religious grounds. Prohibitions on same-sex marriage are unconstitutional, according to *Schwarzenegger*, because they invoke reasons that are constitutionally inadmissible.

Or consider that in its jurisprudence on sex discrimination, the Court deems unconstitutional those laws and policies that rest on the idea that males must be breadwinners and females caregivers. Seen through the lens of liberal neutrality, this doctrinal logic also illuminates the positive argument of this book. Here, the conception of the good is the idea that with a particular sex comes certain kinds of gendered attributes. The idea that males must act or be a certain way and females must act or be another way entails a gendered conception of what it means to be a worthwhile male or female. Equal protection means that government does not have the power to compel these kinds of orthodoxies on its members, or so this book argues.

A law based on simple dislike of or hostility toward a particular group is also not publicly justifiable. Such dislike cannot in principle be accepted by all. It is not based on anything other than the idea, for instance, that being black or being gay is inherently inferior or disgusting. Again, in cases such as *Romer*, the Court has held that laws and policies may not be based on this kind of animus. This is, as Cass Sunstein suggests, a "naked preference."[50] It is naked, because there is nothing underlying the preference except mere dislike or hostility. Laws are arbitrary in so far as they are based on this kind of animus – animus that can take its aim at any group or any one. The Court can deploy this logic to invalidate racist laws and policies in the same way it can invalidate homophobic ones.

---

[48] *Schwarzenegger* at 930–1
[49] *Schwarzenegger* at 931
[50] Sunstein 1984

This suggests that there is some synergy between liberal neutrality and the Equal Protection Clause, something that has gone largely unnoticed by political theorists and constitutional legal scholars. In the recent Ninth Circuit Court of Appeals case upholding *Schwarzenegger* even the dissenting judge concedes that interests such as "animus, negative attitudes, fear, a bare desire to harm, and moral disapproval . . . alone will not support the constitutionality of a measure" under the Equal Protection Clause.[51] Rather than making the constitutional objection to prohibitions on same-sex marriage or laws such as Jim Crow rest on the language of identity or suspect class and the problems that accompany it, the Court does better to focus on those reasons that constitutional law already deems inadmissible. Legal equality is not so much about ensuring that government docs not discriminate against certain groups (e.g., racial minorities, women, gays and lesbian). Legal equality is about ensuring that laws and policies are not based on certain kinds of reasons. Under this approach, prohibitions on same-sex marriage are unconstitutional not because they discriminate against gays and lesbians (i.e., discriminating against a particular suspect class) but because they invoke a particular religious conception of the good life. Similarly, laws like Jim Crow are unconstitutional not because they discriminate against blacks – or any racial group, for that matter – but because they rest on animus or hostility, which can take aim at any group or any one.

In expounding on this alternative account of equality under the law, I conceptualize the Equal Protection Clause as a ban on constitutional powers. The current approach views the Equal Protection Clause as saying that the state may not discriminate on the basis of certain classes or identity affiliations. I call this the "identity approach." The approach I work out in this book views the clause as saying that the state does not have the *power* to act on certain kinds of reasons. I call this a "powers review." There are two types of powers: grants of powers and limits on powers. For instance, Section 8 of Article I grants Congress various powers including the power to tax and spend and to "regulate Commerce" among the states.[52] Contrastingly, Section 9 of

[51] *Perry v. Brown* (9th Cir. 2012) at 1102, concurring dissenting
[52] Article I, Section 8, U.S. Constitution

that article specifies powers forbidden to Congress. These forbidden powers include passing ex post facto laws or granting titles of nobility. Section 10 specifies powers forbidden to the states including the power to enter into a treaty, alliance, or confederation. In *McCulloch v. Maryland* (1819), the state of Maryland imposed a tax on the Second Bank of the United States. The Supreme Court held that a national bank was within the power of the federal government to establish. It then posed the question of "whether [the] power [to tax the bank] can be exercised by the respective States."[53] The Court held that it could not, reasoning that the "power to tax involves the power to destroy."[54] This represents the scope of state power with regards to taxing federal instrumentalities.

Similarly, we ought to understand the Equal Protection Clause as a ban on the state's power to act on certain kinds of reasons. The clause is best understood as any other clause that limits the power of government. That means that if a law is based on animus or a certain conception of the good life, the state exceeds its power in enacting it. While the discourse of powers often invites distinctions between the federal and state government, my argument is not about federalism but rather the language of powers that often accompanies it. The powers review I propose is one that applies to all government power – federal or state. By adopting it, we better ensure equality under the law.

A powers review avoids the four problems that arise with the identity approach, or so this book argues. First, because a powers review does not require identifying suspect classes, it avoids placing the Court in a position of determining which groups are constitutionally "in" and which are "out." Because the focus is simply on the purpose or underlying rationale of the law, there is no need to engage in a suspect class analysis. It does not matter which group the law discriminates against. What matters is whether the law is based on a constitutionally inadmissible rationale. This relieves the need for the Court to constitutionally elevate certain classes or groups above others.

Second, unlike the identity approach, the language of powers attaches to the state rather than the relevant group. This stands to

[53] *McCulloch* at 430–1
[54] *McCulloch* at 431

mitigate the sting of the counter-majoritarian difficulty, because the Court is not invalidating the law on behalf of a particular identity group or class but on behalf of the polity itself. A powers review points to the way in which the polity itself has gone astray – going beyond *its* powers. A law that is based on animus or hostility is simply outside the scope of government power just like a law granting a title of nobility is outside of Congress' powers. The Court frames the constitutional objection in more inclusive terms. A constitutional objection to granting a title of nobility does not concern a particular class or group of individuals. It concerns everyone. A policy of "separate but equal" is unconstitutional not because it fails to take into account the interests of blacks but because the state goes beyond its powers in enacting it: such a policy is based on racial animus. Similarly, if the state exceeds its power in prohibiting same sex-marriage (such a prohibition is based on a religious conception of the meaning of marriage), this is not the concern of just gays and lesbians. We all have an interest in making sure that the state does not go beyond its constitutional powers, in this case banning marriages between individuals of the same sex.

Third, if the Court focuses on invalidating laws based on hostility, strict scrutiny is not necessary in order to do the equality work. The Court can easily distinguish between laws like Jim Crow and laws like affirmative action, precisely because only the former are based on hostility, in this case a bare desire to harm a racial group. For instance, affirmative action policies are often based on rationales about increasing racial diversity. No searching scrutiny is necessary to realize that such policies are not based on animus. By specifying the content of those reasons that are constitutionally inadmissible, higher scrutiny is no longer necessary. And without strict scrutiny, the Court does not perversely rationalize racist beliefs, leaving the relevant polity the constitutional freedom to pass policies that seek to remedy the status of racial minorities.

Fourth, this turn to powers avoids the subjective nature of the scrutiny approach. There is no language of "compelling" or "narrowly tailored" that too easily invites individual justices to decide cases on ideological grounds. Defining what is an important versus a compelling purpose is rightly left to the relevant democratic body. The Court need not engage in this inquiry focusing only on whether the law invokes a constitutionally inadmissible rationale. A powers review makes clear that an invidious or illicit purpose is one that, for instance, is based on animus or hostility. This rightly captures the Court's role under the Equal Protection Clause. The tiers-of-scrutiny framework endows the Court with the *additional* task of deciding whether a purpose is compelling, important, or simply legitimate. This invites a justice to appeal to ideological considerations. A powers review entails a conceptually prior question about whether the law invokes a constitutionally inadmissible rationale. If the law does invoke such a rationale, the Court ought to strike it down. If the law does not invoke such a rationale, the Court ought to uphold the law.

The framework that the state exceeds its powers by acting arbitrarily is not new. It has roots in administrative law[55] and even the common law.[56] As one scholar of the common law puts it: "The special strength of the common law, as a foundation for constitutional government, lies in its inherent commitment to rationality and equality."[57] This doctrine of *ultra vires* ("beyond the powers"), then, is not simply one in which a department or agency exceeds its constitutionally proscribed roles. The principle is also substantive, pointing to a requirement that rule of law be constrained by a rule of reason. As T. R. S. Allan explains,

> [T]he particular legal orders or official decisions concerned must be justified by reference to publicly-avowed objectives.... [T]he rule of law constitutes a bulwark against the deprivation of liberty through exercise of arbitrary power. It encompasses principles of procedural fairness and legality, equality and proportionality. Fully articulated, the rule of law amounts to a sophisticated doctrine of constitutionalism, revealing law as the antithesis of arbitrariness or the assertion of will or power.[58]

This tradition of conceptualizing deprivations of liberty as a case of arbitrary power stands at the core of my analysis.

In fact, my argument has an interesting kind of affinity with the republican definition of freedom. Consider here Philip Pettit's account

---

[55] *See, e.g.*, Bressman 2003, Levin 1997
[56] *See generally* Jenkins 2003, Kalscheur 2006
[57] Allan 1999: 239
[58] Allan 1999: 222–3

of freedom as nondomination. As Pettit puts it, "One party dominates another just so far as they have the capacity to interfere on an
arbitrary basis in some of the other's choices."[59] In a recent volume on
republicanism and political theory, Quentin Skinner describes this neo-
Roman theory of liberty as the "absence of arbitrary power."[60] The
emphasis on power rather than those identity classifications that are off
limits to state action informs the approach I propose here. Alexander
Hamilton famously argued in Federalist #84 that a Bill of Rights to
the Constitution was unnecessary: "For why declare that things shall
not be done which there is no power to do?"[61] Rather than frame an
equal protection violation as an instance in which the state discriminates against a suspect class or an identity marker, we do better to
frame the violation as an instance in which the state exceeds its power
by invoking a constitutionally inadmissible rationale. This importantly
renders the Equal Protection Clause a structural feature of the Constitution – a limit on state power, rather than an embodiment of equal
rights.

A prohibition on same-sex marriage is unconstitutional not because
it harms gays and lesbians or discriminates on the basis of sexual
orientation but because the state exceeds its powers by prohibiting this
kind of marriage. There is no need to say that such a prohibition fails
to treat gays and lesbians as equals, because the state does not even
have the power to limit marriage in such a way. It does not have the
power to act on some particular religious view of marriage or a belief
in the intrinsic goodness of certain relationships over others.

In drawing from *Lawrence*, Randy Barnett implicitly connects this
argument to the powers framework I work out in this book:

> [*Lawrence*] rejected an open-ended conception of the police power
> of states and found that the particular purpose of the statute
> was illegitimate or improper. This is analogous to finding a fed-
> eral statute unconstitutional because, however effective it might
> be, its purpose is not among the enumerated *powers* in Article I,
> Section 8.[62]

[59] Pettit 1997: 272
[60] Skinner 2008: 83
[61] Cooke 1961: 579
[62] Barnett 2008: 1495 (emphasis added)

Now under the alternative approach I work out in this book, the Equal
Protection Clause is not a grant of power but rather a limitation on state
or governmental power. But I take Barnett's emphasis on powers as an
important conceptual step in realizing that the state does not have the
power to enact legislation based on an unconstitutional purpose just
as Congress does not have the power to pass ex post facto laws or
confer titles of nobility. I argue that the Equal Protection Clause is
best understood, then, as a limit on the kinds of reasons government
may invoke. This is what it means to treat individuals equally. This
reframing may appear as a mere rhetorical modification in the way the
Court invalidates laws and policies. This is undoubtedly true. But I
argue that this change from a discourse of identity to a discourse of
powers has important normative and political implications. It avoids
the problems that come with invoking identity while providing a more
robust check against equality infringing laws and policies.

There are three important caveats to my argument. First, this book
is not strictly about moral philosophy or justice but constitutional law
and its relationship to political theory. It is also not a comprehensive objection to the language of identity. This book critiques the suspect class doctrine by revealing constitutional law's preoccupation with
identity to do the equality work as problematic, expounding on a better
framework for understanding equal protection. After all, justice may
well require that a polity pass all kinds of laws or legislation: laws about
redistribution, affirmative action, or child care.

The Constitution does not generally require that a state or federal
government do something, only that when it does, it acts within certain
constitutional constraints. The Equal Protection Clause is a limit on
state action: "No State shall. . . . " This means that the constitutional
question is not about what equality requires but what *violates* equality
under the law. In elucidating a powers review, then, this book expounds
on those reasons that constitutional law already deems inadmissible.
This relieves an explicit need to defend some conception of what reasons or rationales count as publicly justifiable. After all, the Equal
Protection Clause is a limit on state action pointing to what the state
may *not* do. Explaining what reasons or rationales are constitutionally
outside the scope of state power is sufficient in outlining this kind of
review.

This in part explains why the tiers-of-scrutiny framework is unnecessary, or so this book argues. There is no need to define what is an important versus a compelling state purpose as long as the Court invalidates those laws and policies that rest on a constitutionally inadmissible rationale. The equal protection analysis is by its very terms a negative inquiry – about what the state may not do. The Court need only decide whether the state goes beyond its power by invoking a constitutionally inadmissible rationale. Requiring that the Court *also* decide whether the law's purpose is compelling or just important is therefore unnecessary and problematic. It invites ideological considerations by needlessly expanding the purview of the Court's role under the Equal Protection Clause.

Second, the book's focus is only on understanding equality under the law. I realize that the logic of a powers review may relieve the need to invoke certain constitutional rights. After all, if the state does not have the power to act on a particular conception of the good life, laws that regulate consensual sexual activity are automatically unconstitutional. The state exceeds its powers in passing them. The Court therefore does not need to invoke a constitutional right to privacy to strike down these laws. I do not engage this kind of argument, in part because I have already done so elsewhere.[63] The point of this book is to flesh out the Court's commitment to a powers review with regard to the Equal Protection Clause. If such a review has implications for other constitutional doctrines, I leave that to be worked out at another time. So, even if a law passes the Equal Protection Clause and does not invoke a constitutionally inadmissible rationale, it may well violate other provisions or rights contained in the Constitution.

Third, my argument is not simply about uncovering or establishing a fixed or originalist understanding of that clause. It will not suffice to argue that the Court ought to strike down legislation by looking to what "equal protection" originally meant. If that were the case, our inquiry would simply be a historical one. Originalism's failure as a method of constitutional interpretation is clearest in considering two cases: *Loving v. Virginia* (1967), a case that invalidated state antimiscegenation laws, and *Bolling v. Sharpe* (1954), a case decided the same day as

---

[63] *See* Bedi 2007, 2009

Brown that invalidated racial segregation in the District of Columbia. First, although there may be an originalist defense of *Brown*,[64] there is no similar evidence that the Equal Protection Clause even contemplated application to social legislation such as prohibitions on interracial marriage. Equality of such social rights was not part of the original understanding of that clause.[65] But the idea that *Loving* was wrongly decided – that the Constitution would not invalidate antimiscegenation laws – seems beyond the acceptable limits of constitutional interpretation. Second, and even more definitively, because the District of Columbia is a federal instrumentality, the Equal Protection Clause of the Fourteenth Amendment does not even apply; that clause applies only to states ("No State shall . . . "). Rather, the relevant provision for federal legislation is the Fifth Amendment. That amendment demands that no person shall be "deprived of life, liberty, or property, without due process of law."[66] In *Bolling*, the Court states that "it would be unthinkable that the same Constitution would impose a lesser duty on the Federal Government."[67] But "unthinkable" is not the same as in accord with originalist principles. As Jack Balkin, directly questioning Justice Antonin Scalia's practice of constitutional interpretation through the paradigm of originalism, argues:

> Consider this: in 1791 [when the Fifth Amendment was ratified] black people were held in slavery. It's hard to argue that this clause, interpreted according to the expectations of the late eighteenth century generation that framed it, prevents the federal government from engaging in racial discrimination. . . . If Justice Scalia believes that *Bolling* is correct, it can't be because of his originalist views. Rather, it is, as he would say, a case where courts just made new rights up.[68]

And Justice Scalia had an opportunity to weigh in on the constitutional status of federal laws that discriminate on the basis of race when considering a Congressional remedial affirmative action law in

---

[64] *See generally* McConnell 1995, 1996
[65] *See* Avins 1966, Frank and Munro 1950; *see also* Balkin 2005: 221–6
[66] Amendment V, U.S. Constitution
[67] *Bolling* at 500
[68] http://balkin.blogspot.com/2009/10/scalias-biggest-problem-isnt-brown-its.html

Adarand Constructors, Inc. v. Peña (1995). Scalia not only joins the majority opinion – along with Justice Clarence Thomas – holding that federal racially discriminatory laws must receive strict scrutiny but also writes a separate concurrence to make clear that this standard is indeed stringent. Reading the doctrine of strict scrutiny into the Fifth Amendment flies in the face of originalism.[69] Originalism cannot be the basis of modern equal protection doctrine and its focus on tiers of scrutiny, a doctrine that even the most conservative members of the Court have endorsed.

The current debate over equal protection is not about history or some fixed understanding of the text. Although some version of originalism may still be relevant for other provisions in the Constitution, it is simply a nonstarter for understanding legal equality. The "meaning of the equal protection guarantee," according to Laurence Tribe, is a "debate not so much over what the Constitution's text says" but "over the Constitution's invisible, unstated presuppositions about the purposes of demanding various forms of equality under law."[70] This book seeks to make clear this seemingly "invisible" and "unstated presupposition" by working out a powers review. In *Harper v. Virginia Board of Elections* (1966), the Court struck down a Virginia poll tax under the Equal Protection Clause. Justice William Douglas, writing for the Court, stated that in "determining what lines are unconstitutionally discriminatory [under equal protection], we have never been confined to historic notions of equality."[71]

This book deploys political theory both to criticize current doctrine and to inform a more salutary one. I argue that at its best, the Court's equal protection jurisprudence is about a powers review, one that limits the state's power to act on certain reasons. In the *Partial Constitution*, Cass Sunstein insightfully argues that American constitutional law is indeed about a "republic of reasons." Importantly, the "required reason must count as a public regarding one. Government cannot appeal to private interest alone."[72] Although Sunstein does not deploy this

---

[69] *See generally* Lemieux 2007
[70] Tribe 2008: 118
[71] *Harper* at 669
[72] Sunstein 1993: 17

distinction between public and private reasons to rethink equal protection doctrine, his theory importantly highlights the centrality of
justification. Again, this book's focus is only on the Equal Protection
Clause. I elucidate an equal protection framework grounded in the
language of powers instead of identity.

   To that end, this book is in three parts. Part I criticizes the identity-
centered interpretation of the Equal Protection Clause and fleshes out
one grounded in the idea that the government does not have the power
to invoke certain constitutionally inadmissible rationales. I argue that
instead of the conventional suspect class doctrine and its tiers-of-
scrutiny framework, the Court is better off with a powers review, a
review that is already immanent in constitutional law. Part II applies
this analysis to the category of race. It challenges the Court's use of
strict scrutiny for those laws that discriminate on the basis of race, suggesting that such scrutiny is both problematic and unnecessary. Part
III considers the cases that conventionally arise under the categories of
sex and sexual orientation, arguing that here too the Court does better
to adopt a powers review and avoid the language of identity.

PART I: IDENTITY VERSUS POWERS

Chapter 1 argues that the Court's use of the suspect class doctrine to
understand equal protection is susceptible to political theory's critiques
of identity. The Court looks to four primary criteria to determine
whether a group counts as a suspect class: history of discrimination,
immutability, political powerlessness, and irrelevance. I argue that by
invoking these criteria to strike down legislation, the Court exemplifies
four core problems with the language of identity, problems that track
each prong of this doctrine: the history of discrimination reinscribes the
very oppression groups seek to end, immutability reifies the boundaries
of the relevant identity group, political powerlessness exacerbates the
counter-majoritarian difficulty, and irrelevance problematically masks
the reality that identity is often salient in our contemporary world.
Ultimately, I argue that by elevating these groups to suspect status, the
Court turns out to stigmatize them. It forces individuals who belong

to these groups to highlight the way they are different from everyone else.

Chapter 2 fleshes out a powers interpretation of the Equal Protection Clause, one that deems certain kinds of reasons or rationales constitutionally inadmissible. Drawing on some of the synergy between constitutional doctrine and liberal neutrality, I argue that a powers review contains three important justificatory constraints. The state may not (1) act on justifications that invoke certain conceptions of the good life, (2) that are based on mere animus or hostility, or (3) that are proffered in bad faith. I look to the Court's jurisprudence to tease out and elaborate on these constraints. With regard to bad faith, I suggest that under a powers review, the constitutional debate will not be about which reasons are inadmissible but about whether the law or policy is *actually* based on one of them. For instance, the disagreement in the Ninth Circuit case upholding *Schwarzenegger* was about whether Proposition 8 was truly based on a constitutionally inadmissible rationale. Taken together, these justificatory constraints, I argue, better capture equality under the law, avoiding the problems often associated with the identity approach.

PART II: RACE

Chapter 3 considers and challenges the Court's use of race as the paradigmatic identity category that constitutes a suspect classification. This chapter argues that the Court perversely rationalizes racism by deploying the doctrine of strict scrutiny. By imposing such a high bar on laws and policies that explicitly discriminate on the basis of race, the Court gives credence to the otherwise illegitimate claims of racism. After all, why does the Court need searching scrutiny to realize that racist laws and policies are based on animus. Constantly suggesting that strict scrutiny is necessary to do so only legitimates racist beliefs. Adding insult to injury, strict scrutiny jeopardizes remedial legislation, which seeks to remedy the effects of racism. In fact, Justice John Marshall Harlan's dissent in *Plessy v. Ferguson* (1896) does not impose any kind of higher scrutiny, strict or otherwise. Whereas *Plessy* upheld

racial segregation in railway cars, Justice Harlan importantly concludes that such segregation is unconstitutional precisely because it was
based on racial animus. He rightly applies the constitutional standard
outlined in that case, a standard that informs a powers review: "[E]very
exercise of the police power must be reasonable, and extend only to
such laws as are enacted in good faith for the promotion of the public
good, and not for the annoyance or oppression of a particular class."[73]
This is the *ultra vires* doctrine I seek to resuscitate.

Chapter 4 analyzes the more difficult case of racial profiling and its
use of statistical analysis in light of my analysis. I argue that here too
a powers review is sufficient to invalidate laws and policies that profile
racial minorities for criminal activity. I focus on the constitutionality
of laws that would seek to profile blacks for certain kinds of drug
crimes. I argue that this kind of racial profiling is often indeed based on
animus, because such profiling cannot be rational. Even if individuals
of a particular racial group are more likely to offend than individuals of
another (premise 1), this does not make such profiling rational. Simply
put, for profiling to be rational, it must actually seek to reduce crime
(premise 2). Drawing from Bernard Harcourt's insightful and novel
analysis of the irrationality of racial profiling,[74] this chapter argues that
these two premises cannot both be valid. That is, the more the first
premise is true, the more the second is false. It is the socioeconomic
disadvantage faced by racial minorities that explains why premise 1 may
be true. And because racial profiling will not alter this disadvantage (in
fact, it will most likely make a bad situation worse), it does not stand
to reduce crime, thereby undermining premise 1.

PART III: SEX AND SEXUAL ORIENTATION

Chapter 5 interrogates the underlying theory of intermediate scrutiny
drawing from the distinction between sameness and difference feminism. Sameness feminism contends that males and females are essentially the same, just as different racial groups are essentially the same.

[73] *Plessy* at 550
[74] Harcourt 2007

Difference feminism contends that the sexes are essentially different. By deploying intermediate rather than strict scrutiny for those cases invoking sex or gender, the Court problematically accepts the difference theory of feminism. In doing so, the Court has upheld sexist policies of sex segregation and male-only military conscription. But there is an alternative reading of the Court's jurisprudence on gender, one that informs a powers review. In a series of cases including *Frontiero v. Richardson* (1973), *Weinberger v. Wiesenfeld* (1975), and *Califano v. Goldfarb* (1977), the Court struck down policies that rest on the idea that females must be caregivers and males breadwinners. Accordingly, the idea that males or females must act or be a certain way is a conception of the good that the Court already deems constitutionally inadmissible. A powers review eschews both different and sameness feminism invalidating those laws that rest on the idea that there is an appropriate relationship between sex and gender. I argue that this informs Catharine MacKinnon's account of dominance.

Chapter 6 concludes by bringing the identity framework I criticize and the powers review I defend to a head in the case of same-sex marriage. The chapter considers the constitutional implications of taking seriously a powers review. I argue that this review stands to challenge marriage laws themselves, inviting a slippery slope to the disestablishment of marriage. Just as a limitation on same-sex marriage is about the moral or religious superiority of one set of couplings (a heterosexual conception of an appropriate or good relationship) over another (a homosexual one), so too are limitations on adult incestuous or plural marriage. Here too the state seeks to privilege one conception of the good (a two-person, non-blood-related union) over another (a three-person or a blood-related union). In fact, marriage itself is kind of orthodoxy, as recent contemporary political theory makes clear. By deeming individuals "married," the state does more than simply permit these individuals to avail themselves of the legal benefits, burdens, and responsibilities that come with a civil union. The state proclaims that this kind of relationship is morally special, that it entails a conception of the good that individuals ought to pursue. Those who live alone, with their siblings, or with an unmarried partner fall short of this state-sanctioned ideal. By taking sides in a very personal decision about what constitutes the good life, the state violates a powers review, or so this chapter suggests. Taking such a review to its logical constitutional conclusion means that the state exceeds its power in marrying individuals. Although this may point to an extreme, even counterintuitive implication of a powers approach, I argue that it illuminates an important constitutional argument, one that brings the issue of same-sex marriage into sharper focus.

Part I IDENTITY VERSUS POWERS

1   SUSPECT CLASS AND THE DILEMMA OF IDENTITY

What does it mean for laws and policies to violate equal protection? This is the motivating puzzle of this book. At its core, this book is about how the Court strikes down democratically enacted laws and policies. The ability of the Court to uphold legislation does not trigger pressing normative and political concerns about legitimacy or judicial review. After all, the counter-majoritarian difficulty arises when the Court invalidates, rather than upholds, laws and polices. Alexander Bickel defines this difficulty as one in which the Court "thwarts the will of representatives of the actual people of the here and now; it exercises control, not in behalf of the prevailing majority, but against it."[1] It is a difficulty precisely because the Court *thwarts* rather than affirms majority sentiment. This tension is at the center of judicial review in a constitutional liberal democracy: on one hand is our commitment to democratic rule, and on the other hand is our commitment to ensuring liberty and equality. When a court strikes down laws in the name of liberty or equality, it acts in a counter-majoritarian fashion.

Most scholarly work focuses on solving this difficulty – on establishing why a Court ought to have the ability to strike down laws and policies. Scholars aim to provide an answer to the question of why judicial review is important, even necessary, to liberal democracy. I assume its importance in this book. My focus is not on *why* a court ought to have the ability to strike down laws and policies. I examine *how* a court does so. Even if the Court reaches the "correct" result, it matters how it arrives at that conclusion. This book analyzes the framework the Court deploys to invalidate democratically enacted laws and

---

[1] Bickel 1962: 17

policies under the Equal Protection Clause. I suggest that the language the Court deploys in striking down legislation is of critical importance. Currently, the Court enforces equal protection by deeming certain identity markers or classifications off limits to state regulation. This is why laws and policies that invoke these markers receive a form of higher scrutiny. Central to this framework is the suspect class doctrine. Those groups that constitute suspect classes inform the list of prohibited classifications. For instance, laws that discriminate on the basis of sex and race receive higher scrutiny because women and racial minorities constitute a suspect class.

Although critiques of identity are well established, scholars have largely ignored their relationship to constitutional jurisprudence. On one hand, constitutional legal scholars focus on the doctrine with little or no attention to its political weaknesses. On the other hand, political theorists focus on difficulties with the language of identity with no attention to constitutional doctrine and, in particular, the suspect class framework. That is, there is no sustained treatment of the political problems posed by how the Court defines what counts as a suspect class. This chapter fills this gap by arguing that the suspect class doctrine invokes the problems often associated with identity.

Central to this argument is the assumption that the Court's equal protection doctrine often frames the relevant debate. The Court trades in the language of identity or class, but scholars and advocates often speak in the language of equal rights. For instance, constitutional jurisprudence frames a prohibition on same-sex marriage as an issue of sexual orientation discrimination. It entails determining whether gays and lesbians constitute a suspect class. Its corresponding political debate is over ensuring the equal rights of gays and lesbians. After all, empirical work in political science codes this debate as one about "gay rights."[2] Even a recent First Circuit Court of Appeals opinion invalidating the Defense of Marriage Act, a law that does not recognize same-sex marriage at the federal level, characterizes decisions such as *Lawrence* and *Romer* as ones in which "gay rights" prevailed.[3] This is

---

[2] *See, e.g.*, Lax and Phillips 2009, Pinello 2003
[3] *Massachusetts v. U.S. Dept. of Health and Human Services* (1st Cir. 2012) at 8

why Evan Gertsmann argues that the "Court fulfills its proper role in a constitutional democracy when it protects the rights of unpopular individuals and minorities even when doing that frustrates the will of the majority."[4] This debate in turn is often framed as either for or against gay marriage, for or against gay rights. Whether the claim is that such a prohibition violates the equal rights of gays and lesbians or discriminates on the basis of sexual orientation, the logic is the same: such a claim *invalidates* discriminatory laws and policies on behalf of a particular identity group. It frames the constitutional objection in terms of identity.

The Equal Rights Amendment, an amendment that was approved by the House and Senate in 1972 but ultimately failed to garner the requisite number of state ratifications, informs this logic. Section 1 of the proposed amendment reads: "Equality of rights under the law shall not be denied or abridged by the United States or by any state on account of sex."[5] Although the amendment speaks in the language of equal rights or the "equality of rights," it makes clear that such rights shall not be denied on account of an identity affiliation – here, a person's sex. That is, it specifies what classification or identity marker is constitutionally special. Under this conventional view of equality under the law, a sexist law would violate the equal rights of women just as a homophobic one would violate the equal rights of gays and lesbians. The language of equal rights cannot avoid the language of identity. The question will always be the equal rights of *whom*.

This chapter argues that this logic, this emphasis on suspect class or its equal rights political analog, is problematic. I am not concerned, then, with ethnocultural group rights, rights that seek an affirmative response from the state in terms of self-governance or accommodation.[6] Multiculturalism's primary concern is over such rights. When scholars criticize group rights, they often mean ethnocultural rights.[7] This book is only about criticizing the Court's appeal to identity and its equal rights analog to strike down laws and policies.

---

[4] Gerstmann 2008: 163
[5] House Joint Resolution 208, 92d Congress, 2d Session (1972)
[6] *See, e.g.*, Kymlicka 1995, Parekh 2000, Shachar 2001, Young 1990
[7] *See, e.g.*, Barry 2001, Kukathas 2003

This chapter comprises two parts. First, I briefly point out that the conventional understanding of public reason treats equality under the law as a commitment to equal rights, a commitment that invariably implicates identity. Second, and this is the main focus of the chapter, I argue that the criteria the Court deploys to determine suspect class status inform extant critiques of identity. Ultimately, I argue that there is a deep dilemma with the suspect class framework, with *how* the Court strikes down equality-infringing laws and policies. On one hand, it is clear that racial minorities, women, and gays and lesbians require constitutional protection given the kind of discrimination each has faced. On the other hand, by elevating these groups to suspect status, the Court stigmatizes them. It forces individuals who belong to these groups to highlight the way they are different from everyone else, or so this chapter argues.

PUBLIC REASON AND EQUAL RIGHTS

John Rawls's account of political liberalism provides one of the most robust philosophical defenses of liberal public reason.[8] Most scholarly work on political liberalism analyzes it. But Rawls also makes clear that public reason translates into a set of "constitutional essentials."[9] Although this part of his argument is often neglected, it informs mine. He suggests that such essentials are of two kinds:

a. fundamental principles that specify the general structure of government and the political process; the powers of the legislature, executive, and the judiciary; the scope of majority rule; and
b. equal basic rights and liberties of citizenship that legislative majorities are to respect: such as the right to vote and to participate in politics, liberty of conscience, freedom of thought and of association, as well as the protections of the rule of the law.[10]

---

[8] Rawls 1996 [1993]: 1997
[9] Rawls 1996 [1993]: 227
[10] Rawls 1996 [1993]: 227

The first concerns the powers of government; the second concerns the rights a majority may not violate. Obviously, (b) encompasses both individual rights such as the rights to privacy, free speech, or religion as well as the right to be treated equally. There is a difference between an individual right and its identity counterpart. A law may violate an individual right but still treat individuals equally. Consider a law that prohibits the possession of handguns. Such a law may violate a constitutional right to bear arms, but it does not violate legal equality. My book does not concern individual rights, something my previous work has analyzed.[11] The focus here is on what Rawls calls "equal rights." This is how public reason conceptualizes equality under the law. Rawls himself makes clear that public reason includes "gay and lesbian rights."[12] Again, although the suspect class framework does not explicitly characterize the Equal Protection Clause as a claim of equal rights, it trades in the language of identity or class. In the same way, the Equal Rights Amendment invokes sex as the constitutionally relevant suspect classification. These are all conceptually the same kind of claim. They seek to invalidate laws and policies on the basis of identity.

It is worth noting that Rawls does not include the difference principle (i.e., the commitment to justifying social and economic inequalities) as part of these constitutional essentials. Liberals may certainly debate the necessity of addressing social and economic inequalities at the constitutional level,[13] but such a discussion is beyond the scope of this book. My analysis is only about equal protection, not equality writ large. It is about ascertaining what principle ought to guide the Court in striking down legislation that violates equality under the law.

Relevant here is that Rawls indeed separates public reason into commitments of powers on one hand (a) and equal rights or identity on the other (b). This captures the distinction between the powers approach I elucidate in this book and the suspect class or identity approach I criticize. The discourse of equal rights invokes the language of identity. Under this logic, the problem with homophobic, racist,

[11] Bedi 2007, 2009
[12] Rawls 1997: 788
[13] *See generally* Estlund 1996

or sexist laws is not that they violate everyone's rights but that they fail to ensure equal rights *for gays and lesbians, for racial minorities,* or *for women,* respectively. This is why Rawls describes constitutional essentials as including gay and lesbian rights. As long as we speak in the language of rights – equal or otherwise – there is no way to avoid making the constitutional argument about a particular identity group. This is why James Nickel characterizes these identity claims as "universal rights applied to minorities" (URAM).[14] Although Nickel's concern is with human rights and not constitutional essentials, his framing informs my argument here. If the infirmity with Jim Crow is that it does not apply a certain kind of universal right to racial minorities, this makes the protest about identity. Importantly, the white majority could not make a URAM claim on behalf of itself in challenging racist legislation. As applied to whites, there is no infraction of any alleged universal right. I argue that if we operationalize public reason in terms of equal rights, we cannot avoid invoking identity. When a court strikes down equality violating laws under (b), it must do so on behalf of a particular group. I call this the "identity approach."

SUSPECT CLASS AND THE CRITIQUE OF IDENTITY

The Court endorses the identity approach through its interpretation of the Equal Protection Clause. This is a three-step process. First, and this step is often not made explicit, the law must discriminate against a group or a kind of status. This is the threshold requirement for an equal protection violation under the suspect class framework. Laws that discriminate against behavior or "doing something" do not generally trigger the conventional understanding of equal protection. A law, for instance, that makes it a crime to criticize the government, to use contraception, or to possess firearms does not discriminate against any particular class of individuals. Although such laws may violate individual rights to free speech, privacy, or a right to bear arms, they do not trigger a possible constitutional concern over equality under the law. This initial doctrinal step is not easy to meet. According to the Court,

[14] Nickel 2007: 154

the law must explicitly invoke a group or class. It will not suffice for a law simply to have a disparate impact on a particular set of individuals.[15] This step requires that the "the decisionmaker... selected or reaffirmed a particular course of action at least in part 'because of,' not merely 'in spite of,' its adverse effects upon an identifiable group."[16]

Second, and this step is central to my critique of the Court's doctrine, the law must discriminate against a *suspect* class. It must discriminate against a particular kind of group. There are many groups in society: racial groups, the local Parent Teacher Association (PTA), gays and lesbians, women, a simple book club, blondes, or those with a particular eye color. Most are not suspect classes. Cass Sunstein argues that the core purpose of the Equal Protection Clause is "an attempt to protect *disadvantaged* groups from discriminatory practices, however deeply engrained and longstanding."[17] This step seeks to elevate certain groups or affiliations but not others to suspect status – treating them as constitutionally "special." Currently, whereas racial minorities and women are "in" (they count as protected disadvantaged groups), gays and lesbians are "out" (they do not count as a suspect class). Scholarly work has argued that they ought to count as one, thereby rendering sexual orientation a suspect classification under the Equal Protection Clause.[18] Attorney General Eric Holder argues that gays and lesbians meet the relevant criteria for suspect status in his letter to Congress justifying the administration's decision not to defend the Defense of Marriage Act in court:

> The Supreme Court has yet to rule on the appropriate level of scrutiny for classifications based on sexual orientation. It has, however, rendered a number of decisions that set forth the criteria that should inform this and any other judgment as to whether heightened scrutiny applies: (1) whether the group in question has suffered a history of discrimination; (2) whether individuals "exhibit

---

[15] *Washington v. Davis* (1976) (holding that a police officer test that had a disparate impact on blacks did not constitute a presumptive equal protection violation)

[16] *Personnel Administrator of Mass. v. Feeney* (1979) (holding that automatic preference for veterans that had a disparate impact on women did not constitute a presumptive equal protection violation) at 279

[17] Sunstein 1988: 1163 (emphasis added)

[18] *See, e.g.*, Ackerman 1985, Ely 1980, Feldblum 1996, Steiker 1985, Sunstein 1988, Yoshino 1996

obvious, immutable, or distinguishing characteristics that define
them as a discrete group"; (3) whether the group is a minority or
is politically powerless; and (4) whether the characteristics distinguishing the group have little relation to legitimate policy objectives
or to an individual's "ability to perform or contribute to society"
[citations omitted].[19]

The four criteria that underlie the Court's suspect class framework are
history of discrimination,[20] immutability,[21] political powerlessness,[22]
and irrelevance.[23] And in fact, the Second Circuit Court of Appeals
invalidated the Defense of Marriage Act by declaring that gays and
lesbians count as a suspect class, reasoning that sexual orientation is a
suspect classification.[24]

Third, once the Court determines that a group has met these criteria, rendering it a suspect class, laws that invoke the relevant classification or identity marker are subject to higher scrutiny.[25] This
relationship between suspect status and heightened scrutiny is the cor-
nerstone of modern equal protection jurisprudence. Again, under current case law, laws discriminating on the basis of race,[26] alienage,[27] and
national origin[28] get strict scrutiny: the Court asks whether the law is
narrowly tailored to serve a compelling state purpose. Laws discriminating against sex get intermediate scrutiny[29]: the Court asks whether
the law is substantially related to serving an important governmental
purpose. Those laws that do not invoke a suspect classification merely
receive rational review, the most deferential standard of review. Under

---

[19] Letter from the Attorney General to Congress on Litigation Involving the Defense of
Marriage Act, 2/23/2011; http://www.justice.gov/opa/pr/2011/February/11-ag-223.html
[20] *See, e.g., City of Cleburne v. Cleburne* (1985) at 441; *San Antonio v. Rodriguez* (1973) at
28; *Frontiero v. Richardson* (1973) at 684–5
[21] *See, e.g., City of Cleburne v. Cleburne* (1985) at 440–4; *Frontiero v. Richardson* (1973) at
685–7
[22] Ibid; *see also Graham v. Richardson* (1971) at 372
[23] *See, e.g., Frontiero v. Richardson* (1973) at 686
[24] *See Windsor v. U.S.* (2nd Cir. 2012). The Court has agreed to review this case along with
the Ninth Circuit Court of Appeals decision invalidating Proposition 8 in its 2013 term.
[25] I have argued in my previous work that the Court conflates class with classification by
having its list of suspect classes inform its list of suspect classifications; Bedi 2013
[26] *See, e.g., Bolling v. Sharpe* (1954); *Loving v. Virginia* (1967); *Grutter v. Bollinger* (2003)
[27] *See Graham v. Richardson* (1971)
[28] *See, e.g., Korematsu v. United States* (1944)
[29] *See, e.g., Craig v. Boren* (1976)

rational review, the legislation must only have a legitimate purpose, and the means must be rationally related to that purpose.

The Subjectiveness of the Tiers-of-Scrutiny Framework

This framework means that certain laws receive greater or more searching scrutiny than others. It is obvious that a purpose that is "compelling" is more important than one that is merely "legitimate." But this framework does not define "compelling," "legitimate," or "narrowly tailored." These are only relative descriptions leaving the tiers-of-scrutiny framework a subjective doctrine. Although it may have comparative value in deciding cases (a law struck down under intermediate scrutiny ought to be struck down under its strict scrutiny counterpart), it does not have any actual content. This leaves the Court to fill in the framework as it sees fit. For instance, the Court has defined the meaning of "compelling" in radically different ways. In *Korematsu v. United States* (1944), the Court upheld Japanese interment, reasoning that national security constitutes a compelling purpose under strict scrutiny. In *Grutter v. Bollinger* (2003), it upheld Michigan's race-based affirmative action policy, reasoning that racial diversity in higher education constitutes a compelling purpose under a similar level of scrutiny. Dissenting in *Grutter*, Justice Thomas chastises the Court for failing to treat the compelling purpose standard as a strict one. For him, almost no reason will pass strict scrutiny, precisely because "only those measures the State must take to provide a bulwark against anarchy, or to prevent violence, will constitute a 'pressing public necessity.'"[30] Is achieving racial diversity in higher education really as compelling as national security? This question is difficult to answer because nowhere does the Court define what is compelling or even what is merely, under a lower standard of review, legitimate.[31]

Simultaneously, *Grutter* held that a plus system, in which racial minorities receive a plus factor in the admissions system along with a range of other characteristics, is "narrowly tailored." This kind of individualized assessment fulfills the means requirement of strict scrutiny.

---

[30] *Grutter* at 353, dissenting
[31] *See generally* Fallon 2007

But in *Gratz v. Bollinger* (2003), the Court held that a point system akin
to quotas is not narrowly tailored, failing strict scrutiny. Ian Ayres and
Sydney Foster argue that these decisions turn the narrowly tailored
requirement on its head.[32] If a narrowly tailored option is the least
restrictive one – that is, the option that uses the "smallest racial preference" – quotas may be superior to an individualized assessment.[33]
Quotas may be the most precise and transparent way of achieving racial
diversity. Under the rubric of individual assessment, admission officers
may end up using race more often than under a system in which a certain number of seats have been assigned for particular racial minorities.
By not having to quantify "its preferences," an individualized assessment need not "'tell' courts how much of a racial preference it is
giving."[34] This option could turn out to sneak in a large quantity of
racial preference. The Court's real concern, then, may be a simple
distaste for quotas not some theory of tailoring.

To add insult to injury, the Court imposes intermediate scrutiny (a
middling standard between strict and rational review) for laws discriminating on the basis of sex. Here the law must seek to accomplish an
"important" purpose rather than a "compelling" one, and it must be
"substantially related" to that purpose rather than "narrowly tailored."
But what's the difference between important and compelling? With no
theory to anchor these tests, individual justices can simply decide for
themselves whether the law meets them. The intermediate standard
has added even more complexity but no real content to the Court's
scrutiny framework.

Empirical political science makes clear that Court decisions are
often influenced by ideology or preference.[35] Although no theory of
constitutional adjudication is immune to such ideological decision making, we ought to, *ceteris paribus*, favor a constitutional method of adjudication that is less prone to it. Yet, the tiers-of-scrutiny framework
easily invites justices to decide cases on ideological grounds. It does
not provide guidance as to what "compelling" or "legitimate" means,

---

[32] Ayres and Foster 2007; *see also* Ayres 1996
[33] Ayres and Foster 2007: 519
[34] Ayres and Foster 2007: 519
[35] *See, e.g.*, Epstein and Knight 1998; Segal and Spaeth 1993, 2002

only that when a law invokes race, it ought to receive a more searching scrutiny.[36] Imagine if I were to send you into a room with the following possibilities: briefly search the room, search the room carefully, or search the room very thoroughly. This may provide you relative guidance as to how thoroughly you should search, but it does not tell you what you are searching *for*. These search descriptions are subjective, because they do not provide substantive content. The scrutiny framework does not tell the Court what counts as a compelling or legitimate purpose, perversely leaving justices to decide for themselves what such words mean – to decide for themselves, for instance, whether racial diversity is compelling or whether quotas are narrowly tailored. This invites ideological and policy considerations that are best left to the relevant democratic polity.

It will not suffice to suggest that the aim of this framework is to "smoke out" laws and policies that have an invidious or illicit purpose.[37] After all, what does "invidious" mean? This formulation of the test is subjective, too. If the Court applies a more searching scrutiny to uncover laws that are invidious or illicit, this requires that there be a clear definition of such terms. For if we make clear what reasons or rationales are constitutionally inadmissible, we may not need higher scrutiny. The core problem with imposing an ever-increasing level of scrutiny is that equal protection doctrine does not specify what the Court is looking for. Higher scrutiny is an empty or subjective framework that does not provide adequate constitutional guidance in deciding actual cases.

Recognizing some of this doctrinal confusion, Suzanne Goldberg challenges the tiers-of-scrutiny framework.[38] She seeks to put in its place a single standard of review. There is much to admire in her approach. She streamlines the current test to propose one that focuses on the plausibility of the means, understood contextually, and any bias in the ends.[39] But her test does not fully explain what "plausible" or "bias" means. And in proposing this alleged alternative, Goldberg

---

[36] *See generally* Fallon 2007: 1321–5
[37] *City of Richmond v. Croson* (1989) at 493. *See also* Fallon 2007: 1308–11, Matthews and Sweet 2011: 805, Rubenfeld 1997: 436–7
[38] Goldberg 2004a
[39] Goldberg 2004a

still treats a ban on "class legislation" as crucial to equal protection doctrine.[40] Her account, like the tiers-of-scrutiny framework, does not go far enough in solving the subjectiveness problem.

This is does not mean that the scrutiny framework is a free-for-all. As a statistical matter, if a law receives higher scrutiny, it will likely be struck down (although there is no guarantee). According to Adam Winkler, between 1990 and 2003, 73 percent of all race-conscious laws subjected to strict scrutiny in federal courts were struck down.[41] This means that the scrutiny framework often turns out to be doctrinal shorthand for whether a law will be upheld or struck down. As one scholar suggests, heightened scrutiny is strict "in theory and fatal in fact," whereas rational review is "minimal scrutiny in theory and virtually none in fact."[42] Because the third step in the conventional equal protection analysis has no substantive content, it is the higher level of scrutiny that generally dooms the law. Such scrutiny has often become an end in itself rather than an alleged means to smoking out what an individual justice may consider as an illicit rationale or reason.

As a practical matter, then, the most important step turns out to be the second: deciding which groups or classes are suspect. For once a class becomes suspect, laws and policies that discriminate against that classification receive higher scrutiny. And when the Court imposes strict scrutiny, it will strike down at least three out of four of these laws. All the constitutional action is about determining suspect status, about whether a particular group meets the four relevant criteria. If the group at issue does not count as a suspect class, the Court will most likely uphold the challenged legislation. This is what is at stake in the conventional interpretation of the Equal Protection Clause.

For instance, in *Lyng v. Castillo* (1986) the Court upheld a congressional law that did not treat a group of distant relatives as a household for purposes of food-stamp eligibility. The Court did not subject the law to heightened scrutiny, reasoning that "close relatives are not a 'suspect' or 'quasi-suspect' class. As a historical matter, they have not been subjected to discrimination; they do not exhibit obvious, immutable,

---

[40] Goldberg 2004a: 528–32
[41] Winkler 2006: 839
[42] Gunther 1972: 8

or distinguishing characteristics that define them as a discrete group; and they are not a minority or politically powerless."[43] Contrastingly, Holder's memorandum argues that gays and lesbians ought to count as a suspect class precisely because they meet these criteria.

Four Criteria for Suspect Status

This chapter focuses on these criteria, arguing that they invite the problems often associated with invoking identity. Critiques of identity are common in contemporary political theory, feminist theory, queer studies, critical race theory, and poststructuralism. Canvassing the full range of this criticism is beyond the scope of this chapter. Dividing my analysis into four parts, I point to the way in which the criteria for suspect class status exemplify four core problems with the language of identity, problems that track each prong of this doctrinal logic: (1) the history of discrimination reinscribes the very oppression groups seek to end, (2) immutability reifies the boundaries of the relevant identity group, (3) political powerlessness exacerbates the counter-majoritarian difficulty, and (4) irrelevance problematically masks the reality that identity is often salient in our contemporary world. These problems, I argue, are unavoidable as long as the Court insists on deploying the suspect class framework to do the equal protection work. This is the core dilemma of conceptualizing equality under the law in terms of identity.

History of Discrimination Reinscribes Oppression

One of the criteria the Court deploys to determine suspect status is a history of discrimination. The Court asks whether a group has suffered from discrimination or oppression. This doctrinal requirement perversely reaffirms the very exclusion that suspect class status seeks to counter. Again, there are countless groups in society, including the Rotary club, gays and lesbians, women, racial minorities, and brunettes. Obviously, it does not make sense to speak in terms of the equal rights of brunettes or the rights of those with a particular eye

---

[43] *Castillo* at 638

color. No current or historical exclusion is based on these characteristics or, for that matter, on PTA membership. A law that discriminates on the basis of PTA membership or hair color would thus not receive heightened scrutiny by the Court. These do not count as suspect classes or groups.

Consider that in *San Antonio Independent School District v. Rodriguez* (1973), the Court upheld the Texas local property tax system challenged by a group consisting of economically poor families. With regard to the Equal Protection Clause, the Court held that this group does not count as a suspect class. The Court reasoned that those who brought the class action constitute a "large, diverse, and amorphous class, unified only by the common factor of residence in districts that happen to have less taxable wealth than other districts."[44] In turn, this "class is not saddled with *such* disabilities, or subjected to *such* a history of purposeful unequal treatment, or relegated to *such* a position of powerlessness as to command extraordinary protection from the majoritarian process."[45] Simple discrimination is not sufficient to garner suspect class status. There must be a more pronounced history of discrimination. This prong of the analysis requires a significant level of oppression over time for the group to constitute a protected class under the Equal Protection Clause.

It is under this constitutional standard that scholarly work argues that gays and lesbians ought to count as a suspect class.[46] In his memorandum to Congress, Eric Holder argued that "most importantly, there is, regrettably, a significant history of purposeful discrimination against gay and lesbian people, by governmental as well as private entities, based on prejudice and stereotypes that continue to have ramifications today."[47] This argument of oppression is crucial for a group to gain constitutional protection under the Equal Protection Clause. In fact, according to Holder, it is the "most important" consideration.

In this way, a group proclaims its rights (politicizes its identity) precisely *because* it has been subjugated; those who are members of the

---

[44] *Rodriguez* at 28
[45] *Rodriguez* at 28 (emphasis added)
[46] *See* note 18
[47] Letter from the Attorney General to Congress on Litigation Involving the Defense of Marriage Act, 2/23/2011. http://www.justice.gov/opa/pr/2011/February/11-ag-223.html

PTA or have brown hair have not suffered such oppression. The force of a constitutional objection based on identity trades on the group's exclusion. Wendy Brown provocatively characterizes this as a form of *ressentiment*:

> In its emergence as a protest against marginalization or subordination, politicized identity thus becomes attached to its own exclusion . . . because it is premised on this exclusion for its very existence as identity. . . . But in so doing, it installs its pain over its unredeemed history in the very foundation of its political claim, in its demand for recognition as identity.[48]

So when the Court invalidates a law or policy by invoking identity, it invariably invokes this subjugation. In objecting to discriminatory laws and policies through identity claims, the group trades on its victim status. To elevate and distinguish itself as a suspect class, the group has to invoke its own history of oppression. The constitutional definition of a suspect class cannot escape this charge of *ressentiment*, precisely because it requires a history of discrimination. In proclaiming that a law violates the equal rights of gays, blacks, or women, and this is Brown's charge, these groups seek to curry the Court's sympathy in their "demand for recognition."

In constitutional parlance, the "demand for recognition" is nothing other than the demand for suspect class status and hence heightened scrutiny. Again, current constitutional doctrine does not deem sexual orientation a suspect classification. Constitutional advocates who seek to bring gays and lesbians under the conventional logic of equal protection doctrine highlight the violence, discrimination, and hatred that gays experience. The plaintiff's trial brief in *Perry v. Schwarzenegger* (N.D. Cal. 2010) goes to great lengths to underscore this oppression:

> [Gays and lesbians] have been executed for being homosexual, classified as mental degenerates, targeted by police, discriminated against in the workplace, censored, demonized as child molesters, excluded from the United States military, arrested for engaging in private sexual relations, and have repeatedly had their

[48] Brown 1995: 74

fundamental state constitutional rights stripped away by popular vote.[49] ... Discrimination against gay and lesbian individuals
in the United States has deep historical roots, stretching back at
least to colonial American times.[50] ... Gay and lesbian individuals also continue to face violence motivated by anti-gay bias. The
FBI reported 1,260 hate crime incidents based on perceived sexual orientation in 1998, and 1,265 in 2007. In 2008, a national
coalition of anti-violence social service agencies identified 29 mur-
ders motivated by the assailants' hatred of lesbian, gay, bisexual, or
transgender people.[51]

There is no denying the reality of this experience of discrimination,
violence, and antipathy. But in making these claims, which the brief
buttresses with expert testimony and statistics, legal advocates straightforwardly seek the Court to acknowledge the pain gays and lesbians
experience, and these advocates do so in the context of litigation that
seeks to overturn a prohibition on same-sex marriage. The more
painful and violent the history of discrimination, the more constitutional law ought to protect that group, or so this argument contends.

Brown's charge is that the very violence that oppresses a minority
is perversely appealed to in order to gain equal protection for them. It
is as if the oppression provides a constitutional good; here, a claim that
sexual orientation is indeed a suspect classification. The constitutional
requirement of a history of discrimination to trigger suspect status
means that every legal brief submitted on behalf of gays and lesbians
must rehearse this history of oppression. This is troubling precisely
because it is this oppression that the identity group seeks to end.

I am not simply suggesting that there is an irony in requiring a history of discrimination to be constitutionally protected from it. Rather,
the group invokes such discrimination to differentiate itself from others – blonds, a book club, or the PTA. In so differentiating themselves,
individuals of such groups must see themselves as first and foremost
victims of oppression. That is *who* they are, at least in so far as the Constitution is concerned. But these individuals are also human beings,
sharing the same desires, needs, and hopes as everyone else. Groups

---

[49] Plaintiff's Findings of Fact and Conclusions of Law, 9-CV-2292 (2010) at 144
[50] Ibid. at 148
[51] Ibid. at 151–2

who seek suspect class status must downplay these similarities focusing only on their differences – in this case, their victimhood status. Legal briefs do not seek to highlight the way these groups are like everyone else. That would be antithetical to the suspect class framework. This is because the point of this framework is to constitutionally elevate certain groups above others. The point is to explain why these groups are different from blonds or members of the PTA. The suspect class analysis does not invite the Court to consider all the ways in which gays and lesbians are like heterosexuals. That would undermine the purpose of this framework, a framework that requires that groups differentiate themselves from others to gain suspect class status.

To be sure, I am not suggesting that gays and lesbians or racial minorities "get over" this discrimination. In fact, it is the suspect class framework that stands to invite the charge that such groups are "playing the victim card." After all, they must characterize themselves as victims to be constitutionally protected under the Equal Protection Clause. My point is that the conventional constitutional logic of invalidating legislation on the basis of identity or class "is premised on" the group's exclusion. Exclusion is deployed to elevate the group constitutionally. Victimhood must be placed front and center to gain suspect class status.

If we simply reject this criterion, avoiding the need for groups to characterize themselves as victims above all else, all groups are perversely placed on the same constitutional footing. Without the marker of historical discrimination, blonds, PTA members, gays and lesbians, and racial minorities all become suspect classes. This turns the tiers-of-scrutiny framework on its head. Again, it is undeniable that certain groups have suffered from a history of discrimination. We problematically downplay that discrimination, even ignoring it, if the Court deems all and any kind of group a suspect class, deploying such a framework willy-nilly. Yet by focusing on that discrimination as current constitutional doctrine does, we downplay the way in which all individuals, no matter their group affiliation, are essentially the same. This is the dilemma that the suspect class framework creates. It cannot escape this vicious circle of victimhood and recognition. Without victimhood, there is no constitutional recognition. With victimhood, there is recognition but at the cost of forcing individuals in these groups to see themselves as victims rather than as just human beings like everyone else.

Immutability Reifies Identity

It is not just that gays and lesbians, racial minorities, and women must highlight their victimhood status – differentiate themselves from others; they must also claim that their differences are immutable. That is, the suspect class doctrine requires that there be some distinguishing or obvious trait that marks off the class. This trait cannot be one that an individual can simply alter or change like PTA membership or membership in a book club. There has to be some permanent, biological, or fixed nature to the trait, a trait that defines the class. This is why the Court requires that this trait be immutable. But this requirement of immutability points to the way in which identity reifies the relevant group while denying the experiences of individuals. It forcibly clumps individuals together under the banner of "women," "gay," or "black," making these differences fixed and static.

Drawing from Marxist and Foucauldian accounts of power, Brown also highlights the problematic way in which the language of identity views group membership in primordial terms. If the boundary or trait that defines the group must be fixed, those invoking identity to challenge legislation must invariably speak for a particular group: women, gays and lesbians, or blacks. As one scholar puts it: "Primordial identity is based on features that cannot be changed or questioned, they appear to be given by nature."[52] In doing so, the group's experiences become "natural" and set, often excluding the needs and desires of others.[53] For instance, championing *women's* equality – women's rights – often leaves out the experiences of poor women or women of color.

In turn, if membership in the class is immutable, this often denies the reality of intersectionality: ways in which individuals do not fit neatly into one group or another.[54] Kimberle Crenshaw's intersectionality objection to nondiscrimination law informs the essentializing

[52] Tempelman 1999: 17–18
[53] Brown 1995: 131, 2002: 427; *see also* Markell 2003
[54] *See, e.g.,* Appiah 2005, 1994, Crenshaw 1989, Ford 2002, Jordan-Zachery 2007, Alexander 2002

nature of identity. Crenshaw considers class action suits where employers discriminated against black women. At issue in these cases was
whether black women could be certified as a class to challenge their
discrimination as *black women* under employment law. In each case,
the court rejected class certification, because black women could neither make a claim on behalf of women (because white women were
not discriminated against) nor blacks (because black men were not
discriminated against). Crenshaw criticizes laws and policies, most
notably nondiscrimination legislation, for treating the listed identity
categories as bounded and fixed.

She argues that:

> Underlying this concept of discrimination is a view that the wrong
> which antidiscrimination law addresses is the use of race or gender
> factors to interfere with decisions that would otherwise be fair or
> neutral.... This narrow objective is facilitated by the top-down
> strategy of using a singular "but for" analysis to ascertain the effects
> of race or sex. Because the scope of antidiscrimination law is so
> limited, sex and race discrimination have come to be defined in
> terms of the experiences of those who are privileged *but for* their
> racial or sexual characteristics. Put differently, the paradigm of
> sex discrimination tends to be based on the experiences of white
> women; the model of race discrimination tends to be based on the
> experiences of the most privileged Blacks.[55]

In this way, the identity categories come to represent the experiences of only certain individuals or subgroups: in this case, white
women or black men. Now, Crenshaw's example is statutory and not
constitutional. She focuses on the language of identity in nondiscrimination legislation. I readily concede that the problem of intersectionality
arises with such legislation. However, my argument is about constitutional essentials, about how the Court deploys identity at the constitutional level to strike down laws and policies. Laws and policies may well
have to categorize on the basis of identity affiliation. In fact, this kind
of categorization may be necessary to do the antisubordination work.
This kind of work is rightly left to the relevant legislature. This book
criticizes the way the *Court* invokes identity to strike down laws and

---

[55] Crenshaw 1989: 151; *see also* Brown 2002: 426–7

policies. Making the Constitution and, in particular, the Equal Protection Clause about identity places the problem of intersectionality at the level of higher law. By deploying the suspect class inquiry and the immutability requirement that accompanies it to review legislation, the Court, composed of unelected judges who have life tenure, reifies a set of experiences. It is one thing to have legislatures make the difficult decisions about categorizing on the basis of identity. To place this inquiry on judges, as the conventional equal protection logic does, is more troubling.

Constitutionally, it makes it difficult for those who stand at the intersection of two distinct suspect classes to object to discriminatory laws and policies. Consider a law that discriminates against black women. One could very well argue that the law does not discriminate against a racial minority because it does not discriminate against all black individuals. And it also does not discriminate against women because it does not discriminate against all women. Does the Court, then, need to create a new suspect class – those encompassing black women – to meet this problem? And what happens when laws discriminate against lesbians but not gay men? Or black lesbians but not others? As long as the constitutional objection under the Equal Protection Clause is characterized in terms of suspect classes, this problem is seemingly unavoidable. There will always be a need to identify another suspect class when the current ones do not capture all individuals "within" that group. This is because the suspect class inquiry requires that there be a class, a common understanding of what it means to be in that identity group, what it means to share a distinguishing trait.

Brown argues that even when identity is attuned to diverse experiences, the nature of its legal recognition is one that is often ontologically given.[56] Identity claims are seen as things or objects. That is, constitutional law recognizes the identity group as already existing even though the boundaries of membership may be far from fixed. And this is exactly how the Court engages in its suspect class inquiry. The class – women or racial minorities – exists prior to the Court's declaration that they ought to be protected by the Equal Protection Clause and its

---

[56] Brown 1995: Ch. 3; *see also* Zivi 2005

conventional focus on heightened scrutiny. It is as if the suspect class is "out there" to be found and deemed important for purposes of equality under the law. If these groups exist prior to the individual, they leave individuals at the mercy of such membership boundaries. Understood in such fixed terms, identity claims undermine individuality.

This only further emphasizes the way individuals from these groups are different from everyone else. By prioritizing the class or group over the individual, the suspect class inquiry reinforces difference rather than underscoring commonality. It binds individuals to what Kwame Anthony Appiah calls identity "scripts," scripts that outline what it means to be black, gay, or a woman.[57] This binding only highlights the way *these* individuals are indeed different from everyone else.

Recent contemporary theory posits a more fluid and voluntary understanding of identity.[58] It repudiates the fixed conception of identity, arguing that such affiliations be seen as voluntarily chosen, even open to contestation and debate. This view of identity seeks to privilege the individual over the group. As Seyla Benhabib describes it:

> An individual must not be automatically assigned to a cultural, religious, or linguistic group by virtue of his or her birth. An individual's group membership must permit the *most extensive form of self-ascription and self-identification*; there will be many cases when such self-identifications are contested, but the state should not simply grant the right to define and control membership to the group at the expense of the individual. It is desirable that at some point in their adult lives individuals be asked whether they accept their continuing membership in their communities of origin.[59]

Yet this understanding of identity is at odds with the Court's immutability requirement for suspect class status. In *Plyler v. Doe* (1982), the Court invalidated a Texas law that prohibited children of undocumented immigrants from attending public school. The Court reasoned that the children of such immigrants constitute a kind of suspect class because they did not voluntarily choose their status as being

---

[57] Appiah 2005
[58] *See, e.g.*, Benhabib 2002, Gilroy 1993, Hall 1992, Parekh 2000
[59] Benhabib 2002: 131 (emphasis added)

undocumented.[60] However, the Court made clear that undocumented noncitizens who are adults do not count as a suspect class. "Unlike most of the classifications that [it has] recognized as suspect," the Court argues that an individual becomes an undocumented noncitizen "by virtue of entry into this country."[61] Their status as such is "the product of *voluntary* action."[62] If an individual may simply join a group, thereby "permitting the most extensive form of self-ascription and self-identification," as a constitutional matter the group cannot be a suspect class. This suggests that the relevant trait that defines the group is hardly fixed. In his memorandum to Congress, Eric Holder makes clear that the "scientific consensus accepts that sexual orientation is a characteristic that is immutable."[63]

Although recent legal scholarship criticizes the immutability requirement for being too rigid,[64] it does not thereby endorse a robust, voluntary conception of identity I have outlined here. For instance, David Richards, who is critical of the immutability requirement, argues for an understanding of sexuality that is similar to its religion counterpart. He suggests that just as religion need not be a biological accident of birth – individuals leave, join, debate, and reconsider their faiths – so too should we view sexuality. He says that

> The constitutional protection of religion never turned on its putative immutable and salient character . . . but on the traditional place of religion in the conscientious reasonable formation of one's moral identity in public and private life. . . . Claims by lesbian and gay persons today have . . . exactly the same ethical and constitutional force. . . . [T]hey are in their nature claims to a self-respecting personal and moral identity in public and private life through which they may reasonably express and realize their ethical convictions of the moral powers of friendship and love in a good, fulfilled, and responsible life.[65]

[60] *Plyler* at 219–21
[61] *Plyler* at 219, fn. 19
[62] *Plyler* at 219, fn. 19 (emphasis added)
[63] Letter from the Attorney General to Congress on Litigation Involving the Defense of Marriage Act, 2/23/2011. http://www.justice.gov/opa/pr/2011/February/11-ag-223.html
[64] *See, e.g.*, Halley 1994, Helfand 2009, Richards 1999, Stein 2001a
[65] Richards 1999: 93

This conception of sexuality moves toward a more fluid variety, but it does not go far enough. Richards still accords special status to it. He directly equates "gay identity" to religious identity, arguing that antigay positions are similar to ones that would despise a non-Christian religion.[66] Identity for him has "ethical force." Now, the Court has no need to hold that religious affiliation constitutes a suspect class, because the Free Exercise Clause of the First Amendment provides the constitutional hook for invalidating laws that discriminate on the basis of religion.[67] This is why as a doctrinal matter the Court has not had to reconsider immutability in light of religious affiliation. Laws that discriminate on the basis of religion would violate the Free Exercise Clause. Relevant to the criterion of immutability, Richards's point is that we can understand gay identity as a kind of religious affiliation. No one is born a particular religion. In fact, individuals often convert, leave, and even abandon their faith.

But this does not mean that religious affiliation is like membership in the PTA or a simple book club. These groups, to name just a few, are open to the "most extensive form of self-ascription." Here, individuals exist before such groups. We do not view such associations as anything other than mere voluntary collections of individuals, collections that individuals are free to reject, accept, or revise. But on Richards's account, they do not embody the normative and hence special role afforded to religion and, by comparison, sexuality.

This is precisely why he views sexuality in religious terms. Just as religion constitutes us in an important and deep way, so too does sexuality. The Sikh's decision to wear a turban is unlike the decision to wear a hat just as a gay man's decision to be intimate with another man is not the same as preferring vanilla to chocolate ice cream.[68] Although Richards's argument is about sexuality, it points to a more general view of identity. This view is not grounded in biology but in the idea that identity plays a central and formative role in our lives.

---

[66] Richards 1999: 93

[67] Amendment I, U.S. Constitution

[68] In his classic economic analysis of sex, Richard Posner considers sexuality akin to such a preference; Posner 1992: 123

This view is a familiar one in political theory. Bhikhu Parekh argues that cultural communities are unlike voluntary associations, in that "we are deeply shaped by our cultural communities and derive our values and ideals from them."[69] They shape and inform our identity rather than vice versa, providing preconditions to choice.[70] For example, as Alasdair MacIntyre writes, "[a]s such, I inherit from the past of my family, my city, my tribe, my nation, a variety of debts, inheritances, rightful expectations and obligations. These constitute the given of my life, my moral starting point."[71] Although these scholars focus on eth-nocultural rights, their characterizations have implications for under-standing immutability. Religious practices and identity are immutable because they are normative or "ethical" unlike affiliation in a vol-untary association or a mere preference. There is something special about religion, in the same way as there is something special about identity.

Currently, the Court does not consider gays and lesbians a suspect class.[72] But state supreme courts, including those of Iowa and Cali-fornia, have held that gays do count as a protected group under their respective state constitutions. These courts have invalidated their state prohibitions on same-sex marriage. In fact, although they shy away from the language of biological immutability, the Iowa and California state decisions still do not endorse a fully voluntary notion of sexuality. The California Supreme Court reasons: "Because a person's sexual orientation is so integral an aspect of one's identity, it is not appro-priate to require a person to repudiate or change his or her sexual orientation in order to avoid discriminatory treatment."[73] It is simply unfair for the state to ask gays and lesbians to change whom they are attracted to. Similarly, the Iowa Supreme Court contends that with a prohibition on same-sex marriage, "gay and lesbian individuals cannot

---

[69] Parekh 2000: 33
[70] *See, e.g.*, Kymlicka 1995, 1989, MacIntyre 1984, Taylor 1994
[71] MacIntyre 1984: 220
[72] Federal courts of appeals have argued that they are a suspect class: *Watkins v. U.S. Army* (9th Cir. 1988) (concluding that gays constitute a suspect class invalidating the military's explicit ban on homosexuals; this was before the military's Don't Ask, Don't Tell policy); the case was overturned en banc by the full Ninth Circuit. *Watkins v. U.S. Army* (9th Cir. 1989); *Windsor v. U.S.* (2nd Cir. 2012)
[73] *In re Marriage* (Ca. 2008) at 98

simultaneously fulfill their deeply felt need for a committed personal relationship, as influenced by their sexual orientation."[74] The Iowa Court goes on to say that being gay is "so central to a person's identity that it would be abhorrent for government to penalize a person for refusing to change [it]."[75]

Similarly, Jonathan Quong argues that identity claims ought to be seen as fundamental interests, similar, in fact, to an interest not to be murdered. These fundamental interests are

> logically prior to other interests: securing your fundamental interests is required before you can even begin to pursue your various *preferences*. Not being murdered, for example, is obviously a much more fundamental interest than going to the movies; in fact, it must logically be of higher priority to me, since I won't be able to go to the movies if I get murdered along the way.[76]

Hence, if an identity claim is "central to the claimant's sense of self, then the claimant will ground his argument by saying that a *fundamental* interest of his is at stake because the practice is so important to his identity."[77] This is exactly the view of sexuality that the Iowa and California decisions endorse.

The conventional interpretation of legal equality forces a court to proclaim that being gay is a fundamental rather than a contingent aspect of identity.[78] The Iowa and California opinions seem to close off a voluntary and open conception of identity. Gay individuals cannot alter their deeply felt attraction and love for someone of the same sex, and thus it is problematic to ask them to give it up. If such desire were not so deep-seated, perhaps the state could ask individuals to "prefer" someone of the opposite sex. Neither the Iowa nor California opinion uses the locution "sexual preference." Scholarly work that criticizes prohibitions on same-sex marriage invariably adopts the language of "sexual orientation" rather than "preference."[79] Consider

---

[74] *Varnum v. Brien* (Iowa 2009) at 30
[75] *Varnum v. Brien* (Iowa 2009) at 30
[76] Quong 2002: 310 (emphasis added)
[77] Quong 2002: 313
[78] *See, e.g.,* Nussbaum 2010: 120–32, Richards 2005, 1999, Roosevelt 2006.
[79] *See, e.g.,* Koppelman 2002, Nussbaum 2010, Richards 2005, 1999, Roosevelt 2006, Wolfson 2004

also that every major gay and lesbian organization characterizes the issue as one of combating discrimination on the basis of "sexual orientation."[80] This is telling. Preference implies the full range of choice; orientation does not. Orientation suggests that being gay is a fixed trait. The language of orientation undercuts a robust notion of "self-ascription" problematically reifying the identity group in line with the foregoing critique.

Ultimately, the conventional logic says that gays and lesbians cannot help who they are. They are simply, as a popular Lady Gaga song proclaims, "born that way."[81] This perversely stigmatizes the gay condition, fueling the nature–nurture debate.[82] The immutability requirement compels gays to see themselves as unfortunate victims of desires, desires that nature has foisted on them. Why can't such a desire be a mere preference? What is so problematic about simply preferring to date those of the same rather than opposite sex? These questions are unavoidable if we insist on deploying a suspect class analysis. This is why I prefer to deploy the language of "sexuality" to avoid this kind of critique.

As long as suspect class status requires that the identity affiliation – racial, sexual, or gender – is central to individuals in a way that other affiliations or preferences are not, it runs the risk of reifying them. My direct concern is not whether as a sociological matter identity affiliations provide unique contexts or preconditions for choice. This analysis is about the way in which equal protection jurisprudence views identity as importantly different from other voluntary associations or preferences. This view of identity would not be met by membership in the PTA, a book club, or one of many voluntary associations. These associations do not count as suspect classes. They are ordinary affiliations, failing to trigger the special "ethical convictions" that arise with religious or sexual identity. Simply put, the conventional

---

[80] Lambda Legal http://www.lambdalegal.org/issues/employment-workplace/; International Gay and Lesbian Human Rights Commission http://www.iglhrc.org/cgi-bin/iowa/theme/2.html; Human Rights Campaign http://www.hrc.org/issues/workplace/equal_opportunity.asp; GLAD (Gay and Lesbians Advocates and Defenders) http://www.glad.org/rights/c/anti-lgbt-discrimination

[81] Lady Gaga, "Born This Way." Streamline, Interscope, Kon Live (2011)

[82] *See generally* Stein 2001a

understanding of equal protection does not deem a suspect class as a voluntary collection of individuals. This runs the risk of essentializing the class, leaving individuals unable to contest, revise, or even reject it. In so doing, this threatens to undermine a robust notion of individuality.

But if the suspect class doctrine genuinely jettisoned the immutability requirement, treating the desire for someone of the same sex like any other preference, this would undermine the doctrine. It would leave all groups and affiliations on the same normative footing. If all groups – the PTA or the Rotary Club – thereby receive suspect class status, the Court would have to subject all legislation that discriminates against any group or preference to heightened scrutiny.

This undermines the very language of a suspect class. There is a normative and political cost in treating identity categories such as race, sex, and sexuality like any other voluntary affiliation. For a group to proclaim that the law has violated its rights, there must be a set of experiences that bind its members, experiences that exist prior to the individual. Otherwise, how would individuals find commonality to be a constitutionally protected class? In describing this dilemma in the particular case of women's rights, Linda Zerilli notes: "posited as a unified category given in advance of politics, 'women' generates exclusions; posited as a site of 'permanent openness and resignifiability,' 'women' precludes the possibility of speaking collectively."[83] The more we "open up" the boundaries of the identity group, the less powerful the impact of the identity claim.[84]

Treating identity as a mere preference confounds the suspect class framework. If there is no category of blacks, women, or gays and lesbians that exists prior to the individual, how can constitutional jurisprudence proclaim that *their* rights have been violated? How can the Court proclaim the existence of a suspect class to strike down discriminatory laws and policies if we deconstruct these identity groups? To be sure, "downgrading" sexual orientation to a preference does permit a robust notion of self-ascription, privileging the individual over the group. But if sexuality is a preference, and so can be easily changed,

---

[83] Zerilli 2005: 170
[84] *Cf.* Leeb 2008

why couldn't the state ask individuals to *prefer* someone of the opposite sex?[85]

Cass Sunstein argues that immutability ought not to be a lodestar for suspect class status.

> [I]t should not matter, for Equal Protection purposes, if skin color or gender could be changed through new technology. After all, discrimination on the basis of race would not become acceptable if scientists developed a serum through which blacks could become white.[86]

What, then, should matter? According to Sunstein, the "real question is whether legislation disadvantaging the relevant group is peculiarly likely to rest on illegitimate grounds; heightened scrutiny is a way of testing whether it does."[87] But by once again insisting on the use of heightened scrutiny, Sunstein must explain which groups trigger it. Doing so requires a list of criteria that would mark out those groups or classes that are "in" for constitutional protection and those that are "out." Jettisoning the immutability requirement would mean that a wide variety of voluntary associations and preferences now count as suspect classes. This would stand to undo the very idea of heightened scrutiny because all groups would be on the same constitutional footing. By failing to repudiate heightened scrutiny, Sunstein cannot escape the class-based focus of this clause.[88]

So, on one hand, deeming identity special threatens individuality, an individual's ability to revise, reject, or accept membership in the suspect class. On the other hand, deeming identity ordinary leaves the Court unable to proclaim that the law has violated their rights as a class. If there is nothing special about race, sex, or sexuality, the language of class seems to unravel. How can we even speak in the constitutional language of a suspect class if such a class does not really exist, only a group of disparate individuals akin to a voluntary book club? If constitutional jurisprudence insists on deploying an immutable

---

[85] *Cf.* Bedi 2007
[86] Sunstein 1994: 9
[87] Sunstein 1994: 9
[88] *See also* Balkin 2011: 234–7

or fixed nature of identity to object to laws and policies, this dilemma is inescapable.

Group Political Powerlessness Exacerbates the Counter-Majoritarian Difficulty

Political powerlessness is another important criterion to determine whether a group constitutes a suspect class. In a footnote in *U.S. v. Carolene Products Co.* (1938), the Court reasoned that we should be wary "when legislation appears on its face" to discriminate against "discrete and insular minorities."[89] Whereas a history of discrimination is a historical fact (i.e., whether individuals have been discriminated on the basis of a particular trait), political powerlessness is a present condition. It is about the failure of the demos to represent the interests of a particular class. For instance, in *Graham v. Richardson* (1971), the Court held that noncitizens constitute a suspect class, invalidating welfare legislation that discriminated between citizens and noncitizens. The Court cited *Carolene Products* reasoning that noncitizens are "a prime example of a 'discrete and insular' minority."[90] Obviously, by definition, noncitizens do not have political power. They cannot vote in state and federal elections.

John Ely famously expounds on this "discrete and insular" argument contending that the Court's role is to ensure that the democratic process represents all citizens.[91] Under this view, laws such as Jim Crow or a prohibition on same-sex marriage are democratically deficient, because they do not take into account the interests of racial minorities or gays and lesbians, respectively. In those cases in which the law discriminates against subordinated minorities, the Court ought to impose heightened scrutiny to ensure that the interests of the class are being taken into account. Central to Ely's account of judicial review is determining which groups or classes the Court ought to be worried about with regard to representation. Ely considers the case of individuals such as himself who have high blood pressure. He argues that it would be:

[89] *Carolene Products* at 153, fn. 4
[90] *Graham* at 372
[91] Ely 1980: 101–4

nonsense to treat a disqualification based on high blood pressure
as constitutionally suspicious. It is true that a majority of people
do not have it and probably are unaware of the extent to which
they are surrounded by people who do. It is also true, however, that
there are a good number of us – about 35 million in the United
States – interacting with you daily, perhaps even marrying your
children, and should one of you even announce your overdrawn
stereotype, let alone try to legislate on the basis of it, you would
rightly expect us to say "Hold it, Lester, there are lots of us with
high blood pressure who don't fit your generalization," or to bear
the consequences of keeping silent.[92]

However, according to Ely, it is appropriate to treat gays and lesbians
as a suspect class:

The reason homosexuals don't say "Hold it, Lester, *I'm* gay, and
my wrist's not the least bit limp," is that because of the prejudices of many of the rest of us there would be serious social costs
involved in such an admission. It is therefore a combination of the
factors of prejudice and hideability that renders classifications that
disadvantage homosexuals suspicious.[93]

If the Court's role is to step in when the majority fails to represent
the interests of a group, this requires that the law single out those
groups whose interests may not be represented. So, while the majority
will represent the interests of those with high blood pressure or those
with a certain hair or eye color, it may fail to represent the interests
of gays and lesbians. This is what makes gays and lesbians a "discrete
and insular" minority. The "discrete and insular" criterion is central
to Ely's representation-reinforcement theory of judicial review. It is
precisely because a majority may not represent a group's interests, for
instance, acting on negative stereotypes, that suspect status and hence
higher scrutiny are triggered.

But if the Court strikes down laws and policies by invoking this
"discrete and insular" argument, constitutional discourse has the
potential to exacerbate the counter-majoritarian difficulty. Most scholarly work on this difficulty seeks to extinguish it. Scholars challenge

[92] Ely 1980: 163
[93] Ely 1980: 163

both assumptions of the counter-majoritarian difficulty. On one hand, they argue that when the Court invalidates laws and policies, it reflects rather than contravenes majoritarian preferences.[94] On the other hand, they argue that legislative decisions often do not reflect majority preferences.[95]

What has been undertheorized in this literature is an analysis of how the Court strikes down laws and policies. By invoking identity, and in particular the discrete and insular criterion, I argue that the discourse of rights exacerbates the sting of the counter-majoritarian difficulty. In striking down democratically enacted legislation, the Court is already acting counter to the majority. This is what makes the counter-majoritarian difficulty a difficulty. But the discrete and insular criterion makes this difficulty worse, because the Court strikes down legislation by invoking a particular group or suspect class. The Court invalidates a law for failing to take into account the interests of a particular group. This frames the constitutional objection in possibly divisive terms. Scholarly work suggests that identity rights have the potential to frustrate deliberative democracy.[96] Much of this work primarily takes aim at ethnocultural rights encompassing rights to self-government and accommodation,[97] rights with which this book is not concerned. Now this is not to imply that groups make no contribution to democracy. Amy Gutmann suggests "mutual identification makes political organization easier," aiding in aggregating and mobilizing individuals.[98] My focus is on the democratic deficiency of constitutional objections to discriminatory laws and policies grounded in the language of identity.

To contend that a prohibition on same-sex marriage is invalid because it harms gays and lesbians makes the discourse about a particular group. According to the standard view of deliberative democracy, an objection ought to "be recognizably moral in form and mutually acceptable in content."[99] Said differently, deliberative democracy

---

[94] *See, e.g.*, Ackerman 1993, Dahl 1957, Graber 2002, Powe 2000
[95] *See e.g.*, Lemieux and Watkins 2009: 36–7, M. Shapiro, 1966
[96] *See, e.g.*, Elshtain 1993, Quong 2002, Schlesinger 1992, Simon 1999, Waldron 2000
[97] *See* Quong 2002, Waldron 2000
[98] Gutmann 2003: 57
[99] Gutmann and Thompson 1996: 57

requires that we advance arguments that all can reasonably accept, an argument that runs through the literature on public reason.[100] It rules out arguments that are sectarian or based on self-interest. A focus on gays and lesbians, however, seems to undermine this deliberative requirement. Jean Bethke Elshtain puts it (provocatively to say the least) in the following way: "To the extent that citizens begin to retribalize into ethnic or other 'fixed-identity groups,' democracy falters. Any possibility for human dialogue, for democratic communication and commonality, vanishes as so much froth on the polluted sea of phony equality."[101]

The logic of this discourse separates members in a polity. It makes the constitutional objection about the interests of a particular group, not the interests of all.[102] This is exactly what Ely's representation-reinforcement theory of judicial review does. It invites the Court to invalidate laws and policies that do not take into account the interests of a particular group – namely, a "discrete and insular" minority. This straightforwardly makes the constitutional objection not about the interests of all citizens but the interests of a particular class. This stands to frame the objection in terms that do not apply to everyone but only to those individuals in the constitutionally elevated group or class.

Perhaps those who are unsympathetic to deliberative democracy will simply not care that the Court exacerbates the sting of the counter-majoritarian difficulty by invoking the suspect class doctrine. They may suggest it is perfectly fine that the Court is making a bad situation worse by invoking the interests of a particular group. This is what a court ought to do. But this response is shortsighted. We ought to care not just about the result – finding racist and homophobic laws unconstitutional – but how the Court arrives at it. This is because irrespective of one's position on the value of deliberative democracy, the conventional suspect class framework stands to invite the "special rights" retort. It invites the charge that "judicial activism" is afoot. We all ought to care about this precisely because this kind of retort poses

---

[100] *See, e.g.*, Ackerman 1980, Forst 2002, Habermas 1990, 2001, Larmore 1987, Rawls 1996 [1993]; *see also* Scanlon 1998: 202
[101] Elshtain 1993: 75
[102] *See* Mason 2010

political problems for court decisions that invalidate equality-infringing laws and policies.

If a ban on same-sex marriage is unconstitutional because it discriminates against a certain "discrete and insular" class, that group seems to benefit.[103] This, in turn, invites detractors to say that if we are singling out gays and lesbians for recognition, why not other groups? This triggers the "us" versus "them" pathology of the "special rights" retort, a retort that is often made by those who defend prohibitions on same-sex marriage.[104] By emphasizing the interests of a minority, the conventional logic highlights the counter-majoritarian difficulty. It suggests that the Court is not taking into account the interests of all, only those of the relevant group in striking down a prohibition on same-sex marriage. After all, this is the point of Ely's argument.

The "special rights" retort is seemingly powerful because it turns the minority into the oppressors and the majority, who passed the discriminatory legislation, into their victims.[105] The retort threatens to make constructive debate difficult if not impossible.[106] In his criticism of conventional equal protection theory, Christopher Kutz puts this point in the following way: "[the language of group identity] threatens to (and does) invite a politics of zero sum, interest group competition, rather than a politics of common aspiration and collective achievement."[107] In *Romer v. Evans* (1996), the Court invalidated a Colorado amendment that prohibited local ordinances from protecting gays and lesbians as a class. Colorado sought to justify the state amendment by arguing that the provision "does no more than deny homosexuals special rights."[108] In his dissent, Justice Scalia affirms this line of reasoning. He takes aim at the "discrete and insular" argument suggesting that gays are far from powerless:

> [B]ecause those who engage in homosexual conduct tend to reside in disproportionate numbers in certain communities [citations

---

[103] *See* Gerstmann 1999: 38–9
[104] *See generally* Cahill 2004: 70–2, Goldberg 1995
[105] *See generally* Dudas 2005, 2008, Goldberg-Hiller 1998, Goldberg-Hiller and Milner 2003, Schacter 1994
[106] Bybee and Gosh 2009: 144–5
[107] Kutz 2003: 9
[108] *Romer* at 626

omitted], and of course care about homosexual-rights issues much more ardently than the public at large, they possess political power much greater than their numbers, both locally and statewide. Quite understandably, they devote this political power to achieving not merely a grudging social toleration, but full social acceptance, of homosexuality.[109]

By making the constitutional objection to antigay laws about the political powerlessness of gays and lesbians, the Court invites this kind of retort – one in which gays turn out to be the oppressors and the majority their victims. The language of identity frames the objection in divisive terms.

To be sure, it will not suffice to say that this is about equal rights, not special rights. For once we frame the equal protection violation in terms of identity, we cannot escape the special rights retort. Evan Gerstmann makes a powerful case that prohibitions on same-sex marriage violate a "fundamental right to marry the person of his or her choice."[110] He argues that this does not amount to a "special" rights claim.[111] Rather, this argument is about "equality instead of difference," framed "in terms of aspiration instead of victimhood."[112]

But same-sex marriage detractors would no doubt say that gays and lesbians are not being denied equal rights under a regime that prohibited same-sex marriage. They, like everyone else, have a right to marry someone of the opposite sex, if they so choose. They simply may not marry someone of the same sex. After all, the ban is on same-sex marriage, not gay marriage. A gay man may marry a lesbian. Similarly, a ban on plural marriage does not deny individuals equal rights. Such a ban just says that no one may marry more than one person.

The only way to avoid this conclusion is to argue that gays are born with the desire to be with someone of the same sex; this is a fundamental desire, unlike plural marriage enthusiasts, an argument I consider in more detail in the final chapter. Being gay is not a choice, whereas preferring to marry more than one person is. The Court

---

[109] *Romer* at 646
[110] Gerstmann 2008: 116
[111] Gerstmann 2008: 116
[112] Gerstmann 2008: 116

must reason that gays and lesbians are constitutionally special in a way that plural marriage enthusiasts are not. Therefore, gays and lesbians simply cannot choose to marry someone of the opposite sex. Being gay has "ethical force." But in making this argument, we invariably invite the "special rights" retort and the problems with the criterion of immutability.

Under the conventional equal protection challenge, a prohibition on a same-sex marriage does not violate the equal rights of everyone. That is the important point. After all, heterosexuals may still get married. Such a prohibition only violates the equal rights of *gays and lesbians*. This is a "universal rights applied to minorities" (URAM) argument. Here, the universal right is a right to marry. A straight majority could not make a URAM claim on behalf of itself in challenging such homophobic legislation. As applied to heterosexuals, there is no infraction of any alleged universal right. This is crucial, for it means that gays and lesbians must proclaim that their rights – and not anyone else's – are being violated. Gays and lesbians must single themselves out as a group worthy of constitutional elevation under the suspect class framework. In doing so, we invite detractors to make the minority (here, gays and lesbians) out to be the oppressors.

In turn, the identity approach has the potential to cause a democratic backlash. When the Hawaii Supreme Court became the first court explicitly to question the constitutionality of a prohibition on same-sex marriage in 1993 under a state constitution,[113] many states amended their constitutions or passed statutes declaring marriage between same-sex couples void or invalid. The federal government passed the Defense of Marriage Act, the federal law that does not recognize valid same-sex marriages under state law. When the California State Supreme Court invalidated that state's prohibition on same-sex marriage on grounds of sexual orientation discrimination, it invited Proposition 8, a state amendment overturning the decision.

Consider that *Brown* did not desegregate schools. Even *Brown II* (*Brown v. Board of Education* (1955)) failed to do so, proffering the standard of "all deliberative speed."[114] Gerald Rosenberg's classic work

---

[113] *Baehr v. Lewin* (Hawaii 1993)
[114] *Brown II* at 301

on the subject contends that these decisions caused retrenchment from
the American South.[115] What is interesting for purposes of this chapter
is that *Brown* informs the core feature of the logic of special rights.
Justice Warren's short opinion focuses on the fact that segregation in
education was (surprise, surprise) bad for black children:

> To separate them from others of similar age and qualifications
> solely because of their race generates a feeling of inferiority as to
> their status in the community that may affect their hearts and minds
> in a way unlikely ever to be undone. The effect of this separation
> on their educational opportunities was well stated by a finding in
> the Kansas case by a court which nevertheless felt compelled to
> rule against the Negro plaintiffs.[116]

The constitutional infirmity with segregation, then, is its effect on black
children. The interests of black children were not taken into account.
This makes the objection about identity – here, the law's effect on a
racial minority.

By doing so, Justice Warren invites the majority at that time to
view the decision's logic as imposing black preferences over white
ones, failing the deliberative requirement that we advance arguments
that all can accept. The objection to segregation is made in terms of
an identity claim – here, the deleterious effects of segregation on a
racial minority. This all too easily invites racists to balk, contending
that the Court's holding does not concern the democratic majority,
only the relevant identity group in line with the "discrete and insular"
argument.

I am not making a mere causal claim here: had the Court invalidated racial segregation on an alternative approach, this would have
been more efficacious than doing so on the basis of identity. Independent of its effects (or lack there of), *Brown* stands as an iconic,
"symbolic" case in constitutional jurisprudence.[117] This book questions this significance by critiquing not the holding but the reasoning
deployed by Warren's opinion, an opinion that makes the constitutional objection about identity. The logic of *Brown* is flawed precisely

---

[115] Rosenberg 1991; *see also* Klarman, 1994a, 1994b
[116] *Brown* at 494
[117] Rosenberg 2004; *see also* Bork 1990: 77

because it frames the objection in terms of a particular group or class. In so doing, it is conceptually linked to the special rights retort.

And this identity-based logic stands at the center of the constitutional objection to prohibitions on same-sex marriage. Rosenberg criticizes it, suggesting that

> [s]ame sex marriage proponents had not built a successful movement that could persuade their fellow citizens to support their cause and pressure political leaders to change the law. Without such a movement behind them, winning these court cases sparked an enormous backlash. They confused a judicial pronouncement of rights with the attainment of those rights.[118]

Although Rosenberg does not connect this backlash to the retort of "special rights," his logic informs my analysis here. If a prohibition on same-sex marriage is problematic because it discriminates against gays and lesbians, this makes the argument about that particular identity group. It permits detractors to view (perversely to be sure) gays as the oppressors, imposing their preferences on the straight majority. From a democratic perspective, this will invariably make it more difficult to persuade fellow citizens about the unconstitutionality of such a prohibition. The conventional logic pits *them* (gays and lesbians) against "us" (everyone else).

This failure to persuade may lie in the fact that, as Rosenberg argues, rights claims are often empty. Like the tiers-of-scrutiny framework, they also turn to be devoid of content, inviting subjective considerations. This is why Rosenberg characterizes rights claims as mere preferences, preferences that can be for anything:

> It follows from this definition of rights as preferences that arguing for or protecting certain practices by calling them rights will have no effect on the evaluation of that practice. Since rights are merely a label that adds nothing to the underlying claim, what matters is the substance of the claim, not how it is labeled. So, for example, Supreme Court decisions finding a constitutional right to

---

[118] Rosenberg 2006: 813; *see also* Klarman 2005; for an argument that scholars overstate the backlash thesis with regard to gay rights, see Keck 2009

something should make no appreciable difference in how Americans react to whatever practice has been constitutionalized.[119]

Proponents of same-sex marriage will view the desire to marry someone of the same sex as a rights issue. Opponents will view it as just a preference akin to the desire to marry more than one person or the desire to marry one's adult sibling. The point is that there is no genuine way to decide who is "correct," precisely because rights claims are empty. So when a court invalidates a prohibition on same-sex marriage by taking into account the interests of gays and lesbians but does not invalidate prohibitions on plural marriage or adult incestuous ones, detractors will invariably view the decision as affirming special rights, as a problematic instance of "judicial activism." After all, the Court seems to care about some groups but not others. The "discrete and insular" criterion invites the Court to do just that, treating certain groups as constitutionally special but not others.

Irrelevance Ignores the Salience of Identity

The final criterion the Court deploys to determine whether a group is suspect is whether the group's characteristic is irrelevant to one's ability to contribute to society.[120] For instance, in *Frontiero*, a plurality of the Court held that "the sex characteristic frequently bears no relation to ability to perform or contribute to society."[121] Similarly, in *Windsor v. U.S.*(2nd Cir. 2012), the appeals court held that gays and lesbians count as a suspect class.[122] In *Windsor*, the court made clear that sexual orientation is a trait that is irrelevant to one's ability to contribute to society: "homosexuality has no relation to aptitude or ability to contribute to society."[123]

The criterion of irrelevance is in one sense uncontroversial. It is undoubtedly true that being black or gay or a woman bears no relationship to one's ability to contribute to society. There is nothing

---

[119] Rosenberg 2009: 13
[120] I argue elsewhere that this criterion is inconsistent with its "discrete and insular" counterpart; Bedi 2013
[121] *Frontiero* at 686
[122] See also note 72
[123] *Windsor* at 182

intrinsic about race, sex, or sexuality – or for that matter, hair or eye color – that bears on one's abilities. However, to suggest that race and hair color are irrelevant characteristics masks the way in which race is still salient in our society. We do not live in a color-blind world. Even if race does not intrinsically track a kind of hierarchy or status, many individuals certainly believe it does. It is a social fact that we do not view race as we do hair or eye color, precisely because it matters whether one is black, white, or brown. This goes for sex and sexuality as well. Many (and maybe even most) individuals still believe that sex intrinsically tracks certain kinds of abilities or characteristics. Males ought to be masculine, aggressive, and breadwinners, and females must be feminine, passive, and caregivers. We unfortunately live in a world where such characteristics have salience, which turns out to subordinate women or racial minorities

A recent experiment by two economists showed that racist views still pervade the labor market.[124] In the experiment, résumés were sent to various help-wanted ads in Boston and Chicago. The study randomly assigned to each résumé a name suggesting that the applicant was white (e.g., Emily, Greg) or black (e.g., Lakisha, Jamal). If employers considered race to be irrelevant like hair or eye color, the callbacks should have been roughly equal for both groups. But, as it turns out, the résumés with white-sounding names received 50 percent more callbacks than their black counterparts. In fact, the study found that this disparity was "uniform across occupation, industry, and employer size."[125] This means that even though race is irrelevant to one's ability to contribute to society, many still believe it is relevant. Racism, then (both current and past), has put racial minorities at a social, economic, and, of course, political disadvantage. This is why they are a "discrete and insular" group. Adopting a color-blind or formal equality approach prevents the relevant legislature from altering or, at a minimum, even mitigating this disadvantage. Erwin Chemerinksy criticizes the formal equality approach for just this reason, arguing that the "Court has failed to realize that there is a world of difference

---

[124] Bertrand and Mullainathan 2004
[125] Bertrand and Mullainathan 2004: 991

between the government using race to subordinate minorities and using race to benefit minorities and advance equality."[126]

Ultimately, there is a deep tension between an emphasis on irrelevance and an emphasis on being "discrete and insular." On one hand, "discrete and insular" assumes a norm of antisubordination. It identifies those groups that are indeed political minorities in the democratic process. The Court's role is to ensure that laws and policies adequately represent the interests of women, racial minorities, or gays and lesbians. But by invoking the interests of a particular group, the Court exacerbates the counter-majoritarian difficulty. It makes the constitutional objection about a particular group.

On the other hand, irrelevance assumes a commitment to formal equality. It problematically elides the fact the certain identity categories have salience. Treating race, sex, or sexuality as irrelevant problematically invites a constitutional commitment to formal equality where laws and policies ought to be race, sex, or sexuality blind. Legal scholars (and most notably critical legal scholars) have criticized the doctrinal emphasis on formal equality.[127] By suggesting that these characteristics are irrelevant, the Court forecloses the possibility of deploying these very categories to remedy subordination. After all, it is difficult for laws and policies to combat racial or sexual inequality and subordination without invoking race or sex.

In interpreting the Equal Protection Clause, scholarly work ultimately endorses either the "discrete and insular," antisubordination argument or its irrelevance, formal equality counterpart.[128] The clause seems beset by these two norms of equality, norms we will revisit throughout the book. Both are problematic. The discrete and insular argument needlessly makes the constitutional objection about a particular group or class, and its irrelevance counterpart problematically masks the need for invoking identity. An equal protection framework that triggers higher scrutiny for laws and policies that discriminate against a subordinated group exacerbates the counter-majoritarian

[126] Chemerinsky 2010: 269
[127] *See, e.g.*, Gotanda 1991, Parker 1996, Siegel 2000, Law 1984, Littleton 1987, Fiss 1976
[128] *See, e.g.*, Colker 1986, Balkin and Siegel 2003

difficulty. It makes the constitutional objection about the interests of a particular class rather than the interests of all. A framework that triggers higher scrutiny for all laws and policies that invoke race or sex or any other such characteristic draws too broad of a constitutional brushstroke. It calls into question policies such as affirmative action, policies that seek to remedy the status of subordinated racial minorities. The next chapter expounds on an alternative understanding of legal equality.

2   A POWERS REVIEW

By making the equal protection objection about suspect classes, the Court needlessly invites the problems that come with invoking identity. I say "needlessly," because there is a better way to understand equality under the law, a way that avoids the dilemma of identity. Constitutional law already deems inadmissible certain kinds of reasons or rationales, what I call a "powers review." This kind of review is already immanent in the Court's jurisprudence. Once we focus on it, the Court no longer needs higher scrutiny, strict or otherwise. The central insight of a powers review is that laws and policies are unconstitutional not because they discriminate against a particular class or on the basis of a particular identity classification (e.g., race, sex, or sexuality) but because they are based on reasons that are inadmissible. A powers review is a constitutional review of the state's power to pass laws and policies under the Equal Protection Clause. This chapter outlines the logic of this approach, leaving Parts II and III to expound and clarify it.

The core problem with the tiers-of-scrutiny approach is that it does not make clear what counts as an inadmissible rationale or reason. Drawing on some of the synergy between liberal neutrality and constitutional doctrine, this chapter argues that these rationales include animus or a particular moral or religious conception of the good life. Once we realize that laws and policies are unconstitutional if they are based on such rationales, we no longer need heightened scrutiny. By explaining what the Court is looking for when it seeks to invalidate legislation under the Equal Protection Clause, such scrutiny turns out obsolete. This is the crucial implication of teasing out the nature of a powers review.

Like a rational review standard, a powers review also applies to all laws and policies. And like rational review, it does not require that the law discriminate against a particular class. This book looks in part to those cases in which the Court strikes down laws under rational review because in such cases the law invokes a constitutionally inadmissible rationale. But a powers review is not mere shorthand for the current rational review standard. The current standard does not make clear that the Court's role is simply to invalidate those laws that invoke such inadmissible rationales. The language of rational review, like intermediate or strict scrutiny, asks the Court to decide whether a purpose or rationale is legitimate, important, or compelling, in addition to deciding the requisite tailoring requirements. A powers review does not frame the constitutional question as ascertaining what qualifies as a legitimate rationale. The Court itself never makes clear what counts as a legitimate rationale. It is hard to decipher what the constitutional definition of "legitimate" means. If anything, as one scholar rightly remarks, the "guidance the Court has provided has more often focused on what is illegitimate."[1]

In this way, the rational review standard may be a powers review only half-consciously realized. Constitutional law already recognizes that certain kinds of reasons are illegitimate under this standard. Those rationales that are illegitimate – animus or mere moral considerations – are therefore constitutionally inadmissible. Fully appreciating this, as this chapter seeks to do, means that the Court does not need the rational, intermediate, and strict scrutiny framework to invalidate equality infringing laws and policies. Invalidating laws that invoke a constitutionally inadmissible rationale is sufficient. The thrust of this chapter is that the Court does not need a more searching examination to decide that laws are based on such inadmissible justifications.

Liberal neutrality holds that there are certain kinds of reasons that are nonpublic. Laws and policies ought not to be based on them. This is what Lawrence Solum calls an "exclusionary" account of public reason or public justification. It is "exclusionary" because it does not permit all justification to count as legitimate.[2] Ronald Den Otter powerfully expounds on this "exclusionary" approach by arguing that it

[1] Forde-Mazrui 2011: 303
[2] Solum 1993

is "the best interpretation of an ideal of public justification."[3] I fully
realize that drawing the line between public and nonpublic reasons can
be controversial. Again, this book is not about defending this line in
any philosophical or abstract way. Rather, and this has gone largely
unnoticed by scholarly work, I seek to show that constitutional law,
in line with some features of liberal neutrality, already excludes certain kinds of reasons from the realm of lawmaking. Under a powers
review, the constitutional prohibition that no state shall "deny to any
person . . . equal protection of the laws" means that a state may not
act on these reasons. What are these reasons? Current constitutional
doctrine holds that the state may not act on justifications that invoke
certain conceptions of the good life or that are based on mere animus
or hostility, or so this chapter argues. Central to enforcing these justificatory constraints is ensuring that the state does not proffer a reason in
bad faith. After all, if the state can simply "come up" with a reason or
justification for a law after the fact; it can undo a powers review. This
chapter works out each of these constraints.

CERTAIN CONCEPTIONS OF THE GOOD LIFE

First, and this may be the most salient feature of liberal neutrality, a
powers review rules out reasons that are based on certain conceptions
of the good life.[4] John Rawls defines a conception of the good as what
"is valuable in human life."[5] This is a belief about what counts as a
good, appropriate, or worthwhile life.

> Thus, a conception of the good normally consists of more or less
> determinate scheme of final ends, that is, ends we want to realize
> for their own sake. . . . [6]

A conception of the good is a belief about privileging a certain way of
living over another for its own sake. Often, these conceptions of the
good are based on religious or moral doctrines. Public reason contends

---

[3] Den Otter 2009: 139
[4] *See, e.g.*, Ackerman 1980, Den Otter 2009, Larmore 1987, Rawls 1996 [1993], Raz 1986:
    110–57, Solum 1993
[5] Rawls 1996 [1993]: 19
[6] Rawls 1996 [1993

that these conceptions are illegitimate grounds for state legislation. That is, the state may not pass laws and policies grounded in the belief that a particular way of life is *intrinsically* better than another. These beliefs are perfectionist ones, because they point to what counts as a decent or virtuous existence. They seek to articulate how we as individuals can live more perfect lives. Precisely because individuals may disagree over the inherent worthiness of certain ways of living over others, such beliefs are not in principle shareable by all. Liberal neutrality eschews them.

This does not mean that the state should be "neutral regarding its effect on various conceptions the good."[7] Laws and policies may well adversely affect a particular conception of the good. For instance, a law that prohibited assault would no doubt affect someone who believes that assaulting others is a worthwhile life. Liberal neutrality is about the justification of laws and policies not their effect on individuals. As Jonathan Quong puts it:

> So long as the *reasons* underlying the central principles of the state are acceptable to all reasonable citizens, then the liberal principle of legitimacy is realized. Again, because reasonable people disagree about the good life, the state will have to eschew any appeals to conceptions of the good in justifying its core principles. Put another way, only *public reasons* – reasons that are acceptable to all reasonable citizens – can legitimate the coercive use of state power over its citizens.[8]

So, a law that prohibits assault would be legitimate as long as it was based on reasons that could genuinely be shared by all such as preventing harm.[9] The crucial point is that this kind of law does not rest on the belief about the inherent goodness of a particular way of life. Rather, it rests on the idea that not assaulting others has extrinsic or public benefits, benefits that accrue to others not simply to the person who fails to assault.

Under a powers review, the state violates the Equal Protection Clause when it passes legislation on the idea that certain ways of life are good "for their own sake." This, in turn, is often based on moral or

---

[7] Quong 2004: 233
[8] Quong 2004: 233; *see also* Larmore 1987: 44
[9] *See generally* Bedi 2009

religious precepts. In *Lawrence v. Texas* (2003), the Court invalidated same-sex sodomy laws, reasoning, in part, that "morals legislation" is unconstitutional. Writing for the majority, Justice Anthony Kennedy held that sodomy is protected under a constitutional right to privacy. Most of the opinion focuses on this argument. I do not analyze it here. Relevant to the powers review I elucidate, the Court also holds that a law fails rational review if based solely on moral considerations. Toward the end of the opinion, Justice Kennedy quotes Justice John Paul Stevens's dissent in *Bowers v. Hardwick* (1986), an earlier case that had upheld sodomy laws. *Lawrence* explicitly relies on Stevens's words to invalidate the sodomy statute:

> Our prior cases make two propositions abundantly clear. First, the fact that the governing majority in a State has traditionally viewed a particular practice *as immoral is not a sufficient reason for upholding a law prohibiting the practice*; neither history nor tradition could save a law prohibiting miscegenation from constitutional attack. Second, individual decisions by married persons, concerning the intimacies of their physical relationship, even when not intended to produce offspring, are a form of "liberty" protected by the Due Process Clause of the Fourteenth Amendment. Moreover, this protection extends to intimate choices by unmarried as well as married persons.[10]

This is the crux of the *Lawrence* decision. It not only expands the right of privacy to include gay sex but also, relevant to a powers review, deems constitutionally inadmissible laws and policies prohibiting a practice based simply on the idea that a majority finds it immoral.

By quoting Stevens's dissent, the *Lawrence* Court informs a powers review where such moral rationales are unconstitutional. The opinion states that morality is "not [a] sufficient reason for upholding a law prohibiting the practice [of sodomy]."[11] It does not say that laws that interfere with fundamental rights such as the right to privacy may not be based on morals. In fact, the Court states that the gay sodomy statute furthers no "legitimate state interest."[12] This is undoubtedly

[10] *Lawrence* at 577–8 (quoting *Bowers* at 216 (1986), dissenting) (emphasis added)
[11] *Lawrence* at 577
[12] *Lawrence* at 578

the language of rational review – applying to all laws and policies. The majority could have said that the statute furthers no "compelling state interest," thereby leaving the door open for perfectionist rationales to justify non-fundamental-interest-violating laws, but it did not.

The Court did not subject the sodomy law to heightened scrutiny under this prong of the analysis. Rational review was sufficient to invalidate it. The powers review I propose here informs what constitutional law already recognizes as the "police powers" of the state. Traditionally, these powers have included the health, safety, and morals of the public.[13] *Lawrence* repudiates the morals component of these powers.

But this argument is not solely present in *Lawrence*. Suzanne Goldberg spends an entire article arguing that *Lawrence* merely makes explicit this ban on morals legislation, a ban that was already immanent in the Court's earlier jurisprudence.[14] Goldberg argues that:

> Rather than representing a break with tradition, *Lawrence* reflected the Court's long-standing jurisprudential discomfort with explicit morals-based rationales for lawmaking. Notwithstanding its ubiquitous rhetorical endorsements of government's police power to promote morality, it turns out that the Court has almost never relied exclusively and overtly on morality to justify government action. Indeed, since the middle of the twentieth century, the Court has never relied exclusively on an explicit morals-based justification in a majority opinion that is still good law.[15]

This book takes seriously Goldberg's argument in working out the implications of a powers approach. So although the state may act on reasons relating to health and safety, it may not act on only moral justifications, an argument I elaborate on in my previous work.[16] Important here is that morals legislation can be understood as legislation based on a conception of the good life – in this case, the belief that gay sex is morally wrong or intrinsically inferior to its heterosexual counterpart. Morals legislation is legislation that is not based on extrinsic or public benefits but on the idea that a particular way of life is simply better for

---

[13] Brest et al. 2006: 430
[14] Goldberg 2004b
[15] Goldberg 2004b: 1234–1236
[16] Bedi 2009: Ch. 7, 2005

the individual who practices it. Morals legislation is best understod as legislation based on perfectionist reasons.

Lawrence makes clear that "[t]hese matters, involving the most intimate and personal choices a person may make in a lifetime . . . are central to the liberty protected by the Fourteenth Amendment."[17] This liberty entails the freedom "to define one's own concept of existence, of meaning, of the universe, and of the mystery of human life."[18] This "concept of existence" looks an awful like a conception of the good life. The language of "mystery" and "meaning" point to the idea that these beliefs are not about what has extrinsic or public benefits. Hence, the Court's concession in an earlier case that homosexuality counts as a "victimless" crime.[19] Rather, these beliefs are about what lives have intrinsic value, beliefs that *Lawrence* holds the state may not impose on its members. Under this reading, *Lawrence* informs a core idea of liberal neutrality that individuals ought to be free to define their "own concept of meaning."

Justice Scalia's dissent supports this reading of *Lawrence*. Justice Scalia focuses on the real import of the decision when he writes that most "of the [majority] opinion has no relevance to its actual holding – that the Texas statute 'furthers no legitimate state interest which can justify' its application to petitioners under rational-basis review."[20] Justice Scalia believes that the majority opinion renders constitutionally suspect laws "against fornication, bigamy, adultery, adult incest, bestiality, and obscenity."[21] In so far as these laws are based on the idea that some way of living is worthwhile for its own sake, Scalia may be right. The final chapter connects this kind of slippery slope argument to a powers review. In particular, that chapter analyzes the constitutionality of the ban on plural marriage in light of the argument of this book.

In fact, Justice O'Connor's concurrence in *Lawrence* focuses just on the meaning of the Equal Protection Clause. For her, the question is "whether, under the Equal Protection Clause, moral disapproval is a legitimate state interest to justify *by itself* a statute that bans

---

[17] *Lawrence* at 574
[18] *Lawrence* at 574
[19] *Bowers v. Hardwick* (1986) at 195
[20] *Lawrence* at 586, dissenting
[21] *Lawrence* at 599, dissenting

homosexual sodomy, but not heterosexual sodomy."[22] O'Connor answers in the negative. According to her, "[m]oral disapproval of this group, like a bare desire to harm the group, is an interest that is insufficient to satisfy rational basis review under the Equal Protection Clause."[23] O'Connor importantly articulates moral disapproval and animus as two reasons or rationales that are constitutionally inadmissible. The state does not have the power to act on them under the Equal Protection Clause. She makes clear that the Court has "never held that moral disapproval, without any other asserted state interest, is a sufficient rationale under the Equal Protection Clause to justify a law that discriminates among groups of persons."[24] Although O'Connor says that moral disapproval or animus must be aimed at "groups," the Court makes clear in *Village of Willowbrook v. Olech*, a case I discuss later in the chapter, that animus against a lone individual is also unconstitutional.

By so invaliding morals legislation, the Court effectively suggests that as a constitutional matter, laws and policies may not be based on certain conceptions of the good, on what the state deems as a worthwhile or meaningful life for its own sake. The language of "without any other asserted state interest" points to the idea that the state may not act on perfectionist morals beliefs about what ways of living are intrinsically good. A mere belief that a particular way of life is wrong or "immoral" is not a sufficient reason to ban it. This is why *Lawrence* says the Court's "obligation is to define the liberty of all, not to mandate [its own] own moral code."[25] Laws violate equal protection in so far as they rest on a particular "moral code."

In *Goodridge v. Dep't of Public Health* (Mass. 2003), the Massachusetts Supreme Judicial Court cites this exact line from *Lawrence*, holding that Massachusetts's ban on same sex marriage violates that state's constitution.

> Many people hold deep-seated religious, moral, and ethical convictions that marriage should be limited to the union of one man and

---

[22] *Lawrence* at 582, concurring (emphasis added)
[23] *Lawrence* at 582, concurring
[24] *Lawrence* at 582, concurring
[25] *Lawrence* at 571

one woman, and that homosexual conduct is immoral. Many hold
equally strong religious, moral and ethical convictions that same-
sex couples are entitled to be married, and that homosexual persons
should be treated no differently than their heterosexual neighbors.
Neither view answers the question before us. "Our obligation is to
define the liberty of all, not to mandate our own moral code."[26]

Goodridge makes clear that the court's role is to avoid appealing to
contested religious and moral views in deciding the constitutionality of
a ban on same-sex marriage.

The conventional suspect class understanding of equal protection
requires that the law single out a particular class. Again, this is the
first step of the tiers-of-scrutiny approach. The sodomy law at issue in
Lawrence singles out behavior – in this case, consensual sexual activity between individuals of the same sex. But although this distinction
between behavior and class is crucial to the suspect class framework, it
is irrelevant under a powers review. This kind of review focuses simply on the kinds of reasons the state may not deploy in justifying laws
and policies. It does not matter whether the law regulates behavior or
singles out a particular group or even a lone individual, as I suggest
later. At its best, equality under the law is not about status or class. It is
about those reasons that are constitutionally inadmissible, reasons that
can underlie any kind of legislation including the sodomy law struck
down in *Lawrence*.

But we need not look just to cases like *Lawrence* to illuminate the
way in which constitutional law has some synergy with liberal neutrality.
The Establishment Clause in the First Amendment ("Congress shall
make no law respecting an establishment of religion") provides a constitutional hook to rule out conceptions of the good based on religious
considerations. Edward Foley, one of the few scholars who recognizes
the connection between public reason and nonestablishment,[27] argues:

> The Establishment Clause, properly construed, is the Constitu-
> tion's textual embodiment of this idea of political liberalism: the
> basic purpose of including the Establishment Clause within the Bill

---

[26] *Goodridge* at 312
[27] *See also* Greenawalt 1995: 62–71; Schweber 2012: 184

of Rights was to prohibit the new federal government from developing an allegiance to any of the various religious belief-systems that then existed, or that might come to exist, within American culture.[28]

The Court has interpreted the Establishment Clause to embody a commitment to religious neutrality. Even if liberal political theorists may disagree over the legitimacy of invoking religious justifications for laws and policies (an argument I do not engage here), it is hardly controversial that such justifications are generally unconstitutional in the United States.[29]

The Court's jurisprudence looks to three tests in determining whether a law violates the Establishment Clause: "First, the statute must have a secular legislative purpose; second, its principal or primary effect must be one that neither advances nor inhibits religion [citations omitted]; finally, the statute must not foster 'an excessive government entanglement with religion' [citations omitted]."[30] This chapter primarily focuses on the first test, the requirement that the law have a secular purpose. After all, if the law fails this test, it clearly violates the Establishment Clause. Michael Perry argues that this principle of non-establishment means that "laws for which the only discernible rationale is an offending religious rationale" are constitutionally illegitimate.[31]

In *Epperson v. Arkansas* (1968) (invalidating an Arkansas law that forbade the teaching of evolution in public schools), the Court affirms this core principle arguing that the "First Amendment mandates governmental neutrality between religion and religion, and between religion and nonreligion."[32] In *McCreary County v. ACLU* (2005), the Court held that a Ten Commandments display in a courthouse violated the Establishment Clause. The Court made clear that this standard of neutrality is one of purpose or justification:

When the government acts with the ostensible and predominant purpose of advancing religion, it violates that central Establishment

---

[28] Foley 1992: 963–4
[29] *See generally* Perry 2009
[30] *See generally Lemon v. Kurtzman* (1971) at 612–13
[31] Perry 2009: 114
[32] *Epperson* at 104

Clause value of official religious neutrality, there being no neutrality
when the government's ostensible object is to take sides.[33]

Laws or policies based on the idea that a particular religious way of
life is superior to another are unconstitutional. This is why Justice
O'Connor famously suggests that by favoring such a religious way of
life, the state sends a message to "nonadherents" that they are "outsiders, not full members of the political community, and an accompanying message to adherents that they are insiders, favored members."[34]
By acting on such private reasons, the state separates individuals in a
polity. Rather than finding reasons that all – adherents and nonadherents – can share, the state endorses a particular religious conception of
the good life.

There is an underlying logic that connects cases like *Lawrence* to
the cases decided under the Establishment Clause. Laws and policies
based on only moral reasons are unconstitutional for exactly the same
principle as laws based on religious considerations. Both point to a
doctrinal commitment that legislation must have in the language of a
pivotal case concerning public funds and religious schools, a "secular
legislative purpose."[35] Just as we may disagree about what kind of
sexual and intimate life is worthwhile "for [its] own sake," so too may
we disagree about the importance and relevance of faith in our own
lives. After all, *Lawrence* describes this freedom as the liberty to define
one's own concept of "meaning, of the universe, and of the mystery
of human life." The state ought to remain neutral with regard to such
conceptions of the good. It does not have the power to act on the basis
of them.

This illuminates the similarity between laws that seek to regulate
sexuality and religion. This similarity is not, as David Richards argues,
about the fact that sexuality is integral to a person's identity in the
same way as religion. Of course, sexuality may be integral to individuals, but, again, it need not be. This misses the crucial point about

---

[33] *McCreary* at 860
[34] *Lynch v. Donnelly* (1984) at 688, concurring (upheld city's display of Nativity scene under
      the Establishment Clause); *see also Lee v. Weisman* (1992) at 601, concurring (held that
      school prayer delivered by religious figure violated the Establishment Clause)
[35] *Lemon v. Kurtzman* (1971) (invalidating Pennsylvania law that provided supplemental
      compensation to nonpublic school teachers) at 668; *see generally* Koppelman 2002

the reasons underlying legislation. Once we turn away from analyzing the behaviors themselves (e.g., the decision to sleep with a person of the same sex or the decision to worship a particular God) and toward the reason or rationale that underlies legislation regulating such behaviors, the similarity becomes evident. Laws that prohibit a certain religious practice or a certain consenting sexual practice are based on perfectionist reasons. They are based on the idea that a certain sexual way of living is inherently better than another or that a certain way of life is sinful or contrary to some religious doctrine. These kinds of reasons that are based on conceptions of the good life are ruled out by the Constitution, or so this analysis suggests. Religious neutrality constitutes a specific commitment to the more general principle of liberal neutrality.

And tellingly, the Court does not impose higher scrutiny in its Establishment Clause cases. The idea of heightened scrutiny is not even relevant to this line of jurisprudence. The Court interprets the clause to invalidate laws and policies that are based on religious rationales, and thus it does not need to invoke a more searching examination. The Establishment Clause inquiry is not empty, precisely because religious neutrality anchors it. Similarly, we need only specify the equal protection inquiry as one that ensures that the state does not act on constitutionally inadmissible rationales. Once the Court acknowledges its own commitment to a powers review; there is no need for heightened scrutiny.

I suggest that our doctrinal commitment to nonestablishment ought to inform our understanding of equal protection. Consider that the reasons underlying a prohibition on same-sex marriage are most likely religious in nature (an argument I take up in more detail in the last chapter). Michael Perry concedes that if any laws violate a principle of nonestablishment, such prohibitions do.[36] Admittedly, no court has explicitly affirmed such an argument under the Establishment Clause. But the Court could incorporate the nonestablishment principle into its interpretation of the Equal Protection Clause, an interpretation that already seems to ban morals legislation. In fact, I demonstrate later that *Perry v. Schwarzenegger* (N.D. Cal. 2010) is the first federal court to do so.

[36] *See also* Simson 2012, Stone 2009

Even though *Lawrence* concerned a criminal prohibition in which the law severely restricted liberty, it would be a mistake to understand a powers review as applying only in cases of such severe infringement. After all, bans on same-sex marriage do not criminalize behavior; they simply prohibit the state from recognizing certain kinds of relationships. But this does not suddenly render such bans constitutional, as I argue in the final chapter. A powers review is about the reason or rationale underlying the legislation, legislation that may be criminal or civil in nature.

In *Cleburne v. Cleburne Living Center* (1985), a case that arose under the Equal Protection Clause, the Court invalidated a city ordinance that required a permit to establish a home for the mentally challenged. This was not a criminal law but a simple permit requirement. Nevertheless, without imposing any kind of higher scrutiny, the Court invalidated the requirement holding that the state may not single out a particular living arrangement for adverse treatment. The city did not require a permit for homes used for other purposes such as "apartment houses, multiple dwellings, boarding and lodging houses, fraternity or sorority houses, dormitories, apartment hotels, hospitals, sanitariums, nursing homes for convalescents or the aged."[37] The Court refused to deem the mentally challenged a suspect class. Without imposing any kind of higher scrutiny, the Court held that under the Equal Protection Clause, there were no "legitimate interests" that justified treating a certain living arrangement – in this case, a home for the mentally challenged – differently from others.[38] The Court concluded "that requiring the permit in this case appears . . . to rest on an irrational prejudice against the mentally retarded."[39]

The city permitted many others kinds of living arrangements, many other purposes for using a dwelling. Individuals could start a fraternity or a hospital with no sanction needed from the state. But they could not start a home for the mentally challenged without obtaining a permit. The Court held that because there was no legitimate reason justifying this kind of disfavor of a particular living arrangement, such a policy

[37] *Cleburne* at 447
[38] *Cleburne* at 442–8
[39] *Cleburne* at 448

violates the Equal Protection Clause. This affirms the principle that equality under the law limits government's power to act on the idea that a particular way of life is intrinsically inferior – in this case, a home for the mentally challenged.

In *West Virginia v. Barnette* (1943), the Court held that a law forcing students to recite the Pledge of Allegiance was unconstitutional. Although the case arose under the First Amendment, the Court articulates a more general proposition about our Constitution that informs this ban on favoring a particular way of life for its own sake:

> If there is any fixed star in our constitutional constellation, it is that no official, high or petty, can prescribe what shall be orthodox in politics, nationalism, religion, or other matters of opinion or force citizens to confess by word or act their faith therein. If there are any circumstances which permit an exception, they do not now occur to us.[40]

This language suggests that the state may not compel its citizens to follow certain kinds of orthodoxies or ways of living. Although *Barnette* arose from a free exercise challenge to the flag salute, the Court did not to base its decision on the fact that this kind of compelled salute violates a right to religion. The issue does not, as the Court reasons,

> turn on one's possession of particular religious views or the sincerity with which they are held. While religion supplies appellees' motive for enduring the discomforts of making the issue in this case, many citizens who do not share these religious views hold such a compulsory rite to infringe constitutional liberty of the individual. It is not necessary to inquire whether non-conformist beliefs will exempt from the duty to salute unless we first find power to make the salute a legal duty.[41]

That is, the constitutional inquiry is about whether the state even has the "power to make the salute a legal duty." The Court holds that it does not, because it is a "fixed star of our constellation" that the state may not prescribe what is orthodox in matters of opinion. And,

[40] *Barnette* at 642
[41] *Barnette* at 634–5

as *Barnette* makes clear, the state may not "force citizens to confess by . . . act" their allegiance to this particular way of life or orthodoxy. This informs the holding in *Lawrence* and *Cleburne*. If the state may not compel individuals to salute a flag, it may not compel individuals to lead a particular way of life for its own sake. It may not, for instance, simply favor heterosexuality over homosexuality or simply favor fraternity houses over houses for the mentally challenged.

ANIMUS OR HOSTILITY

Second, a powers review rules out reasons that are based on mere animus or hostility. A law based on simple dislike of or hostility is unconstitutional. It is not based on anything other than the idea, for instance, that being black or being gay is inherently inferior or even disgusting. Disgust is merely an emotion and a particularly visceral one at that.[42] Here, the reason or rationale is not the inferiority of a particular way of life but hostility to a particular group or class. Hating an individual for no other reason than the fact he or she is a member of a group fails a powers review. This is, as Cass Sunstein suggests, a "naked preference."[43] It is naked, because there is nothing underlying the preference except mere dislike or hostility.

The flip side of animus is mere favoritism. A law also violates equal protection, if it seeks to favor an individual for no other reason than he or she is a member of a particular group. This is a kind of naked favoritism. Bruce Ackerman argues that central to liberal theory is the principle that no person "is intrinsically superior to one or more of his fellow citizens."[44] This stands as a justificatory constraint on laws and policies. Cass Sunstein argues, in fact, that "[n]eutrality" is the Constitution's "first obligation": "[g]overnment should not single out particular people, or particular groups, for special treatment."[45] In *American Sugar Refining Company v. Louisiana* (1900), the Court

[42] For a discussion of this notion of disgust, see Nussbaum 2004: Ch. 2
[43] Sunstein 1984
[44] Ackerman 1980: 11
[45] Sunstein 1993: 2

upheld a tax on sugar refineries that exempted "planters grinding and refining their own sugar and molasses."[46] The Court reasoned that this exemption was not "arbitrary, oppressive, or capricious" or a case of "pure favoritism."[47] In *Regents of University of California v. Bakke* (1978), the Court struck down University of California at Davis's affirmative action quota policy that reserved a certain number of seats in the medical school class for racial minorities. Justice Lewis Powell's opinion made clear that "[p]referring members of any one group for no reason other than race or ethnic origin is discrimination for its own sake. This the Constitution forbids."[48] Although I criticize this decision in the next chapter, arguing that race-based affirmative action is not based on animus or favoritism, important here is that genuine racial favoritism or any other kind of favoritism violates the Equal Protection Clause. A law that provides a special benefit to an individual for no other reason than that he or she is a member of that group fails a powers review. Both kinds of justifications – animus and favoritism – are arbitrary, because we cannot all in principle accept them. In the case of animus, those individuals who are members of the "hated" group could not accept such hostility. And in the case of favoritism, those individuals who are not members of the "favored" class could not accept such favoritism.

In *Yick Wo v. Hopkins* (1886), a unanimous Court held that San Francisco authorities did not have the power under the Equal Protection Clause to grant laundromat licenses to whites but deny such licenses to those of Chinese descent. The Court reasoned that executing a law in this manner was an instance of "arbitrary power."[49] The Court made clear that "no reason for [such discrimination] exists except hostility to the race and nationality to which the petitioners belong, and which, in the eye of the law, is not justified."[50] The Court did not impose any kind of higher scrutiny in realizing that this action by government was based on racial animus. The Court did not say that racial discrimination by authorities rendered their action presumptively

---

[46] *Sugar Refining* at 92
[47] *Sugar Refining* at 92
[48] *Bakke* at 307
[49] *Yick Wo* at 370
[50] *Yick Wo* at 374

unconstitutional in line with a principle of strict scrutiny. Rather, the
Court says that there is "no reason" for such discrimination. It is
the underlying rationale that does the constitutional work in a powers
review, not the fact that the law invokes a particular identity classification – in this case, race.

Similarly, the Court struck down a Colorado amendment that
banned protection for gays and lesbians in *Romer v. Evans* (1996)
for precisely the same kind of constitutionally inadmissible rationale.
The amendment prohibited any local or city ordinance from making
discrimination on the basis of homosexuality illegal. The Court struck
down the amendment under the Equal Protection Clause. Because the
Court has yet to deem sexual orientation a suspect classification, it did
not subject the amendment to higher scrutiny. This did not stop the
Court from realizing that the "reasons offered for . . . the amendment"
must be nothing other than "animus towards the class" – in this case,
gays and lesbians.[51] In particular, the Court held that the amendment
raised:

> the inevitable inference that the disadvantage imposed is born of
> animosity toward the class of persons affected. "[I]f the constitu-
> tional conception of 'equal protection of the laws' means anything,
> it must at the very least mean that a bare . . . desire to harm a politi-
> cally unpopular group cannot constitute a legitimate governmental
> interest."[52]

It is not simply the disadvantage imposed by the law that is doing the
constitutional work. Rather, *Romer* makes clear that such disadvantage
is "born of animosity," that such disadvantage is based on hostility
against gays and lesbians. This is what renders the amendment unconstitutional.

The Ninth Circuit Court of Appeals in *Perry v. Brown* (9th Cir.
2012) draws from this logic to invalidate Proposition 8, a state constitutional ban on same-sex marriage. After the California Supreme Court
invalidated that state's ban on same-sex marriage under the California
state constitution,[53] the voters of California amended their constitution

---

[51] *Romer* at 632
[52] *Romer* at 634
[53] *In re Marriage* (Cal. 2008)

by initiative to undo the ruling. Judge Stephen Reinhardt, writing the opinion, reasoned that "taking away" the right of gays and lesbians to marry under the California Constitution violated the Equal Protection Clause.[54] The case did not decide the ultimate issue of whether a state ban on same-sex marriage violates the U.S. Constitution,[55] an issue I take up in the final chapter. Nevertheless, a rational review analysis was sufficient to strike down Proposition 8 in *Perry*, just as it was sufficient to doom Colorado's Amendment 2 in *Romer*:

> Proposition 8 is remarkably similar to Amendment 2. Like Amendment 2, Proposition 8 "single[s] out a certain class of citizens for disfavored legal status. . . . " Like Amendment 2, Proposition 8 has the "peculiar property," of "withdraw[ing] from homosexuals, but no others," an existing legal right – here, access to the official designation of "marriage" – that had been broadly available, notwithstanding the fact that the Constitution did not compel the state to confer it in the first place [citations omitted].[56]

Perry argued that this withdrawal of the right to marry rested on mere "disapproval of gays and lesbians."[57] Simply put, "Proposition 8 enacts nothing more or less than a judgment about the worth and dignity of gays and lesbians as a class."[58] And this judgment, this bare "desire to harm . . . cannot constitute a *legitimate* governmental interest" under rational review.[59]

In fact, even the dissenting judge in *Perry* concedes that interests such as "animus, negative attitudes, fear, a bare desire to harm, and moral disapproval . . . alone will not support the constitutionality of a measure" under the Equal Protection Clause.[60] The dissenting judge ends up upholding Proposition 8, because he believes that the state has shown that other interests relating to responsible procreation justify

---

[54] *Perry* at 1085

[55] "Whether under the Constitution same-sex couples may *ever* be denied the right to marry, a right that has long been enjoyed by a opposite-sex couples, is an important and highly controversial question. . . . We need not and do not answer [this] broader question in this case." *Perry* at 1064

[56] *Perry* at 1080–1

[57] *Perry* at 1093

[58] *Perry* at 1094

[59] *Perry* at 1094

[60] *Perry* at 1102, concurring/dissenting

the ban. I criticize this particular line of reasoning later, suggesting that it is proffered in bad faith. The important point is that even the dissenting judge in this case recognizes that certain justifications are constitutionally off limits under the Equal Protection Clause.

Romer makes clear that the Amendment constitutes "arbitrary discrimination."[61] It is arbitrary, because any group could be subject to such animus. Legislative majorities could turn their hostility or disgust to those with a particular hair or eye color, deeming those with brown eyes or red hair intrinsically inferior. Justice Scalia's dissent in *Romer* fails to appreciate the logic of this approach. He implies that the majority opinion cares only about prejudice against gays and lesbians not against those who for instance "went to the wrong prep school" or eat "snails" or who even hate "the Chicago Cubs."[62] But Scalia simply fails to realize that a powers review is not about groups or classes but the reason or rationale underlying a law. A law based on hostility against those who eat snails or those who hate the Chicago Cubs would be unconstitutional in just the same way as the Colorado amendment.

Daniel Farber and Suzanne Sherry insightfully interpret *Romer* – and by implication *Perry* – as embodying what they call a "pariah principle," a principle that "forbids the government from designating *any* societal group as untouchable."[63] Consider a Colorado amendment that prohibited local and city ordinances from making discrimination on the basis of eye color illegal or a California initiative that defines marriage as a between individuals with a particular color of hair. Replacing these amendments with other group characteristics would not make the amendment any less constitutional. Animus is arbitrary, precisely because any group can be subject to it.

Most notably, this animus is evident in racist laws and policies, a core argument of the next chapter. After all, if mere disapproval of a group can invalidate legislation based on homophobia (mere hostility to gays and lesbians), it can invalidate legislation based on racism (mere hostility to racial minorities). Racist laws and policies are also based on nothing other than a bare desire to harm a particular class,

---

[61] *Romer* at 630
[62] *Romer* at 652–3, dissenting
[63] Farber and Sherry 1996: 258 (emphasis added)

as *Yick Wo* makes clear. Jim Crow and antimiscegenation statutes rest on a "pariah principle," one that singles out blacks as "untouchable." In fact, Akhil Amar argues that *Romer* is best understood as embodying the Constitution's ban on "bills of attainder."[64] The "logic and spirit" of the nonattainder clause prohibits legislative majorities from singling out individuals or groups for who they are and not what they have done.[65] As Amar interestingly points out, the plaintiffs seeking to overturn racial segregation in *Bolling v. Sharpe* (1954) specifically invoked the attainder clause:

> Jim Crow laws, plaintiffs argued, had the purpose and effect of stigmatizing blacks – not for what they did, but for who they were. And that, plaintiffs argued, was a kind of attainder, a legislatively imposed stain and taint.[66]

So although the principle of nonattainder was not invoked in *Romer* or *Perry*, it informs the justificatory constraint that rules out laws and policies based on animus. Consider that the attainder clause is in Sections 9 and 10 of Article I of the Constitution, representing limits on governmental power. A powers review considers the Equal Protection Clause as any other such limit.

In cases like *Romer* and *Yick Wo*, the state based its actions on animus: antigay hostility in one case and racial hostility in another. But even if laws and policies are not based on such animus, they can seek to endorse or affirm it. In *Palmore v. Sidoti* (1984), the Court invalidated a custody decision that awarded custody to a father, because the divorced white mother had remarried a black man. Linda and Anthony Sidoti, both white, were divorced in 1981. At that time, the court awarded custody to the child's mother. She later married a black man, Clarence Palmore. Anthony Sidoti sued to alter the custody agreement, arguing that the child's best interests would not be served by living in an interracial household. The Court conceded that a child raised by an interracial couple "may be subject to a variety of pressures and stresses not present if the child were living with parents of the same racial

---

[64] Amar 1996
[65] Amar 1996: 208
[66] Amar 1996: 208–9

or ethnic origin."[67] The Court made clear that the best interests of the child ought to guide the state's decision. The state concluded that because of the societal presence of such animus, a child would suffer more in an interracial household than a single race one. On this basis, the state gave custody to the father.

The Court overturned that decision, refusing to grant custody to the father. The Court held that the "Constitution cannot control such prejudices but neither can it tolerate them. Private biases may be outside the reach of the law, but the law cannot, directly or indirectly, give them effect."[68] Here, the Court outlines two important interrelated features of a powers review. First, the Court makes clear that such biases are private. They are not constitutionally admissible, because they rest on mere disapproval.

Second, the law may not even seek to endorse or affirm racial animus. This is what I take as the Court's claim that the law may not even "indirectly" take such animus into account. A child in an interracial household may very well suffer because others are racist. The state can seek to ignore such animus, challenge it, or capitulate to it. If the state considers removing the child for his or her own best interests because of such racism, it seeks to capitulate to that animus. In awarding custody to the father, the state may not be basing its decision on hostility against blacks, but it is certainly seeking to endorse such racist beliefs. Racial animus undoubtedly still exists. *Palmore* stands for the principle that the state may not simply surrender to it, as it did by awarding custody to the father.

Similarly, in *Cleburne*, the Court rejected justifications by the city that a home for the mentally challenged required a special use permit because of the "negative attitude of the majority of property owners located within 200 feet of the . . . facility, as well as with the fears of elderly residents of the neighborhood."[69] But the Court argues that "mere negative attitudes, or fear . . . are not permissible bases for treating a home for the mentally retarded differently from apartment

---

[67] *Palmore* at 433
[68] *Palmore* at 433
[69] *Cleburne* at 448

houses, multiple dwellings, and the like."[70] Why? The Court cited *Palmore* reasoning that the law cannot give such "private biases" even "indirect [effect]."[71] Here too the Court holds that government may not surrender to animus – in this case, hostility against the mentally challenged – by requiring a permit.

In contrast, remedial laws and policies such as affirmative action seek to do the exact opposite. They do not seek to surrender to racism. Rather, they seek to challenge, even dislodge such racist beliefs. Justice Clarence Thomas dissents in *Grutter*, arguing that race-based affirmative action is unconstitutional. He argues that affirmative action may have "serious collateral consequences" including "actually impair[ing] learning among black students"[72] or "stamp[ing] minorities with a badge of inferiority."[73] But even if these are indeed the effects or consequences of affirmative action, this is not what such laws aim to do. The *Palmore* principle asks whether the law seeks to surrender to racism. And here it is clear that affirmative action and laws like it do not. In fact, such policies seek to challenge, even counter racist beliefs. Whether these policies are successful or whether they have "collateral consequences" that outweigh the benefits is a legislative or policy choice. The constitutional question is whether the law is based on animus or surrenders to it. The custody decision underlying *Palmore* was not about collateral consequences or costs. In awarding custody to the father, the state was not seeking to dislodge racist beliefs, being fully aware that there may be costs in doing so. Rather, it was precisely seeking to affirm such beliefs in removing the child from an interracial household. After all, the state was seeking to ensure the best interest of the child, interests that, in this case, entailed reinforcing racial animus. To do so, as *Palmore* makes clear, would be to countenance animus indirectly.

Importantly, a "bare desire to harm" need not be directed at groups. A powers review is about the justification of the law, a law that could take aim at individuals as well as groups. In *Village of Willowbrook, et al.*

[70] *Cleburne* at 448
[71] *Cleburne* at 448
[72] *Grutter* at 364, dissenting
[73] *Grutter* at 373, dissenting

v. Olech (2000), a case that is often neglected in scholarly work on equal protection, the Court considers what it describes as an equal protection "class of one" case.[74] Grace Olech, the claimant, asked the village of Willowbrook to connect her to the local municipal water supply. The village conditioned the connection on Olech granting the municipality a thirty-three-foot easement, instead of the standard fifteen-foot easement required of other residents who sought a similar connection. Olech contended that the village treated her differently, because she had filed an unrelated lawsuit against the city. She sued claiming that the village violated the Equal Protection Clause in asking for an additional eighteen feet. Olech did not claim that the city discriminated against her on the basis of an identity classification such as sex, race, or sexuality. That is, there was no claim that the city treated Olech differently because she was an individual of a suspect class or group.

The district court dismissed the suit, precisely for this reason, holding that an equal protection claim must be identity-based for it to succeed. The federal appeals court reversed. The appeals court made clear that a claimant "can allege an equal protection violation by asserting that state action was motivated solely by a 'spiteful effort to "get" him for reasons wholly unrelated to any legitimate state objective.'"[75] In other words, as long as the reason for the action is constitutionally inadmissible (here based on nothing but spite), it violates legal equality. The Court unanimously upheld the appellate decision reasoning that even without such spite, the village's decision to ask for fifteen more feet was "irrational and wholly arbitrary," thereby violating the Equal Protection Clause.[76] And there was no language of higher scrutiny – after all, there was no allegation of discrimination on the basis of race, sex, or any other such classification.

Justice Stephen Breyer's concurrence suggests that it is the addition of animus in the municipality's action that triggers the equal protection violation. The village acted with "vindictive action" or "ill will."[77] Breyer makes clear that the village's decision was not the result of an

---

[74] *Olech* at 564
[75] *Olech* at 564
[76] *Olech* at 565
[77] *Olech* at 566, concurring

unintentional arbitrary exercise of power. Rather, it was done with "an illegitimate desire to 'get' him"[78] or in this case "her." This focus on animus seems particularly important in outlining the meaning of a powers review. Again, cases such as *Romer* and *Yick Wo* point to the presence of hostility or animus as dooming a law under the Equal Protection Clause.

Scholarly work on *Olech* wrestles with the issue of whether animus or hostility is necessary to make out a successful "class of one" claim.[79] That is, should Justice Breyer's concurrence be the controlling principle in these cases? Although I do not seek to answer this question definitively here, consider that many kinds of line drawing are arbitrary: highway speed limits, having to drive on the right side of the road, or the amount of a speeding fine. After all, the state may set the speed limit to sixty miles per hour or sixty-three. These acts do not violate equal protection. To suggest as much may define a powers review too stringently, a definition that would turn out to invalidate too many laws and policies. There is no sense in which hostility underlies the decision to set the speed limit at sixty-five or to require individuals to drive on the right side of the road. This is why animus – directed at a group or an individual – may seem necessary in holding that state action is unconstitutional.

But simply focusing on what a successful "class of one" claim requires misses the forest for the trees. More important, *Olech* makes clear that equal protection doctrine is not simply about classes or groups. It points to an understanding of equality under the law that is at the center of the positive argument of this book. Drawing from *Romer* and Justice Beyer's concurrence in *Olech*, we can tease out the constitutional principle that animus is constitutionally inadmissible no matter whom it is directed at. This highlights the fact that a powers review is not concerned with identity or suspect classes. Whereas the Colorado or California amendments were based on hostility against a particular group – gays and lesbians – the village's easement decision was based on dislike of an individual. From a perspective of a powers review, both actions are unconstitutional.

---

[78] *Olech* at 566, concurring
[79] *See, e.g.*, Araiza 2007, Morrison 2009, Powell 2011

The scholarly work that considers the underlying theory of *Olech* is generally critical or skeptical of it arguing that the decision does not sit well with traditional equal protection jurisprudence and its focus on groups or identity.[80] *Olech* challenges the idea that equality under the law is about protecting suspect classes. *Olech* did not concern a suspect class or discrimination on the basis of identity. The town did not single out Olech because of her race, sex, sexuality, or any other such identity affiliation. The Court also did not subject the town's decision to any kind of higher scrutiny. *Olech* points to an equal protection framework that focuses only on whether the reason or rationale underlying a law or policy is constitutionally inadmissible not whether the law discriminates against a suspect class triggering higher scrutiny.

In *Engquist v. Dep't of Oregon* (2008), the Court reaffirmed the principle that a single individual who is not a member of suspect class may bring an equal protection claim. *Engquist* held that this principle does not apply when the government acts as an employer but only when it acts as a "lawmaker."[81] Even though the Court articulates this limitation (one that I do not discuss here), it argues that

> the class-of-one theory of equal protection on the facts in *Olech* was not so much a departure from the principle that the Equal Protection Clause is concerned with arbitrary government classification, as it was an application of that principle.[82]

This language makes clear that the state does not need to discriminate on the basis of an identity category such as race, sex, or sexuality to trigger an Equal Protection Clause violation. A powers review looks only at the reason or rationale underlying the state's action. If this action is "arbitrary," based on animus or hostility, it is unconstitutional no matter the recipient. This logic informs a powers review, a review that dispenses with the suspect class doctrine and the higher scrutiny that accompanies it. After all, the Court in *Engquist* makes clear that this is not some new or radical interpretation of equal protection but an "application of [it]."

[80] *See, e.g.,* Farrell 2009, Richter 2000, Zick 2001
[81] *Engquist* at 598
[82] *Engquist* at 602

BAD FAITH

Third, a powers review requires that the state not avoid or undermine such a review by simply proffering its rationale for a law or policy in bad faith. Although this constitutes an important, even obvious part of the requirement of liberal public reason, it is often undertheorized by political theorists. If a reason is on its face proper but put forth disingenuously, this cannot accord with public reason. Deploying such reasons willy-nilly would undo the justificatory constraint. Micah Schwartzman makes a robust defense of, as he calls it, a requirement of "public sincerity":

> Citizens and public officials cannot know whether their reasons are shared or otherwise sufficient to support their views unless they subject those reasons to public scrutiny. But if everyone expects others to act strategically by offering insincere reasons, then the epistemic value of deliberation is diminished, if not altogether extinguished. To preserve the significance of deliberation, then, citizens ought to conform with a principle of public sincerity.[83]

Although this constraint of sincerity may seem abstract, it is crucial to a powers review. And the Court is in a position to enforce it. A powers review asks that the Court to determine whether the law's *actual* purpose rather than a conceivable purpose is constitutionally inadmissible.

In passing a statute, individual legislators may have various, even diverging motivations in mind. Most problems with deciphering legislative intent occur when a statute's purpose is unclear or ambiguous.[84] Here, the debates over originalism, history, and principle become relevant, informing various theories on how courts should ascertain legislative purpose. But these debates are not about whether the statute is based on a constitutionally inadmissible rationale such as animus. They entail other institutional or jurisprudential concerns, such as whether the statute intends to exceed legislative authority, whether it aims to apply only to certain transactions or cases, or whether it seeks to have retroactive effect. A powers review does not require determining

[83] Schwartzman 2011: 378
[84] *See, e.g.,* Breyer 2005: 85–102, Dworkin 1986: 313–54, Scalia 1997

what the legislative purpose is. Rather, it requires that courts determine whether the law's purpose is indeed based on a constitutionally inadmissible rationale.

This emphasis on actual purpose is immanent in the Court's equal protection jurisprudence. According to Robert Farrell, this distinction between actual and possible purpose tracks the Court's current contradictory meanings of rational review.[85] Again, although a rational review standard may obliquely intersect with a powers review, it does not specify the kinds of rationales or reasons that are constitutionally inadmissible under the Equal Protection Clause. Crucial to a powers review is determining whether the law's actual purpose involves such a reason. This emphasis on actual purpose may look to what is seen as a kind of rational review "with bite."[86] In *Williamson v. Lee Optical Co.* (1955), the Court upheld an Oklahoma law that prohibited opticians from fitting lenses into frames without a prescription from an ophthalmologist or optometrist. The Court subjected the law to rational review under the Equal Protection Clause because no suspect classification was at issue. It reasoned that the legislature "might have concluded that the frequency of occasions when a prescription is necessary was sufficient to justify this regulation of the fitting of eyeglasses" on grounds of the "health and welfare of the people."[87] The language of "might have concluded" means that the Court did not attempt to consider whether the actual purpose is constitutionally inadmissible.

This distinction between actual and possible purpose came to a head in *United States Railroad Retirement Board v. Fritz* (1980) where the Court upheld a Congressional act that sought to restructure railroad retiree benefits. At issue in the case was a component of the law that preserved already accrued benefits for some employees (those who had some "connection" to the railroad industry) but not others. I submit that at its core the majority and dissenting opinions disagreed about whether to adopt the constraint of bad faith. Both the majority and dissent agreed that rational review was the appropriate standard of review

---

[85] *See generally* Farrell 2011
[86] Pettinga 1987
[87] *Williamson* at 486–7

under the Equal Protection Clause. *Fritz* did not involve discrimination on the basis of a suspect classification. The majority upheld the law holding that such review only requires that "there are plausible reasons for Congress' action" even if "this reasoning [did not] in fact underlay the legislative decision."[88] If there are such plausible reasons, the law does not violate the Equal Protection Clause. The majority concluded that because favoring "career railroader" employees (i.e., those who had some "connection" to the industry) could have been a legitimate purpose for the law, the law is constitutional.[89]

The dissent disagreed, arguing that rational review requires ascertaining if the "actual purpose" of the law is legitimate. The "actual purpose of Congress, rather than the *post hoc* justifications offered by Government attorneys, must be the primary basis for analysis under the rational-basis test."[90] The justification about favoring "career railroaders" was only an after the fact justification.

This inquiry is not about what motivated individual legislators to pass a particular piece of legislation, although such an inquiry may shed light on such motivations. Even the tiers-of-scrutiny approach requires that the Court ascertain purpose. In fact, strict scrutiny requires that the Court decide if the law's purpose is compelling. Any difficulties with the relationship between a legislator's individual motivation and the law's purpose arise for either a tiers-of-scrutiny approach or a powers review.

As a matter of constitutional practice, the Court undertakes this inquiry by analyzing the government's stated purpose for the law and the means deployed by the law to accomplish the alleged purpose. A focus on the means reveals whether a stated purpose is being proffered in bad faith. The Court analyzes this stated purpose by looking not just at what the government claims the purpose is in its court briefs but what the law itself says. And in doing so, the Court can determine whether the actual purpose invokes a constitutionally inadmissible rationale. For instance, in *Fritz*, the dissent looked to the section of the law titled "Principal Purposes of the Bill," a section that stated that the

---

[88] *Fritz* at 179
[89] *Fritz* at 178
[90] *Fritz* at 187, dissenting

law sought to preserve the vested benefits of retirees not to favor career railroaders. But the law did not actually seek to preserve vested benefits. After all, the law specifically dissolved benefits for some retirees but not others.[91] The dissent concluded that the "line-drawing" undertaken by the reconstructing was therefore "arbitrary."[92] Perhaps, as the dissent suggests, the law was kind of favoritism for a certain class of employees, securing a windfall for the railroad labor unions.[93] Whatever it is, the actual purpose of the law cannot be based on it.[94] Such favoritism is constitutionally inadmissible.

The former, more permissive understanding of purpose does not adopt the requirement of "public sincerity." In fact, it invites the kind of post hoc rationalizations that undoes a powers review. If the Court's task is to determine whether there is a conceivable purpose for the law that is not unconstitutional, it can invariably find such a reason or rationale, as the Court did in *Fritz*. The more stringent understanding of purpose takes seriously the requirement of sincerity. The powers review I defend here adopts this understanding. It asks the Court to determine whether the actual purpose is based on a constitutionally inadmissible rationale.

In *Perry v. Brown* (9th Cir. 2012), the majority invalidated Proposition 8 under a rational review analysis, holding that the actual purpose of the amendment was based on animus against gays and lesbians. Central to the court's argument was the fact that other justifications were not proffered in good faith. For instance, proponents of Proposition 8 argued in court documents that the amendment's purpose was to encourage opposite-sex couples to procreate responsibly. Here, the court analyzed whether the purpose put forth in legal briefs and arguments was proffered in bad faith. The majority reasoned that even if this rationale was not unconstitutional, it could not be the *actual* purpose of the amendment. The means deployed by Proposition 8, here removing the label of "marriage" from same-sex couples, have nothing to do with responsible procreation. After all, the amendment does

---

[91] *Fritz* at 186, dissenting
[92] *Fritz* at 471 (fn. 11, 12), dissenting
[93] *Fritz* at 191–2, dissenting
[94] *Fritz* at 470–1, dissenting

not regulate the marriages of opposite-sex couples who do not seek to procreate, only their nonprocreating same-sex counterparts. The amendment's means simply do not fit an alleged purpose of responsible procreation. The court holds that

> We will not credit a justification for Proposition 8 that is totally inconsistent with the measures' actual effect and with the operation of California's family laws both before and after its enactment.[95]

The dissent in *Perry*, however, adopts the more permissive understanding of rational review (even citing Robert Farrell to that effect).[96] The dissent argues that responsible procreation could have been a purpose for the marriage limitation. In doing so, it fails to realize the mismatch between the alleged purpose of such a limitation and the means used to effectuate it.

Consider also Justice Ginsburg's dissent in *Gonzales v. Carhart* (2007) (upholding the partial-birth abortion ban). Here, the Court upheld a federal ban on a particular abortion procedure performed during the second trimester of pregnancy. In pointing out that Congress' alleged justification was put forth in bad faith, Ginsburg dissents, arguing that

> [t]oday's ruling, the Court declares, advances . . . the Government's "legitimate and substantial interest in preserving and promoting fetal life." . . . But the Act scarcely furthers that interest: The law saves not a single fetus from destruction, for it targets only a *method* of performing abortion.[97]

Although preserving life is not an unconstitutional reason or rationale, Congress did not proffer it in good faith. After all, the law only targets a particular method of abortion, leaving a doctor other ways to perform an abortion. Hence the law does not save one fetal life. Ginsburg concludes that *something else* besides preserving life is actually afoot. Ginsburg goes on to suggest:

[95] *Perry* at 1084
[96] *Perry* at 1109
[97] *Gonzales* at 181, dissenting

Ultimately, the Court admits that "moral concerns" are at work, concerns that could yield prohibitions on any abortion. . . . Notably, the concerns expressed are untethered to any ground genuinely serving the Government's interest in preserving life. . . . "Our obligation is to define the liberty of all, not to mandate our own moral code" [citing *Lawrence*].[98]

Although Ginsburg does not deploy the language of powers, she informs a powers review, one that rules out reasons that are based on a particular moral conception of the good. This is why she explicitly cites *Lawrence* to that effect. Because preserving fetal life cannot be the actual purpose of the ban, Congress exceeds its powers by enacting it. If the Court's role is to fetter out laws and policies that are based on constitutionally inadmissible rationales, it must ensure that the state does not subvert this requirement by proffering reasons in bad faith.

In *Cleburne*, the city proffered various rationales for singling out a home for the mentally challenged. The city insisted that "several factors" explained the need for a license in this case, but not in any other.[99] The Court reasoned that these explanations were proffered in bad faith.[100] For instance, the city argued that the license was necessary because the location of the anticipated home was in a flood area and because the "size of the home" and "the number of people" occupying it would be too large.[101] But the Court held that these reasons could not be the actual purpose of the law. This concern "with the possibility of a flood, however, can hardly be based on a distinction between the home [for the mentally challenged] and, for example, nursing homes, homes for convalescents or the aged, or sanitariums or hospitals, any of which could be located on the . . . site without obtaining a special use permit."[102] With regard to size and number of occupants, the Court makes clear that this concern did not apply to homes used for other purposes. Thus, the city "never justifies its apparent view that other people

---

[98] *Gonzales* at 182, dissenting
[99] *Cleburne* at 448
[100] *Cleburne* at 448–50
[101] *Cleburne* at 449
[102] *Cleburne* at 449

can live under such 'crowded' conditions when mentally retarded persons cannot."[103] Ultimately, the Court concludes that "requiring the permit in this case appears to us to rest on an irrational prejudice against the mentally retarded."[104] *Cleburne* and the dissenting opinions in *Fritz* and *Gonzales* point to how the Court can enforce this constraint to determine if the state's actual reason or rationale invokes a constitutionally inadmissible rationale.

AVOIDS CRITIQUE OF IDENTITY

Equality under the law is not about which groups or classes are "in" and which are "out." At its best, it is about which reasons or rationales are constitutionally inadmissible. A powers review ensures that the state does not base laws and policies on animus or on certain conceptions of the good. These justificatory constraints represent the scope of state or government power. And the state cannot avoid them by proffering rationales in bad faith. This interpretation of equal protection relieves the need for a suspect class inquiry and the higher scrutiny that accompanies it. Higher scrutiny is not necessary if the Court seeks to invalidate laws and policies that are based on constitutionally inadmissible rationales. The criteria for determining which groups count as suspect classes are therefore irrelevant.

A powers review reveals that the tiers-of-scrutiny framework has needlessly expanded the purview of the equal protection inquiry. If the law is based on a constitutionally inadmissible rationale, it is unconstitutional. If the law is not based on such a rationale, it is constitutional. That is the extent of the equal protection inquiry. Why does the Court also have to decide whether a purpose is legitimate, important, or even compelling? A powers review avoids the problem of subjectiveness because it does not impose this additional, policy-laden task on the Court. A powers review constitutes a more principled method of constitutional adjudication. I elaborate on this point in the next chapter when analyzing affirmative action.

[103] *Cleburne* at 450
[104] *Cleburne* at 450

Framing the constitutional objection in terms of powers avoids the dilemma of identity. This dilemma arises because the suspect class framework requires that groups explain why they are different or "special" from others to challenge equality infringing legislation. On one hand, it is clear that racial minorities, women, and gays and lesbians require constitutional protection given the kind of discrimination each has faced. On the other hand, by elevating these groups to suspect status, the Court turns out to stigmatize them. A powers review protects such groups not by singling them out. Rather, this approach protects them, protects *all of us* by deeming constitutionally inadmissible certain kinds of reasons or rationales. There is no need to focus on the group or the classification, to single out racial minorities, women, or gays and lesbians if racist or homophobic laws fail from the get-go for invoking a constitutionally inadmissible rationale. This straightforwardly relieves the need to elevate certain groups or affiliations above others, thereby extinguishing the dilemma of identity.

First, a discourse of powers rather than identity stands to mitigate the sting of the counter-majoritarian difficulty. It draws individuals together rather than separating them on the basis of identity. Identity interests naturally attach to the relevant group. Powers attach to the state. A law that is based on a constitutionally inadmissible reason is simply outside the scope of state power. The state exceeds its power by acting on it. There is no need to say that the law violates the equal rights of certain groups. That objection is now moot given this structural interpretation of the Equal Protection Clause. Under a powers review, the emphasis is on the demos itself, not the groups that make it up.

Much democratic theory argues that those who would primarily be affected by a decision should have a say in deciding it.[105] This connects interests with democratic decision making and participation. As Ian Shapiro reasons: "[T]hose whose basic interests are most vitally affected by a particular decision have the strongest claim to a say in its making."[106] Making an issue about an identity group, then, straightforwardly gives that particular group the "strongest claim" in the debate. Ely's theory of judicial review does just that. It asks the Court to invalidate discriminatory legislation that fails to take into account

---

[105] *See, e.g.*, Benhabib 1986, Habermas 1996: 458, Shapiro 1999
[106] Shapiro 1999: 37

the interests of particular minorities. These minorities are those who are "discrete and insular," whose interests are likely not to be taken into account by legislative majorities. Under the "discrete and insular" logic, the failure of Jim Crow stems from the fact that the majority has not considered the interests of racial minorities. This informs the antidemocratic critique of invoking identity or class.

Framing the objection in terms of powers, however, is democracy affirming. Powers flow from the state. When the Court strikes down a law on the basis of powers, it does not do so on behalf of a particular group. It points to the way in which the polity itself has gone astray – has gone beyond *its* powers. For instance, prohibitions on same-sex marriage or laws like Jim Crow invoke constitutionally inadmissible rationales. Whereas the former are based on religious or moral conceptions of the good, the latter are based on mere animus, arguments I elaborate on in the ensuing chapters. The important point is that the Court may strike down such laws and policies without proclaiming that gays and lesbians or racial minorities are a suspect class. It can do so without holding that sexuality or race is a suspect classification. It can do so without exacerbating the counter-majoritarian difficulty. The Court need only say that such laws exceed the power of the state. By acting on reasons that are not constitutionally admissible, the state violates equal protection.

An objection that the state of New Hampshire has exceeded its power of taxation affects all those within the state, just as an objection that Congress has exceeded its power in conferring a title of nobility affects all those within the United States. This kind of constitutional objection is not the province of a particular group. A powers claim endows all within the polity an equal interest in challenging an unconstitutional law. This stands to inform "a politics of common aspiration." It prevents the majority from caricaturing a minority as the oppressors.

In this way, the Court would not be seen as proclaiming or vindicating the equal rights of a particular group. It would not be remedying possible democratic defects in a law by focusing on the relevant identity group or class. Rather than make the defect of a law hinge on a democratic majority's failure to take into account the interests of a subordinated minority, the defect turns out to be presence of a constitutionally inadmissible rationale. The defect stems from the fact that the majority has acted on justifications that are not acceptable to all reasonable citizens such as animus or a particular conception of the good life. Under a powers review, the democratic failure concerns *all* citizens not just the interests of a particular identity group, thereby mitigating the sting of the counter-majoritarian difficulty. Similarly, a law that exceeds a power forbidden under Sections 9 or 10 of Article I does not concern the interests of a particular group of citizens but rather the interests of all. We all have an equal interest in making sure that government does not exceed its constitutional powers.

This may render it easier to persuade those in the polity that, for instance, homophobic legislation is unconstitutional. From a democratic perspective, framing a challenge to a law in terms of powers rather than group or class interests is a more inclusive or democratic argument. This informs a commitment to deliberative democracy rather than undermining it. By "more democratic," I do not mean that a powers review will lessen the frequency with which the Court strikes down legislation. Teasing out this kind of review places significance not simply on the result (the homophobic law is struck down) but rather on *how* the Court arrives at it.

A turn toward a powers review expands the scope of those with normative standing to challenge the law. Normative standing is not identical to legal standing. Even in a conventional powers case, every citizen may not challenge the law. Legal standing requires that a claimant have suffered some injury from the challenged legislation. My argument focuses on the discourse a Court deploys to invalidate a law or policy. An objection grounded in the language of powers instead of identity expands the scope of those whose interests are at stake in overturning the law. It points to a more modest language of judging and thus a more democratic way of striking down legislation. *Brown v. Board of Education* (1954) posed the constitutional issue as the following:

> Does segregation of children in public schools solely on the basis of race, even though the physical facilities and other "tangible" factors may be equal, deprive the children of the minority group of equal educational opportunities?[107]

The Court obviously answers in the affirmative, but it frames the deprivation as one that affects the "minority group" – here, black children.

---

[107] *Brown* at 493

Contrastingly, in *McCulloch v. Maryland* (1819), the Court posed the second issue regarding the constitutionality of Maryland's tax in the following way: "Whether the State of Maryland may, without violating the Constitution, tax that branch [of the United States' bank]?"[108] Here the deprivation is not about the interests of a particular group or about the identity classification the law invokes but about the scope of governmental power, in this case the state's power to tax. In challenging Maryland's tax, James McCulloch, head of the United States Bank in Maryland, was not seeking to vindicate his rights but to argue that Maryland had exceeded its powers in imposing the tax. This is why the Court does not frame the issue as one that affects the interests of a "minority group." This is obvious to any student of constitutional law, because *McCulloch* is a powers case. It is a case that concerns the structure of government affecting the interests of all Americans not just a particular group of them.

By avoiding the "us" versus "them" nature of a suspect class claim and its equal rights analog, a powers review stands to extinguish the "special rights" retort. The language of identity that frames current equal protection arguments cannot avoid this retort. After all, it is a particular group – racial minorities, women, or gays and lesbians – that is seeking to vindicate its rights by challenging racist, sexist, or homophobic legislation. A powers review suggests that the challenge is just like a challenge in *McCulloch*, one in which the argument is not one about rights but about powers. For instance, there is no need to argue that a prohibition on same-sex marriage violates equal rights by failing to apply a universal right – here, a right to marry – to a particular minority. Rather, a powers review suggests that such a prohibition simply exceeds the power of the state. It rests on reasons that are constitutionally inadmissible. The constitutional objection does not hinge on the existence of a suspect class. When the Court invalidates state action as going beyond its constitutional powers, the "special rights" retort is irrelevant. Those who would oppose the decision would be hard-pressed to view it has vindicating a certain group's rights. So although invalidating legislation under a powers review may well invite a disagreement about the scope of state power, it importantly avoids the charge of "special rights." This charge is specious not because of

---

[108] *McCulloch* at 426

any claim of "equal rights" – again, this only reinforces the charge. It is specious once we realize that an equal protection claim is about the scope of state power, not about discrimination against suspect classes.

Second, this focus on powers relives the need to engage in the suspect class inquiry entirely. The Court does not need to identify which classes are worthy of protection when invalidating laws and policies. If equality under the law is about ensuring that the state does not act on constitutionally inadmissible rationales, the Court does not need higher scrutiny or the class approach that accompanies it. By specifying the reasons that are outside of the scope of state power, a powers review enforces equal protection without appeal to classes or groups. It applies to all laws and policies.

With no need for the suspect class inquiry, the Court does not need to affirm the immutability of groups or reinscribe their oppression. Under a powers review, it simply does not matter whether membership in the group is immutable. Identifying which groups are "in" and which are "out" is irrelevant. This framework extinguishes the need to make sexuality a fundamental rather than a contingent aspect of one's identity. For instance, it does not matter whether we treat sexuality as an ordinary preference akin to preferring a certain flavor of ice cream or as something more ethical and substantive. As long as the reasons underlying the law are constitutionally inadmissible, the law is unconstitutional. This, in turn, extinguishes the problem of intersectionality, a problem that arises because individuals do not fit neatly into existing suspect classes. A powers review does not require that the Court proclaim the existence of a particular class to strike down a law. With no list of classes, there is no concern about what to do with individuals who do not fit into one of them. Any possible group or collection of individuals or even a lone individual herself can be subject to laws or policies based on animus à la *Olech*. And if so, the Court can strike them down. The guarantee of equal protection does not hinge on being a member of a constitutionally protected class. It hinges on ensuring that the state does not act on constitutionally inadmissible rationales.

Simultaneously, the Court does not have to invoke a history of discrimination to invalidate equality-infringing laws and policies. Groups do not need to invoke their subordination to persuade the Court to invalidate legislation that discriminates against them. They do not need to rehearse their history of discrimination to gain coveted suspect class status. This relieves the need to raise the specter of oppression, thereby avoiding the vicious circle of victimhood and constitutional recognition. In challenging laws and policies as violating equality under the law, they do not need to elevate themselves above any other group. They need only claim that such laws invoke a constitutionally inadmissible rationale. This does not force these groups to downplay the way in which they are like everyone else. The constitutional attack is about whether the legislation is based on a particular conception of the good life or animus, not about whether it invokes a suspect class or discriminates on the basis of identity.

By not raising the subordinated status of groups, the Court frames the constitutional objection in more fundamental terms. Consider again that Rawls separates public reason into commitments of powers on one hand and equal rights or identity on the other. Powers are conceptually prior to equal rights. If a particular law violates the rights of gays and lesbians or racial minorities, this does not necessarily mean that the state lacks the power to pass the law. Rather, and this is often implicit in constitutional adjudication, a powers inquiry comes first. The Court must initially decide if the state has the power to pass a law. Only after the Court concludes that the state has the power to do so does the Court ask if the law discriminates against a subordinated minority by violating the equal rights of a particular group. What is at stake here is the fundamental or prior nature of a powers claim. Again, as Alexander Hamilton said in criticizing a bill of rights, "[W]hy declare that things shall not be done which there is no power to do?" Why say that a law violates the equal rights of a particular group, when the state does not even the power to enact it. The suspect class framework turns out to be a constitutional afterthought. A powers review represents a structural and hence more basic constitutional review than one that must invoke suspect classes.

Consider *Strauss v. Horton* (Cal. 2009) where the California Supreme Court held that Proposition 8 was not a revision but rather a simple amendment to the California Constitution. In *Strauss*, the opponents of Proposition 8 challenged the state amendment arguing that it was a revision to the state constitution violating constitutional procedures. According to the California constitution, an "amendment" may be done by popular initiative alone,[109] but a "revision" requires a constitutional convention or legislative endorsement before approval by the voters.[110] Proposition 8, titled "Eliminates Rights of Same-Sex Couples to Marry,"[111] was passed by popular initiative with no convention or endorsement.

At issue in *Strauss*, then, was whether Proposition 8 was an amendment or a revision. A revision is more of a change to a constitution than a simple amendment.[112] The distinction under California law is "based on the principle that 'comprehensive changes' to the Constitution [namely a revision] require more formality, discussion and deliberation than is available through the initiative process."[113] What counts as a "comprehensive change"? The court defines it as one that "involves a change in the basic plan of California government," a "change in its fundamental structure or the foundational powers of its branches."[114]

The petitioners conceded that the initiative "does not affect the *governmental plan* or *framework* established by the state Constitution."[115] They conceded that this was not an issue of powers but one about identity or class. Nonetheless, they argued that "the measure . . . should be considered to be a revision because it conflicts with an assertedly fundamental constitutional principle that protects a minority group."[116] David Cruz argues that this is indeed a revision because Proposition 8

> rendered the judiciary incapable of performing its longstanding role of independently enforcing constitutional guarantees to protect vulnerable minority groups, particularly in their exercise of fundamental rights.[117]

The petitioners frame Proposition 8 as a constitutional change that fails to take into account the interests of a minority group: it takes "away"

---

[109] California Constitution, Article XVIII (Sec. 3)
[110] California Constitution, Article XVIII (Sec. 1, 2)
[111] *Strauss* at 410
[112] *See generally* Levinson 1995: 21
[113] *Raven v. Deukmejian* (Cal. 2009) at 349–50
[114] *Strauss* at 478
[115] *Strauss* at 389
[116] *Strauss* at 389
[117] Cruz 2010: 48

the equal rights of gays and lesbians to marry; after all, this was the ballot title of the initiative.

Strauss rejects this claim reasoning that the change must be one that alters the "foundational powers" to count as a revision. Whereas a constitutional change to powers constitutes a revision, a change in protecting a vulnerable minority group does not. Ultimately, the court concluded that Proposition 8 was therefore not a revision but a mere amendment. It was procedurally valid under the California Constitution.

By making the all-too-familiar suspect class argument along with its equal rights analog, opponents of Proposition 8 hoist themselves on their own petard. This argument makes it easy for same-sex marriage detractors to proclaim that the initiative was indeed an amendment and not a revision, an argument that the court accepts. If a revision is only a change to the "foundational powers of the branches," Proposition 8 does not seem to implicate the *powers* of any branch. It merely seeks to limit or even remove gays and lesbians as a suspect class. Once we make same-sex marriage a constitutional issue about identity, there is no way to now suggest that this is really a case of powers.

The argument of this book suggests that the opponents of Proposition 8 would have been better off simply framing the issue as one of powers from the get-go. For if we adopt the argument of this book, Proposition 8 rightly counts as a revision. If the legislature does not have the *power* to act on certain reasons or rationales, Proposition 8 changes the scope of this power. The California constitution now reads: "Only marriage between a man and a woman is valid or recognized in California."[118] The initiative forcefully expands legislative power, because the California legislature must now act on an otherwise constitutionally inadmissible rationale in regulating marriage. In particular, the legislature's definition on marriage will be based on a particular conception of the good life. This, in turn, is a change in "foundational powers." Although the legislative branch did not have the power to act on certain reasons in defining marriage (they were constitutionally inadmissible under the California Constitution), Proposition 8 now says it *must* act on those reasons. This constitutes a revision under

---

[118] California Constitution, Article I. Section 7.5

the logic deployed in *Strauss*. By conceptualizing equal protection as a case of powers, a court may strike down a prohibition on same-sex marriage on a more "foundational" principle – namely, that the state exceeds its power in passing such legislation.

Most constitutional law treatises or casebooks begin with a discussion of constitutional powers and end with a discussion of identity and equal rights.[119] Often, texts are in two volumes to track this distinction.[120] Lee Epstein and Thomas G. Walker's well-known casebook, now in its eigth edition, is in two volumes: the first titled *Institutional Powers and Constraints* and the second *Rights, Liberties, and Justice*.[121] This bifurcation suggests that a framework of powers is prior and more fundamental than one of identity. After all, powers articulate the scope and structure of government; rights come after, articulating those areas or classifications off limits to government regulation. A powers review turns this familiar typology on its head. It posits that an equal protection violation belongs as a case of powers, a violation that is as serious and fundamental as any other powers case. This places legal equality as a more central and hence structural feature of our constitutional framework than what the suspect class discourse suggests.

Third (and I elaborate on this argument in the ensuing chapters but only flag it here), a powers review avoids the weaknesses of both antisubordination and formal equality. Again, this kind of review does not take into account the interests of a subordinated group, asking the Court to invalidate laws and policies on behalf of a particular class. Because powers attach to the state, the Court does not exacerbate the sting of the counter-majoritarian difficulty that comes with a commitment to antisubordination. Simultaneously, a powers review eschews a focus on formal equality. It does not proclaim that invoking identity is categorically unconstitutional. Again, the constitutional infringement does not rest on the presence or absence of identity, only whether a constitutionally inadmissible rationale is afoot. The unconstitutionality hinges on the reason or rationale for the law.

---

[119] *See, e.g.*, Chemerinsky 2011, Stone et al. 2005
[120] *See, e.g.*, Epstein and Walker 2013, 2012 (Vols. 1 and 2); Gillman et al. 2013 (Vols. 1 and 2)
[121] Epstein and Walker 2013, 2012 (Vols. 1 and 2)

For instance, whereas formal equality and its ensuing application of strict scrutiny would deem remedial race-based affirmative action policies unconstitutional, a powers review would not. Simply put, affirmative action does not rest on racial animus, but Jim Crow does. The presence of identity does *not* explain the "world of difference" between these two polices: both policies invoke the category of race. A powers review rightly suggests that the difference is about justification. Whereas Jim Crow is based on mere animus or hostility (i.e., the idea that blacks are intrinsically inferior), affirmative action laws are not. Quite the contrary, remedial laws are based on the idea that racial groups ought to have the same opportunities, resources, and life chances as others. Such laws seek to increase racial diversity. They do not invoke a constitutionally inadmissible rationale.

PERRY V. SCHWARZENEGGER (N.D. CAL. 2010)

A powers review is evident in *Perry v. Schwarzenegger* (N.D. Cal. 2010), the first federal case reviewing a prohibition on same-sex marriage under the Constitution, Proposition 8. Again, Proposition 8 was deemed a proper amendment to the California Constitution but was then challenged under the Equal Protection Clause. Writing the district court opinion, Chief Judge Vaughn Walker struck it down under that clause, holding that a state may not limit marriage to opposite-sex couples. Although the decision was upheld in *Perry v. Brown* (9th Cir. 2012), the appeals court deployed a narrower argument than the district court. The appeals court based its ruling on the fact that Proposition 8 withdrew a legal right afforded to gays and lesbians, a right that the California Supreme Court had earlier upheld. Again, because this "taking away" was based on animus, the appeals court invalidated Proposition 8. I do not focus on this argument here, because it is one that does not decide the ultimate constitutional issue about whether the state may limit marriage to opposite-sex couples. I argue that Judge Walker's opinion, in particular, illuminates the argument of this book. He invalidates prohibitions on same-sex marriage by avoiding the conventional suspect class/tiers-of-scrutiny framework and effectively affirming a powers review.

I realize that this is only a district court opinion. Again, this book is about making explicit an underlying logic that already, in part, motivates constitutional law. If the Court had already worked out all the implications of a powers review – not to mention an analysis of the constitutionality of a prohibition on same-sex marriage – this book would be a simple summary, not an argument. Consider that the Court summarily dismissed a Minnesota Supreme Court decision that upheld that state's ban on same-sex marriage in *Baker v. Nelson* (1972). The Court simply said that such a ban did not raise any federal, not to mention constitutional, issue.[122] That case obviously binds lower courts unless subsequent Court doctrine points to a contrary conclusion. In explaining why such a ban is indeed unconstitutional, Walker looks to subsequent cases like *Lawrence* and *Romer*. This suggests that under current constitutional doctrine, *Baker* is not good law. Walker's opinion confirms as much. In fact, Walker also looks at the Court's Establishment Clause jurisprudence in invalidating Proposition 8. In drawing from it, Walker's opinion illuminates and makes explicit the powers review I defend here, one that suggests that there is indeed a genuine constitutional problem with prohibitions on same-sex marriage.

The opinion does not engage in the conventional identity analysis. The "court need not address the question whether laws classifying on the basis of sexual orientation should be subject to a heightened standard of review."[123] The court concludes that Proposition 8 "cannot withstand rational basis review."[124] Walker does not invoke the suspect class inquiry and the heightened scrutiny that accompanies it. The language of identity and its emphasis on discrimination and immutability are not central to the court's reasoning. The opinion does not proffer a fixed conception of identity because it refuses to base its holding on elevating gays and lesbians as a suspect class under the Equal Protection Clause. Instead, it homes in on the fact that Proposition 8 is based on constitutionally inadmissible rationales:

> A state's interest in an enactment must of course be secular in nature. The state does not have an interest in enforcing private moral or religious beliefs without an accompanying secular

[122] *Baker* at 810
[123] *Schwarzenegger* at 997
[124] *Schwarzenegger* at 997

purpose [citing *Lawrence* and *Everson v. Board of Ed.* (1947)]. Perhaps recognizing that Proposition 8 must advance a secular purpose to be constitutional, proponents abandoned previous arguments from the campaign that had asserted the moral superiority of opposite-sex couples.[125]

The court makes clear that the justification for a law "must of course be secular in nature." This is explicit language informing the idea that a law may not be based on moral or religious conceptions of the good life. The language "of course" suggests that this is an obvious constitutional constraint.

In making this statement about secular purpose, Walker cites *Lawrence* and an Establishment Clause case, *Everson v. Board of Ed.* (1947). *Everson* incorporates nonestablishment against states affirming the principle that the "structure of our government has, for the preservation of civil liberty, rescued the temporal institutions from religious interference."[126] Whereas cases like *Lawrence* stand for the proposition that laws based on certain moral conceptions of the good are unconstitutional, *Everson*, like the establishment cases cited earlier, limits the role of religion in "temporal affairs." Walker illuminates the underlying logic that connects cases like *Lawrence* to the Establishment Clause.

This may be the first time a federal case has read the Establishment Clause into equal protection. Although this may seem a novel constitutional challenge to a prohibition on same-sex marriage,[127] it informs a powers review. In doing so, Walker has made explicit a core argument of this book – namely, that equality under the law rules out laws and policies based on a particular conception of the good life.

In fact, the opinion considers whether the supporters of Proposition 8 have "any evidence" that refusal to permit marriage licenses to same-sex couples furthers a secular purpose such as promoting "statistically optimal" child-rearing households or stability in relationships between "a man and a woman."[128] Considering testimony and briefs submitted by the supporters of Proposition 8 during

---

[125] *Schwarzenegger* at 930–1
[126] *Everson* at 15
[127] *See Rosky* 2011: 956–76
[128] *Schwarzenegger* at 931

trial, Walker concludes these claims are groundless. According to the him, supporters "presented no reliable evidence that allowing same-sex couples to marry will have any negative effects on society or on the institution of marriage."[129] The "evidence at trial . . . uncloaks the most likely explanation for [the proposition's] passage: a desire to advance the belief that opposite-sex couples are morally superior to same-sex couples."[130] Judge Walker argues that any alleged secular rationales for limiting marriage to opposite-sex couples are simply proffered in bad faith. Walker therefore concludes the following:

> In the absence of a rational basis, what remains of proponents' case is an inference, amply supported by evidence in the record, that Proposition 8 was premised on the belief that same-sex couples simply are not as good as opposite-sex couples [citations omitted]. Whether that belief is based on moral disapproval of homosexuality, animus towards gays and lesbians or simply a belief that a relationship between a man and a woman is inherently better than a relationship between two men or two women, this belief is not a proper basis on which to legislate.[131]

Proposition 8, then, is unconstitutional precisely because it rests on reasons that are constitutionally inadmissible – in this case, a particular moral conception about the superiority of one kind of "relationship" over another or even on hostility against gays and lesbians. Walker specifically says that Proposition 8 may be based on the belief that a certain kind of relationship is "inherently" better than another. This language seems to inform the principle that certain conceptions of the good life are inadmissible in justifying laws and policies under the Equal Protection Clause. Walker's opinion illuminates this feature of liberal neutrality.

The opinion recognizes that the demos – here, California citizens – voted for this kind of prohibition on marriage. In asking "whether a majority of citizens could use the *power* of the state to enforce 'profound and deep convictions accepted as ethical and moral principles' . . . through regulation of marriage license," Judge Walker argues that "they

---

[129] *Schwarzenegger* at 999
[130] *Schwarzenegger* at 1002–3
[131] *Schwarzenegger* at 1002

cannot."[132] Similarly, the Court in *McCulloch* asked whether the state had the power to tax a branch of the United States' bank. Both frame the constitutional issue as a case of powers forbidden to government. Walker therefore suggests that whether a prohibition on same-sex marriage discriminates against gays and lesbians is constitutionally beside the point. After all, he has already refused to engage in higher scrutiny and the conventional suspect class inquiry. Why proclaim that such a prohibition discriminates against a group, violating its members' equal rights when the state does not even have the power to enact it, or so Walker's reasoning suggests.

The decision is not about the way in which a prohibition on same-sex marriage discriminates on the basis of sexual orientation by unfairly forcing gays to alter their "deeply felt need" for those of the same sex. It avoids the identity politics that are at the core of the California or Iowa opinions. Importantly, *Schwarzenegger* does not challenge a voluntary, contingent conception of identity. The decision is simply about the scope of state power in passing legislation; in particular, it is about the kinds of reasons the majority may not deploy in justifying laws and policies.

In fact, Walker remarks that even those who are against same-sex marriage recognize that they "must advance a secular purpose" for Proposition 8's constitutionality, thereby abandoning previous rationales entailing the "moral superiority" of opposite-sex couples. This is telling. It means that even those who rally against same-sex marriage recognize that as a *constitutional* matter, the state must act on secular, not merely religious or moral, justifications. So framing an objection to a prohibition on same-sex marriage in terms of powers rather than identity may be a more persuasive strategy.

Framing the issue in this way, recognizing the political virtues of a powers review, may well avoid the emptiness that arises from a claim of equal rights. For Rosenberg, the problem is that such claims do not specify the "substance" of the constitutional objection. By adopting the language of powers, it is clear what underlies the unconstitutionality of a prohibition on same-sex marriage: its invocation of a constitutionally inadmissible rationale.

---

[132] *Schwarzenegger* at 1002 (emphasis added)

This preempts the "special rights" retort, possibly avoiding the
backlash that may accompany it. The constitutional objection is not
about rights. This objection would be appealing, in part, to a longstanding principle of our Constitution that government may not invoke
religious rationales in passing laws and policies. It would not be seen
as creating new constitutional rights but rather enforcing an already
recognized principle of non-establishment. After all, if Proposition 8
supporters already accept that religious rationales are constitutionally
inadmissible, we do better to operate within that framework rather than
needlessly invoke identity and with it the appearance of a "judicial pro-
nouncement" of equal rights. Constitutional objections to limitations
on marriage ought to resist the need to deem gays and lesbians a suspect
class. Politically, a powers review has the potential to draw individuals
together rather than separating them on the basis of a particular class or
identity group. Parts II and III of this book expound on this argument.

Part II   RACE

3   HOW CONSTITUTIONAL LAW RATIONALIZES RACISM

The pathology of deploying identity to ensure equality under the law is most salient to the category of race. This is the paradigmatic case in which identity seems necessary to invalidate racist laws and policies. If I am to succeed in drawing out a powers review as a viable alternative over an identity-based one, I must challenge the doctrine of strict scrutiny. This chapter does so on two fronts: one, I argue that such scrutiny is not necessary to strike down racist laws and policies; two, I argue that such scrutiny perversely affirms the very racist beliefs it seeks to counter. The Court's tiers-of-scrutiny approach and its use of identity have rationalized racism.

In its constitutional jurisprudence on race, the Court subjects laws that invoke racial classifications to the highest level of judicial scrutiny. The most recent case evaluating racial preferences, *Grutter v. Bollinger* (2003), affirms the principle that "all governmental action based on race ... should be subjected to detailed judicial inquiry to ensure that the personal right to equal protection of the laws has not been infringed."[1] If I am to rethink the conventional meaning of legal equality, to view such laws and policies as exceeding the power of government, I must dismantle the edifice of strict scrutiny. This chapter goes beyond the normative criticisms in Chapter 1 contending that the doctrinal requirement of strict scrutiny poses its own pathology in combating racism.

At first glance, the justification for strict scrutiny seems intuitive. Because race is one of those classifications that have been used to subjugate, oppress, and harass, in line with the history of discrimination requirement, we need to be particularly wary of laws that invoke it.

---

[1] *Grutter* at 326 (citations omitted)

After all, we want to make sure that our racist history does not repeat itself. As Cass Sunstein explains:

> When a statute discriminates on its face against blacks, the Court applies a strong presumption of invalidity. One reason for heightened scrutiny is a belief that when a statute discriminates on its face against blacks, a naked preference is almost certainly at work.... The danger that such statutes will result from an exercise of (what is seen as) raw political power is correspondingly increased.[2]

The more stringent the test or the stronger the presumption of invalidity, the less likely the law will be upheld. There is a real cost to deploying it. According to Adam Winkler, between 1990 and 2003, 73 percent of all race-conscious laws subjected to strict scrutiny in federal courts were struck down.[3] Invariably the laws struck down during that period were ones that sought to ameliorate the status of racial minorities, such as an affirmative action policy.

This highlights what is at stake in the constitutional debate over such remedial policies, a debate that started with the decision in *Regents of the University of California v. Bakke* (1978). Constitutional proponents of affirmative action often contend that remedial laws ought not to receive strict scrutiny. This, in turn, would permit the Court to uphold such policies of inclusion rather than invalidate them. Constitutional opponents of affirmative action, on the other hand, remain firm that all race-conscious legislation, whether exclusionary or inclusionary, ought to receive the highest level of scrutiny. This issue is particularly salient given that the Court has recently agreed to revisit the constitutionality of a University of Texas affirmative action policy, upheld by the Fifth Circuit Court of Appeals, in its 2013 term.[4] The Court will undoubtedly impose strict scrutiny in conducting its review. This means that affirmative action policies are in constant jeopardy of being invalidated. This is what is at stake in the debate over scrutiny.

---

[2] Sunstein 1993: 33; *see also* John Ely 1980

[3] Winkler 2006: 839

[4] *Fisher v. Texas* (5th Cir. 2011) (upholding a Texas affirmative action policy in higher education that operates alongside a 10 percent plan in which the top 10 percent of high school students in Texas automatically receive admission to the university). The Court heard oral arguments in the case in October 2012

Now I am not directly concerned with the justice of affirmative action, a question that implicates issues of compensation, social good, or desert. That is, I leave to one side the philosophical debate pertaining to affirmative action.[5] This chapter criticizes a seemingly entrenched principle of constitutional law. It illuminates a hitherto unnoticed perversity with the Court's current strict scrutiny approach, one that, I show, needlessly constrains the kinds of legislation a democratic polity may decide to pass. Again, the Equal Protection Clause is not about which kinds of policies the relevant polity must pass, but rather which ones are unconstitutional.

I argue that the constitutional debate, and in turn the Court's use of strict scrutiny, rests on a dangerous assumption – namely, that racism or racist beliefs may be rational. I define "racism" as mere dislike or hostility to a racial group. For instance, the belief that one race is inferior or superior to another is a racist belief. It rests on animus or hostility. Laws seek to accomplish a racist purpose in so far as they arc based on such beliefs. The regime of Jim Crow is again a central example. The Jim Crow laws rested on hostility against blacks. These laws, then, are arbitrary, and I define them as such, precisely because they are based on the kind of animus that the Court found unconstitutional in *Yick Wo* and *Romer*. This animus, this barc desire to harm, can take aim at any group or even an individual, as was the case in *Olech*. This informs its arbitrary character.

Yet far from neutralizing racism, the Court's equal protection jurisprudence rationalizes it. By scrutinizing such laws more carefully, the Court perversely gives credence to the bogus claims of racism. It suggests that racist laws and policies are based on something other than animus or mere prejudice. Otherwise, why impose strict scrutiny. I do not argue that constitutional doctrine intentionally seeks to legitimatize such claims. I make the more modest claim in this chapter that, via its doctrine of strict scrutiny, constitutional law implies that it is not groundless to claim that race tracks a kind of status or hierarchy. Requiring such scrutiny – flagging racial discrimination with a "red

---

[5] For philosophical arguments supporting affirmative action, *see, e.g.*, Nagel 1973, Thomson 1973; for arguments that such policies are unjust, violating principles of desert, *see, e.g.*, Sher 1979, Simon 1979; *see generally* Rosenfeld 1991

flag" – perversely errs on the side of suggesting that racist beliefs are *not* arbitrary, are not based on animus, that these laws are not based on a constitutionally inadmissible purpose. In choosing a sledgehammer to crack a nut, the Court runs the risk of deeming credible, even sensible, that which is already groundless.

This chapter suggests that constitutional advocates of affirmative action needlessly place themselves in a bind. They accept strict scrutiny for racist legislation – scrutiny that is unnecessary given the irrationality of racism – and then fight against it when championing remedial race-conscious legislation. They would do better to reject this scrutiny outright, turning to a powers review.

This chapter is in three parts. First, I explicate the constitutional debate over affirmative action and its emphasis on the level of scrutiny such legislation should receive. I show that the Court has had difficulty ultimately settling on strict scrutiny. Second, as my main focus, I argue that this debate highlights the perversity of the Court's equal protection doctrine. By requiring such scrutiny, the Court suggests that racist beliefs are more credible than they are. Simultaneously, in accepting strict scrutiny, affirmative action advocates create the very constitutional hurdle they seek to avoid. We do better simply to reject it. After all, if the Court can invalidate legislation based on homophobia, mere hostility to gays and lesbians, without invoking higher scrutiny (as it did in *Romer*, not to mention *Yick Wo*), it can invalidate legislation based on racism – mere hostility to racial minorities. Third, I revisit *Plessy v. Ferguson* (1896) and, in particular, Justice Harlan's dissent to inform the powers framework I elucidate in this book.

THE CONSTITUTIONAL DEBATE OVER AFFIRMATIVE ACTION

According to current constitutional doctrine, laws that discriminate on the basis of race are subjected to strict scrutiny.[6] Under strict scrutiny, the Court requires that racially discriminatory laws must be narrowly tailored to serve a compelling purpose. As laws receive more scrutiny,

---

[6] *See, e.g., Korematsu v. United States* (1944); *Loving v. Virginia* (1967); *Adarand Constructors, Inc. v. Pena* (1995); *Grutter v. Bollinger* (2003); *see also* Robinson 2005: 68

the harder they are to justify. Consider, then, two familiar laws, (B) being passed after (A).

(A) Public facilities and transportation will be segregated on the basis of race. This means that, among other things, blacks must sit at the back of trains and buses.
(B) Blacks will receive some kind a preference in educational admissions or employment hiring.

The constitutional debate over affirmative action centers on the level of scrutiny laws like (B) should receive. On one side are those who advocate a formal notion of equality or race-blindness; on the other side are those such as critical race theorists who advocate an antisubordination or race-conscious conception of it.[7]

Formal equality adherents contend that any law that discriminates on the basis of race is presumptively invalid. It does not matter, according to the principle of formal equality, whether the law discriminates against blacks, as in (A), or discriminates against whites, as in (B). As long as the law categorizes on the basis of race, it should trigger strict scrutiny requiring a pressing purpose. Whether the racial group being discriminated against is a political majority or minority is irrelevant. Michael W. McConnell, a constitutional law scholar and a former federal appeals court judge, characterizes the formal equality rationale in this way: "The principle of equal protection of the laws can be understood as a rule of strict formal equality, requiring all citizens to be treated without regard to race or other morally irrelevant distinctions."[8] Formal equality contends that both (A) and (B) should receive a *strong* presumption of invalidity because they explicitly discriminate on the basis of race.

In contrast, adherents of the antisubordination conception of equality contend that laws like (B) should receive lower scrutiny. As Ruth Colker writes, antisubordination seeks to "eliminate the power disparities between men and women, and between whites and non-whites, through the development of laws and policies that directly redress

---

[7] *See, e.g.,* Balkin and Siegel 2003, Colker 1986, Gotanda 1991, Hellman 2008, Rubenfeld 1997
[8] McConnell 1997: 1282

those disparities."[9] Antisubordination is sensitive to the fact that as a political minority, people of color are at a disadvantage. According to the race-conscious approach, we need *not* be suspicious about laws that discriminate against whites because they constitute the racial majority. In line with Ely's theory of judicial review, because whites are not a subordinated minority (i.e., they do not suffer from a power disparity), laws that discriminate against them are not presumptively problematic.[10] In the case of (B), we do not need the highest scrutiny. In fact, individuals may well need to be treated differently on the basis of race to do the necessary antisubordination work.

This disagreement about conceptions of equality and its corresponding levels of scrutiny is clearest in the Court's first race-based affirmative action case, *Regents of the University of California v. Bakke* (1978). In *Bakke*, the Court analyzed an affirmative action program that benefited a racial minority by disadvantaging a racial majority. At issue was a quota system at the University of California at Davis Medical School that accepted certain students from "disadvantaged" minority groups under a special admission program distinct from its general admission counterpart. Allan Bakke, a white male applicant whom the school rejected, instituted the legal action. At the time of his rejection, four unfilled minority quota spots were still available, and minority admittees had significantly lower GPAs and MCAT scores. Bakke argued that the race-conscious remedial program was unconstitutional.

Justice Powell, whose opinion has come to represent the holding of the case, reasoned that "the guarantee of equal protection cannot mean one thing when applied to one individual and something else when applied to a person of another color. If both are not accorded the same protection, then it is not equal."[11] Powell specifically rejected the claim that strict scrutiny ought not to apply simply because Bakke was a white male and thus not a member of a "discrete and insular" minority.[12] Championing the formal equality approach, Powell makes

---

[9] Colker 1986: 1007; *see also* Young 1990: 197–8
[10] *See generally* Ely 1980
[11] *Bakke* at 290
[12] *Bakke* at 290

clear that all "[r]acial and ethnic classifications . . . are subject to stringent examination."[13] This is the current constitutional principle, one that subjects all governmental classifications of race to strict scrutiny. It is a commitment to race-blindness. A law that burdens any racial group – blacks or whites – ought to receive strict scrutiny. Although the more recent case of *Grutter v. Bollinger* (2003), unlike *Bakke*, upheld race-based affirmative action, it did so by deploying the strict scrutiny test. The formal equality approach remains the controlling constitutional principle, and both policies of inclusion and exclusion receive searching scrutiny.

Yet in *Bakke*, the then-liberal wing of the court rejected this approach. Adopting an antisubordination conception of equality, Justices William Brennan, Byron White, Thurgood Marshall, and Harry Blackmun argued that Davis's affirmative action program ought not to receive strict scrutiny. As Brennan writes, "racial classifications are not *per se* invalid" under equal protection.[14] Davis's policy, as Brennan points out, does not discriminate against a discrete and insular group such as blacks. Rather, the affirmative action program hurts whites – a class that does not need "extraordinary protection from the majoritarian political process."[15] Adherents of an antisubordination understanding of equality accept that a law that discriminates against blacks ought to receive strict scrutiny. But as long as a law discriminates against whites, the political majority, it need not receive such exacting examination. Whites are not a politically powerless minority; thus the Court need not single out laws like (B) for a more compelling purpose.

However, and this is telling, it took the Court almost twenty years since *Bakke* to settle finally on strict scrutiny as the appropriate level of review for laws invoking race. In *Fullilove v. Klutznick* (1980), the Court upheld federal preferences for minority contractors, but the justices disagreed over the appropriate level of scrutiny. In line with their opinion in *Bakke*, Justices Brennan, Marshall, and Blackmun subjected the congressional preference program to a kind of intermediate scrutiny, which was less severe than its strict counterpart. Justices

[13] *Bakke* at 290
[14] *Bakke* at 356, concurring/dissenting
[15] *Bakke* at 357, concurring/dissenting

Powell, Burger, and White also upheld the program but did so under an undefined standard of review. In *City of Richmond v. Croson* (1989) the Court struck down a city law providing set-asides for minority businesses. In doing so, it subjected the law to strict scrutiny. The Court suggested that whereas state/local laws invoking race get the highest level of review, congressional legislation does not. The Court reasoned that "Congress, unlike any State or political subdivision, has a specific constitutional mandate [under Section 5] to enforce the dictates of the Fourteenth Amendment" by passing legislation to remedy racial inequality.[16] The Court reaffirmed this distinction between state/local laws and Congressional legislation in *Metro Broadcasting v. FCC* (1990) (upholding Congressional minority policies adopted by the Federal Communications Commission). *Metro Broadcasting* did not subject the policy to strict scrutiny, imposing again a kind of intermediate scrutiny. The Court made clear that as a matter of constitutional doctrine, such a severe standard of review is appropriate for local and state laws but not for federal legislation. But the Court reversed itself in *Adarand Constructors, Inc. v. Peña* (1995) by holding that a federal policy benefiting racial minorities in federal contracts must receive strict scrutiny. Under *Adarand*, all legislation (local, state, or federal) discriminating on the basis of race receives strict scrutiny. The holding in *Adarand* represents the current constitutional principle. The adoption of strict scrutiny, then, was not an easy or straightforward story.

Grutter, the most recent case analyzing the constitutionality of affirmative action, confirms the principle that all race-conscious legislation requires strict scrutiny. In *Grutter*, the Court upheld University of Michigan Law School's plus system where certain racial minorities receive a "plus" in the admission's process to ensure racial diversity. Unlike *Bakke*, the University did not argue that this program sought to remedy the historical discrimination faced by racial minorities. Rather, the purpose of the policy was to promote diversity in education. The Court concluded, drawing from language in Justice Powell's opinion in *Bakke*, that this purpose was indeed compelling. Writing for the Court, Justice O'Connor reasoned that a diverse student body in the

[16] *Croson* at 490

context of higher education promotes "cross-racial understanding" that "helps to break down racial stereotypes, and enables [students] to better understand persons of different races."[17] Moreover, the Court concluded that a policy of giving individuals of racial groups a "plus" in the admissions process was indeed narrowly tailored. Unlike a quota system deployed in *Bakke*, a plus system is a "truly individualized consideration demand[ing] that race be used in a flexible, nonmechanical way."[18] Under a plus system, race is just one factor among many in the admissions process. Quotas, on the other hand, problematically make the racial classification do all the work.

Important here is that all members of the *Grutter* court agree that a law that discriminates on the basis of race (irrespective of whether it discriminates against a racial majority or minority) ought to receive strict scrutiny. Again, this is why the majority makes clear that all "governmental action based on race – a group classification long recognized as in most circumstances irrelevant and therefore prohibited – should be subjected to detailed judicial inquiry to ensure that the personal right to equal protection of the laws has not been infringed."[19]

The only difference among them is whether this standard was applied correctly. Whereas the five-person majority in *Grutter* concluded that the Michigan policy did pass strict scrutiny, the dissent argued otherwise. Justice Thomas stridently argues that the majority "purports to apply"[20] strict scrutiny but in fact does not. Thomas argues that previous cases have held that "national security" or "a government's effort to remedy past [racial] discrimination for which it is responsible" constitute a compelling purpose.[21] Neither, as Thomas reasons, is applicable here. Thomas makes a good point. If laws discriminating on the basis of race must pass such a high and stringent test, does Michigan's policy really pass it? Or does the majority just pay lip service to the strict scrutiny standard without faithfully applying it? Is racial diversity truly a compelling purpose akin to national security or remedying past *de jure* discrimination? After all, as Thomas

---

17 *Grutter* at 330
18 *Grutter* at 334
19 *Grutter* at 326
20 *Grutter* at 351, dissenting
21 *Grutter* at 351, dissenting

goes on to state, the University of Michigan Law School could simply lower standards to achieve racial diversity. But the law school seeks to both ensure racial diversity and maintain its "elite" status.[22] For him, it strains the strict scrutiny standard to suggest that Michigan's need to maintain its "elite" status constitutes a compelling purpose.[23]

Grutter suggests that racial diversity is indeed compelling enough to discriminate on the basis of race. *Grutter* reasons that a diverse student body in the context of higher education promotes "cross-racial understanding" that "helps to break down racial stereotypes, and enables [students] to better understand persons of different races."[24] In fact, O'Connor's opinion suggests racial diversity is important to military preparedness. She quotes from an amicus brief where "high-ranking retired officers and civilian leaders of the United States military assert that, '[b]ased on [their] decades of experience,' a 'highly qualified, racially diverse officer corps . . . is essential to the military's ability to fulfill its principle mission to provide national security.'"[25] And it is precisely from the "service academies" and other colleges and universities where the military draw its officer corp. Racial diversity at the university level, then, is indeed compelling, at least for the majority in *Grutter*.

But for the dissent, taking strict scrutiny seriously means that laws like (B) are constitutionally doomed. After all, if (B) is subjected to a stringent test of justification – like (A) – it will be harder to justify. And, as a result, the Court will be more likely to strike down such remedial legislation. This is a serious problem. It makes it difficult for the relevant polity to enact laws that aim to remedy the status of subordinated racial minorities. Although *Grutter* upheld affirmative action, the Court's decision to review a recent Texas case suggests that this decision is in jeopardy. Justice O'Connor was part of the majority in *Grutter*. She has been replaced by Justice Samuel Alito, who is likely to side with the more ideologically conservative members of the Court in striking down affirmative action. And the doctrinal tool that

---

[22] *Grutter* at 356, dissenting
[23] *Grutter* at 356, dissenting
[24] *Grutter* at 330
[25] *Grutter* at 331

will permit the Court to do so will be strict scrutiny. Again, between 1990 and 2003, 73 percent of all race-conscious laws subjected to strict scrutiny in federal courts were struck down.[26] Adding insult to injury, invariably the laws struck down in that period were ones that sought to ameliorate the status of racial minorities such as an affirmative action policy. Strict scrutiny unequivocally stymies attempts to remedy the effects of racism. Those who are ideologically conservative will no doubt reason that the strict scrutiny standard is so stringent that achieving racial diversity in higher education is simply not an important enough reason to discriminate on the basis of race. Those who are ideologically liberal are faced with explaining why diversity is indeed compelling.

Moreover, strict scrutiny constrains how a polity accomplishes these remedial goals. For instance, *Grutter* makes clear that "universities cannot establish quotas for members of certain racial groups or put members of those groups on separate admissions tracks."[27] Rather, schools must employ a "plus factor" when providing a preference for racial minorities. This is what it means for such a remedial policy to be narrowly tailored.[28] By rejecting strict scrutiny, we invite other alternatives, including quotas, pluses, or a range of other options. But the high bar of strict scrutiny forecloses such attempts. This is the constitutional puzzle for those who endorse affirmative action polices. They accept strict scrutiny for laws like (A) and then are stuck applying it to laws like (B).

THE PERVERSITY OF DEPLOYING STRICT SCRUTINY

What both sides – race-blind *and* race-conscious advocates – appear to agree on is that a high level of scrutiny is necessary for a law like (A). As Randall Kennedy writes: "Although U.S. Constitutional law is inconsistent, it has now typically and *rightly* chosen to subject to strict scrutiny racial classifications used by public officials."[29] The

---

[26] Winkler 2006
[27] *Grutter* at 334
[28] *Grutter* at 334–5
[29] Kennedy 1997: 148 (emphasis added)

affirmative action debate assumes that strict scrutiny is necessary to strike down laws like Jim Crow.

I argue that this assumption and in turn the constitutional debate over affirmative action rests on a dangerous premise – namely, that racism may be rational. After all, if laws like (A) were (and are) based on a constitutionally inadmissible rationale, we would have no reason to subject them to higher scrutiny. If there is nothing to the belief that skin color tracks inferiority or a kind of status, why do we need the highest scrutiny to invalidate laws like (A)? They rest on animus. So, why does the Court need strict scrutiny to strike them down? In this way, those who simply advocate lower scrutiny for remedial legislation turn out to create the very doctrinal obstruction they seek to avoid. Because they do not challenge strict scrutiny for laws like Jim Crow, they are stuck advocating for a lower level of scrutiny for laws like affirmative action. We do better to reject strict scrutiny from the outset.

The need for strict scrutiny seems twofold. First, because racial minorities are obviously minorities in the democratic process, they are susceptible to majority tyranny. Thus, the Court must be particularly wary of laws that invoke race. Second, and this is obviously related, strict scrutiny is (allegedly) how the Court determines whether a policy is based on a constitutionally inadmissible rationale to distinguish between a remedial law (one of inclusion) and a racist one (one of exclusion).

I argue that each of these reasons fails. Strict scrutiny is not necessary to accomplish either. To claim otherwise – and this is the crucial argument of this chapter – runs the risk of legitimizing racist claims. Consider again Ely's classic defense of judicial review in which the Court's role is to intervene when the democratic system malfunctions.[30] Because certain groups are political minorities in this process (they are "discrete and insular"), the majority may not represent their interests properly. Consequently, we must deem legislation that discriminates against such groups presumptively invalid.[31] This is the justification for deploying strict scrutiny.

---

[30] Ely 1980: 101–4
[31] Ely 1980: Ch. 6

But imagine (given this concern) we discover a country with a history of discriminating against individuals with last names beginning with the letters S through Z, or what I call "letter-ism." Letter-ism is the belief that the first letter of one's last name intrinsically tracks a kind of status or hierarchy. People whose last names begin with such letters have to sit in the back of the bus, drink from different water fountains, and are forbidden from voting. Identification cards ensure that the state knows the first letter of your last name. Those whose last names begin with A through R – assume these last names constitute the majority of individuals – benefit from this system of letter-ism. These individuals have the privilege of being an A–R. In fact, to perpetuate this system, the A–Rs pass laws that prevent marriage between these two groups. Some scientists even generate studies to show that S–Zs are genetically inferior to A–Rs.

Consider then the following analogous set of laws (again with (D) being passed after (C)):

(C) Public facilities and transportation will be segregated on the basis of the first letter of one's last name. This means that, among other things, S–Zs must sit at the back of trains and buses.

(D) S–Zs will receive some kind of preference in educational admissions or employment hiring.

I suspect that our immediate reaction would be that letter-ism is ridiculous. It rests on hostility against S–Zs. After all, it just does not make sense to segregate individuals on the basis of the first letter of their last name in this way. The belief that the first letter of one's last name tracks a kind of status is irrational.

The similarity between letter-ism and racism is all too clear: a "morally irrelevant" characteristic deployed for no other reason than mere animus. And like race, the first letter of one's last name is an allegedly immutable characteristic. After all, it is something one is born with rather than something one has voluntarily chosen. Although the institutional apparatus of letter-ism may work quite well, the decision to pick out the first letter of a last name, like picking out skin color, to segregate and effectuate a letter-ist purpose is arbitrary.

Moreover, a law like (C) also represents a malfunction in the democratic process. Here too the majority is discriminating against a democratic minority. The interests of S–Zs are not being taken into account. Imagine, then, the Court were to analyze (C). Suppose a state suddenly adopted a policy of letter-ism. As a doctrinal matter, discrimination on the basis of letters would *not* get higher scrutiny by the Court because, although immutable, there is no history of discrimination on the basis of letters. Because we do not have a history of letter-ism, the law would not trigger a red flag.

But would the Court need higher scrutiny to reject (C)? What legitimate purpose could there be for such a segregation scheme? Again, I suspect the Court would immediately deem the law irrational, ridiculous or, better, just plain stupid. It would not need to scrutinize the law carefully to realize its actual purpose rests on animus, determining whether the law's means are narrowly tailored to achieve a compelling purpose. Rather, the Court would proclaim that (C) rests on reasons that are arbitrary, that seek to accomplish some letter-ist (and hence arbitrary) purpose. The Court would no doubt invalidate the law, proclaiming that letter-ism does not pass rational review. So, if this review is sufficient to invalidate (C), it *ought to be* sufficient to invalidate (A). To suggest otherwise is to imply that a racist purpose is less arbitrary or more sensible than its letter-ist counterpart. But this is exactly the implication, if the Court singles out race, but not all morally irrelevant characteristics, for higher scrutiny.

Perhaps this misses a crucial difference between letter-ism and racism. Whereas letter-ism was not a historical reality – we did not suffer from such a system of segregation – racist legislation was. As noted earlier, a history of discrimination is crucial to justifying higher scrutiny. It stands as an important criterion to the suspect class inquiry. Am I not disregarding that history, failing to give it due credit in criticizing the tiers-of-scrutiny approach? Because racial minorities constitute a democratic minority, they may not be properly represented in the political process. Given our history with racism in the United States, should we not be on guard with laws that discriminate on the basis of race? Put provocatively, am I not trivializing racism by aligning it with letter-ism?

I concede that racist legislation was a reality unlike its fictive letter-ist counterpart. I concede that we should be worried that a state may once again pass such legislation. In fact, it may even be more likely that a white majority will fail to represent the interests of racial minorities than A–Rs will fail to take into account the interests of S–Zs. But how do we go from these claims (all which are uncontroversial) to contending that higher scrutiny by the Court is necessary? In those instances where the majority does act tyrannically, courts will be crucial in striking down legislation. Obviously, I'm not suggesting that we get rid of courts or their ability to review legislation. This chapter objects to the *comparative* level of scrutiny the Court deploys in invalidating racist laws under the tiers-of-scrutiny approach. If the Court does not need strict scrutiny to invalidate (C) – as a matter of constitutional doctrine it would only receive rational review – the Court does not need it to invalidate (A).

Admittedly, the case of letter-ism is a hypothetical. But consider homophobic legislation such as the Colorado amendment struck down in *Romer*. That law was also based on animus or hostility. And gays and lesbians are also a political minority. The law singled them out for who they are. The Court did not subject the amendment to higher scrutiny by deeming gays and lesbians a suspect class. Again, it reasoned that "if 'equal protection of the laws' means anything, it must at the very least mean that a bare . . . desire to harm a politically unpopular group cannot constitute a legitimate governmental interest."[32] It invalidated the law under rational review. So just as the Court found that the purpose of the antigay ordinance in *Romer* was unconstitutional based on animus, so too may it do so for other policies of exclusion – laws like (A) and (C). This standard is sufficient to invalidate racist legislation. If the Court can deploy rational review to reject laws based simply on homophobic reasons, it can do so for laws based on racist ones.

But, and this is the motivating sting of this chapter, as long as the Court continues to suggest that strict scrutiny is indeed necessary to strike down racist laws, it runs the risk of rationalizing racism. It suggests that unlike homophobia, racism is not based on a "bare desire" to harm a group. The amendment in *Romer* shares the same logic as laws like Jim Crow. The former is based on hostility against gays and lesbians and the latter on hostility against blacks. So why is strict scrutiny necessary in the case of racism but not in the case of homophobia? After all, more than 125 years ago, *Yick Wo* invalidated the racist way in which authorities enforced a law without imposing strict scrutiny.

---

[32] *Romer* at 634

To constantly proclaim that racist laws must still receive heightened judicial inspection for the Court to invalidate them implies that such laws may well not rest on animus, that such laws may very well be legitimate. This is the perverse implication of imposing strict scrutiny.

Perhaps strict scrutiny is a fail-safe doctrinal mechanism. After all, what if we found statistics or evidence to show that blacks were in some relevant way inferior to whites? What if studies suggested that a particular race was indeed deserving of such hostility? In these cases, racist legislation could be considered rational or even legitimate. And here the Court would need higher scrutiny to reject such laws. This line of thinking – one that may unconsciously motivate higher scrutiny – problematically holds out the possibility that there could be evidence that justifies racism. Why do we hold out for that possibility? Do we believe that tomorrow, or at some later date, we will find some kind of evidence justifying racism, that demonstrates – aha! – one race is inferior, less industrious, or less intelligent than another? If we do believe this is possible or we believe that there is some "scientific" evidence out there corroborating racism, then we believe that racism could be rational.

If we believe strict scrutiny is necessary, because racism could be rational, we have rationalized racism. Said differently, in *holding out* for the existence of possible evidence to justify racism, we invariably admit that racism may be legitimate. Rather than holding out for this possibility, we should simply say that it could *never* be the case that such evidence is one day uncovered.

Consider letter-ism. We would not hold out for the possibility that there could be evidence justifying or showing that S–Zs are inferior to A–Rs. Instead, we would categorically rule it out. We would reject as bogus any alleged "scientific" evidence demonstrating the correctness of letter-ism. After all, how could there be evidence suggesting that there is an intrinsic hierarchy underlying last names that begin with different letters. This is the case precisely because letter-ism is irra-tional. But if we are willing to entertain the possibility of such evidence in the case of racism (what if . . . ?) but not in the case of letter-ism, we have accepted that racism could be legitimate; hence my argument is made. Again, either higher scrutiny is unnecessary for racist legislation or racism may make some kind of sense.

If one believes that there may be evidence substantiating the claims of letter-ism, (C) should also receive higher scrutiny. In that case, all laws like Jim Crow that publicly segregate individuals on the basis of a morally irrelevant characteristic (e.g., first letter of last name, hair color, and eye color) would receive such scrutiny. But this is not the current doctrine. Again, I criticize the way in which the Court subjects race but *not* other irrelevant characteristics to strict scrutiny. My argument exposes the perversity of flagging racial discrimination as special. If I choose a sledgehammer to crack a nut, I assume that the nut may be difficult to crack. I err on the side that it may be quite strong. Similarly, by deploying a more stringent test of justification to reject racist legislation but not other such legislation, the Court turns out to rationalize racism.

One constitutional scholar in justifying higher scrutiny seems to imply as much, stating:

> *Indeed, if all race-dependent decisions were irrational, there would be no need for an antidiscrimination principle [higher scrutiny], for it would suffice to apply the widely held moral, constitutional, and practical principle that forbids treating persons irrationally.* The antidiscrimination principle fills a special need because – as even a glance at history indicates – race-dependent decisions that *are rational and purport to be based solely on legitimate considerations are likely* to rest on assumptions of the differential worth of racial groups or on the related phenomenon of racially selective sympathy and indifference.[33]

Yet if letter-ism is just as arbitrary as racism, why would the Court be "duped" into believing that (A) is somehow rational? Why does the Court need higher scrutiny to realize that (A) rests on "assumptions" that are patently illegitimate? If this is the justification for higher scrutiny, the Court has undoubtedly rationalized racism. It has made credible the claim that certain races are inferior to others.

Consider that the first Supreme Court case explicitly subjecting a nonremedial law to strict scrutiny was *Korematsu v. U.S.* (1944). Again, the Court did not settle on this standard for remedial laws until almost fifty years later. In *Korematsu*, the Court upheld a racially

---

[33] Brest 1976: 7 (emphasis added)

discriminatory internment scheme aimed at those of Japanese descent including Japanese Americans, even though the policy was subjected to strict scrutiny. The racism underlying *Korematsu* was not simply a conclusion reached in hindsight. We know that even at that time, the government's fear of rebellion by those of Japanese descent was entirely unfounded.[34] Congress formally apologized in 1988, awarding each detention survivor $20,000.[35] Although the thrust of this chapter is that strict scrutiny is not necessary to strike down racist laws and policies, it is worth pointing out that such scrutiny may not even be sufficient to do so, as the decision in *Korematsu* makes clear.

One of the first cases in which the Court invalidated a nonremedial law explicitly on the basis of strict scrutiny was *McLaughlin v. State of Florida* (1964), followed by *Loving v. Virginia* (1967). *McLaughlin* entailed a challenge to a law that punished only interracial, unmarried couples from living together. Although the Court invalidated the law under the Equal Protection Clause, its reasoning is instructive. The Court began by noting that the law required some "overriding statutory purpose."[36] After all, this is the conventional sledgehammer that constitutional law deploys against laws that discriminate on the basis of race.

The state proffered the reduction of promiscuity as the purpose for the law. The Court reasoned:

> We find nothing in this suggested legislative purpose, however, which makes it essential to punish promiscuity of one racial group and not that of another. There is no suggestion that a white person and a Negro are any more likely habitually to occupy the same room together than the white or the Negro couple or to engage in illicit intercourse if they do. [The law] indicate[s] no legislative conviction that promiscuity by the interracial couple presents any particular problems requiring separate or different treatment if the suggested over-all policy of the [law] is to be adequately served.... This is not, therefore, a case where the class defined in the law is that from which "the evil mainly is to be feared"[37] [citations omitted].

---

[34] *See generally* Irons 1993
[35] Irons 1993: 376
[36] *McLaughlin* at 192
[37] *McLaughlin* at 193–4

The Court concludes that interracial cohabitation is no more likely to result in promiscuity than same-race cohabitation. Even assuming that curtailing promiscuity was the actual purpose of the law, the distinction between same- and other-race cohabitation is irrelevant to accomplishing it. There is "no suggestion" that these means are related to the law's alleged purpose. If that is the case, there is no need to subject the law to exacting scrutiny. The Court could have simply concluded that singling out interracial cohabitation is based on animus against interracial couples just as in *Yick Wo* the authorities acted on animus in refusing to grating licenses to those of Chinese descent. So why does the Court need to deploy a strong presumption of invalidity to strike down laws that single out interracial cohabitation? Again, unless we believe that there is something to the claims of racism, higher scrutiny is unnecessary.

Yet the Court constantly proclaims the need for such higher scrutiny. In *Croson*, the Court suggests that strict scrutiny is necessary to distinguish between policies of inclusion and policies of exclusion. "[Without] searching judicial inquiry into the justification for such race-based measures, there is simply no way of determining. . . . what classifications are in fact motivated by illegitimate notions of racial inferiority or simple racial politics."[38] The Court implies that it is hard to tell the difference between (A) and (B): "no way of determining."

The Court did just that in *Parents Involved in Community Schools v. Seattle School District No. 1* (2007), when it struck down racial integration plans proposed by two school districts by subjecting them to strict scrutiny. In particular, Justice Thomas deploys a high presumption of invalidity to argue that integration is constitutionally equivalent to segregation: "What was wrong in 1954 cannot be right today."[39] Thomas reasons that strict scrutiny is necessary, otherwise "[h]ow does one tell when a racial classification is invidious?"[40] He then cites segregationists who "argued [in *Brown v. Board of Education*] that their racial classifications were benign, not invidious."[41] This concern to

---

[38] *Croson* at 493
[39] *Parents Involved* at 778
[40] *Parents Involved* at 779
[41] *Parents Involved* at 779

distinguish racist policies from nonracist ones may be the most powerful justification for strict scrutiny.

This justification, however, proves my basic point rather than repudiates it. What is so difficult about distinguishing between an arbitrary policy (racial segregation) and one adopted to remedy its effects (affirmative action)? If "notions of racial inferiority" are just as irrational as notions of letter inferiority, it seems easy and straightforward to determine that a law's purpose is based on such beliefs. Why do we need such "searching judicial inquiry"? If laws such as Jim Crow share the underlying structure of homophobic legislation, why does the Court need strict scrutiny to realize that animus is driving such laws and policies?

Of course, those who favored racial segregation claimed that their policies were "benign" and that they rested on "legitimate" beliefs. But why does Thomas give credence to these claims, if they were and are from the get-go baseless like their letter-ist and homophobic counterparts? There is nothing tricky or difficult about realizing that a racist and hence arbitrary purpose is afoot. There is nothing tricky about realizing that laws like the one struck down in *McLaughlin* are based on animus. Strict scrutiny is not necessary. If the Court justifies strict scrutiny on grounds that laws such as Jim Crow could be legitimate, that otherwise it would be hard to tell that such laws are based on mere animus, the court has undoubtedly rationalized racism. Proclaiming that higher scrutiny is necessary to distinguish a racist from a nonracist purpose implies that racist legislation is indeed difficult to distinguish from its legitimate counterpart. For there is no difficulty in realizing that whereas (C) rests on a letter-ist and hence illegitimate purpose, a teacher's decision to arrange students by last name (from A to Z) in a classroom does not. No searching examination is necessary.

In fact, Justice John Paul Stevens who retired from the Court in 2010 suggests that we do not need such heightened scrutiny. In *Cleburne*, Justice Stevens concurs writing that

> [i]t would be utterly irrational to limit the franchise on the basis of height or weight; it is equally invalid to limit it on the basis of skin color.... We do not need to apply a special standard, or to

apply "strict scrutiny," or even "heightened scrutiny," to decide such cases.[42]

Unfortunately, this is not the current constitutional principle with regards to race (after all, this language appears in a concurring opinion). Whereas Stevens suggests that higher scrutiny may not be necessary to invalidate racist legislation, he fails to expose why it is perverse to require it. Perhaps this is one reason legal scholars have been reluctant to abandon the conventional tiers-of-scrutiny approach.[43]

Perhaps the similarity between letter-ism and racism seems so apparent to us because we have the benefit of hindsight. As time goes on, certain kinds of discrimination may be seen as more arbitrary. Suzanne Goldberg argues that strict scrutiny may be a kind of "judicial training" that is initially important for judges to realize the unconstitutionality of racist laws and policies.[44] This line of reasoning suggests that the necessity of strict scrutiny diminishes as time passes. There may be partial truth to this claim. After all, up until the early 1970s, the American Psychiatric Association listed homosexuality as a clinical disorder.[45] With the passage of time many of us (although perhaps not all) would consider antigay legislation to be based on nothing more than mere hostility in line with the holding in *Romer*.

Rather than contradicting my thesis, this kind of justification for strict scrutiny informs it. After all, *Romer* was decided in 1996. No higher scrutiny was needed to combat homophobic legislation, legislation that may have seemed legitimate only twenty years before. Why then is it necessary for racist laws and policies? Put differently, even if strict scrutiny is a kind of training or learning curve for judges, why hasn't that training ended? It wasn't needed in *Yick Wo*. By constantly suggesting that such training is still necessary – as the Court no doubt does by imposing strict scrutiny – the Court rationalizes racism. The Court implies that judges have not (yet) realized that racist laws and policies like their homophobic counterparts are based on nothing other than animus or hostility.

[42] *Cleburne* at 454, concurring; *see also* Goldberg 2004a: 518–25
[43] *Pace* Goldberg 2004a
[44] *See* Goldberg 2004a: 581–2
[45] *See generally* Bayer 1987

Admittedly, because gays and lesbians are not a suspect class, the Court in *Romer* may have had to find a way to invalidate the Colorado amendment without imposing higher scrutiny (something that Justice Scalia criticizes the majority for doing). But that only suggests that the doctrinal tool of strict scrutiny is indeed anachronistic. It is no longer necessary to invalidate racist *and* homophobic legislation.

Perversely, this doctrine has jeopardized much-needed remedial race-based programs. Strict scrutiny first arose for laws like the one invalidated in *McLaughlin* that were based on animus, on the belief that race tracks a kind of status or hierarchy. Such scrutiny, as the training analogy suggests, was not necessary. Yet the doctrine has remained a central edifice of the Court's tiers-of-scrutiny approach. The Court then began to apply this scrutiny to remedial laws, including affirmative action, minority set-asides, and racial integration. Of vital importance, such scrutiny has doomed the vast majority of laws that aim to ameliorate the status of racial minorities. Again, race-conscious laws that were struck down between 1990 and 2003 sought to ameliorate the status of racial minorities. This is a devastating cost to legislatures that seek to remedy racial inequality. The crucial point is that had the Court avoided such scrutiny in the first instance, we would not be burdened with it now.

The doctrine of strict scrutiny lumps policies of exclusion with polices of inclusion, suggesting that they are difficult to distinguish. This permits detractors to conflate laws like (B) with laws like (A). We run the risk of inviting this kind of tactic (i.e., permitting others to align racism with affirmative action) when we rationalize racism. There is a "world of difference" between laws like (A) and laws like (B) once we focus just on the reason or rationale underlying these kinds of policies. Of course, both laws invoke race or racial categories. If equality under the law is about identity, this invariably lumps (A) with (B). The crucial difference is that whereas (A) is based on animus, (B) is not.

Consider that Jim Crow and laws like it were part of a network of policies that sought to keep blacks separate. The law struck down in *McLaughlin* was not some isolated policy but one that existed alongside other kinds of racial segregation. And any court reviewing such a policy would be aware of this fact, one that makes clear the difference between (A) and (B). It is not as if (A) and (B) are on some continuum where there is an ever-decreasing level of animus as one moves from one to the other. In the language of political science, these are dichotomous, not continuous, situations: one is based on animus, the other is not – simple as that.

Even Justice Thomas does not suggest that Michigan's policy is based on hostility against whites, or any racial group for that matter. In fact, none of the dissenting justices in *Grutter* claims that affirmative action is based on the kind of animus that underlies Jim Crow or laws like it. They also do not suggest that affirmative action is a kind racial favoritism, a policy that favors blacks over whites just to favor them. Consider an affirmative action policy that gave preferential treatment to those with last names beginning with S to Z. This would undoubt-edly fail a powers review. It seeks to favor a group just to favor them. But this is not applicable with current race-based remedial legisla-tion. It is undeniable that racism, both current and past, has left racial minorities in a disadvantaged position, economically, politically, and socially. Laws that provide preferential treatment for such minority groups do not favor them simply to favor them. They also do not seek to "stick it" to whites. Such laws do not rest on the kind of hostility that underlies the Colorado amendment in *Romer* or the village's decision in *Olech*. Rather, such laws seek to increase racial diversity or to remedy disadvantage, rationales that have nothing to do with animus or mere favoritism.

Justice Thomas's objection is only that such rationales are "incon-sistent with the very concept of 'strict scrutiny'."[46] This points to the fundamental difficulty with higher scrutiny not with the actual jus-tification or reason underlying affirmative action. Thomas's issue is ultimately about policy not the Constitution. His dissent in *Grutter* points to the fact that reasonable individuals may well disagree about the merits of adopting such policies.

In this way, the doctrine of strict scrutiny invites more ideological influence than a powers review. This may initially seem counterin-tuitive. After all, imposing such a stringent test such as strict scrutiny seems to be less prone to ideological manipulation. The justice is forced to impose a stringent bar of justification in reviewing the law. Brandon Bartels draws on empirical work to conclude as much: "the greater the constitutional scrutiny prescribed by a legal doctrine, the lower

---

[46] *Grutter* at 350, dissenting

the ideological discretion."[47] He suggests that there is evidence for the conclusion that the higher the level of scrutiny, the less impact ideological considerations will have on the decision. Under Bartels's logic, the doctrine of strict scrutiny limits a justice's discretion.

But his conclusion does not distinguish between cases in which a justice seeks to uphold a law and a one where he or she seeks to invalidate it. In fact, the larger empirical literature on the role of ideology in judicial decision-making often does not make much of this crucial distinction. After all, the counter-majoritarian difficulty and the problem of "judicial activism" that often accompanies it only arise when the Court strikes down legislation not when it upholds it. That is, the problem of ideology is more troublesome in those cases in which a justice seeks to invalidate a law on the basis of ideology rather than when he or she seeks to uphold it.

This means it is not just ideological discretion in general that we ought to guard against. Rather, we ought to prefer a legal framework that makes it less likely a justice will *strike down* a law on the basis of ideology. Bartels's data consist of free speech cases, not those that involve racial discrimination. But we can ask the same question about legal doctrine and ideology with regard to affirmative action: which doctrine, a powers review or strict scrutiny, better constrains or mitigates the role of ideology in striking down such racial preferences?

Compared with strict scrutiny, a powers review makes it less likely that a justice will strike them down on ideological grounds. This is because strict scrutiny imposes on the Court a policy-laden inquiry: is there a compelling purpose to engage in affirmative action and is the law narrowly tailored to that purpose? This requires that a justice decide whether ensuring racial diversity is important enough to justify racial quotas or pluses. Unsurprisingly, conservative justices will be more likely to conclude that diversity is not important enough to discriminate on the basis of race. Liberal justices will conclude the opposite. We ought to leave this kind of consideration to the relevant democratic polity. After all, if the legislature has decided to discriminate on the basis of race to increase diversity in universities, it has obviously decided that the relevant benefits outweigh the costs.

[47] Bartels 2009: 489

A powers review only asks the Court to strike down such laws if they are based on a constitutionally inadmissible purpose such as racial animus. This imposes a more basic and straightforward constitutional test, one that carries a steeper argumentative burden. For a justice to strike down affirmative action legislation, he or she must proclaim that some kind of animus or brute favoritism is afoot. Tellingly, none of the dissenting justices in *Grutter* does so. They may conclude that racial diversity is not a compelling enough reason to discriminate on the basis of race. Just because diversity is not important enough does not make it constitutionally inadmissible. Imposing the additional task of deciding whether the law's purpose is important or even compelling needlessly invites ideological considerations. So, although a powers review will invite justices to strike down laws like (A), it will prevent them from invoking ideology to strike down laws like (B).

Those who find affirmative action laws constitutional, then, place themselves in a bind. On one hand, they accept strict scrutiny for racist legislation, scrutiny that is unnecessary given the arbitrary nature of racism. On the other hand, they must somehow contend why such scrutiny is inapplicable with policies of inclusion. This is a false dilemma. We do better to reject strict scrutiny outright.

SUFFICIENCY OF A POWERS REVIEW: REVISITING PLESSY V. FERGUSON (1896)

The powers review I elaborate in this book is even present in *Plessy v. Ferguson* (1896). An infamous case in constitutional history, *Plessy* upheld state-imposed racial segregation in railway cars. Important to this analysis is the standard the Court adopts and the way Justice Harlan applies it in his dissent. Justice Henry Billings Brown's infamous opinion surprisingly poses the correct constitutional standard: "[E]very exercise of the police power must be reasonable, and extend only to such laws as are enacted in good faith for the promotion of the public good, and not for the annoyance or oppression of a particular class."[48] That is, *Plessy* does not characterize the issue as one

---

[48] *Plessy* at 550

about discrimination. It also does not ask whether segregation invokes a suspect classification triggering heightened scrutiny. Informing the justificatory foregoing constraints, the opinion rightly contends that every exercise of power must be "reasonable" and proffered in "good faith." This is the *ultra vires* doctrine I seek to resuscitate: when the state acts arbitrarily, it goes beyond its powers.

Although Justice Brown poses the right question, his answer is incorrect. He goes on to say that in "determining the question of reasonableness," the Court must make "reference to the established usages, customs, and traditions of the people. . . . Gauged by this standard, we cannot say that a law which authorizes or even requires the separation of the two races in public conveyances is unreasonable."[49] Although Cass Sunstein does not connect his analysis to a powers review, he instructively understands the Equal Protection Clause as designed "to eliminate practices" based on tradition.[50] Equality under the law demands that we do not credit the mere fact that a majority found a practice legitimate or even rational. Because the customs and traditions of that time were and are blatantly racist, so too is Brown's reasoning. He finds reasonable the belief that one race is intrinsically inferior or superior to another. But, again, this is simply false. The problem is not with the standard of reasonableness but its application by the majority opinion in *Plessy*.

This is not some hypothetical claim: the Court would have decided differently, if it had realized that racist beliefs are arbitrary. Justice Harlan's undertheorized dissent in *Plessy* rightly holds that the state acts outside of its powers by enacting such a segregation scheme. And, to be sure, Justice Harlan does not deploy any kind of higher scrutiny in his dissent. Harlan reasons that "[e]very one knows that" the purpose of the segregation law was "not so much to exclude white persons from railroad cars occupied by blacks, as to exclude colored people from coaches occupied by or assigned to white persons."[51] For instance, Harlan correctly noted that Louisiana "did not make discrimination

---

[49] *Plessy* at 550–1
[50] Sunstein 1988: 1174
[51] *Plessy* at 557, dissenting

among whites in the matter of accommodation."[52] By looking at other laws that the state had or had not passed, Harlan homed in on the actual purpose of the segregation statute, one that was simply motivated by animus against a group. This was the purpose of Jim Crow and the range of laws encompassing it, including the one struck down in *Brown*. In fact, Harlan says that "[e]veryone" knows that this is the purpose of the law. This is not some difficult judgment requiring a more careful eye, as Thomas perversely suggests more than one hundred years after *Plessy*.

Harlan's dissent effectively adopts the crucial requirement of good faith that animates the powers review I propose here. Again, a powers review requires that the Court ascertain whether the law's actual purpose is based on a constitutionally inadmissible rationale. After all, the Court may well find a conceivable constitutional purpose for a law. For instance, consider the letter-ist scheme outlined in (C). The state could provide some *ex post facto* justification for this scheme. For instance, it could argue that such a scheme increases economic productivity. The point is that this is not the actual justification for the law. Economic productivity is a sham. Proffering such a rationale fails to engage the requirement of good faith outlined in Chapter 2.

Just as Harlan realized that the actual purpose of the racial segregation scheme was animus against blacks, so too is the actual purpose of (C) based on animus against those with last names beginning with S to Z. And to be clear, this animus can take aim at a lone individual as well. Under a powers review, the Court would realize that the purpose of a law like (C) is not economic productivity but rather to discriminate against a group simply to discriminate against it. In particular, the law seeks to achieve some letter-ist end just as Louisiana's segregation scheme seeks to achieve a racist end.

Contrastingly, consider a teacher's decision to arrange students alphabetically by their last name. Like (C), this kind of policy is also based on the first letter of one's last name. Both policies share that one fact. But it is obvious that the former is not based on animus. "Everyone knows" that a teacher's decision to arrange students in such a manner is not based on hostility against those with a last name beginning with

---

[52] *Plessy* at 557, dissenting

Y or Z. This kind of judgment does not require strict scrutiny. Jim Crow and laws like it rested on a network of policies whose justification rested on animus against blacks. The law struck down at issue in *Plessy* was not an isolated one. Again, it existed alongside numerous other policies that ensured blacks were kept separate including public school segregation and antimiscegenation statutes. The existence of such a regime makes clear that a law like (A) is indeed based on racist reasons.

Harlan's dissent realizes that this kind of animus may be aimed at any group informing the arbitrary nature of the segregation scheme upheld in *Plessy*. Harlan goes on to reason:

> It is one thing for railroad carriers to furnish, or to be required by law to furnish, equal accommodations for all whom they are under a legal duty to carry. It is quite another thing for government to forbid citizens of the white and black races from traveling in the same public conveyance, and to punish officers of railroad companies for permitting persons of the two races to occupy the same passenger coach. If a state can prescribe, as a rule of civil conduct, that whites and blacks shall not travel as passengers in the same railroad coach, why may it not so regulate the use of the streets of its cities and towns as to compel white citizens to keep on one side of a street, and black citizens to keep on the other? Why may it not, upon like grounds, punish whites and blacks who ride together in street cars or in open vehicles on a public road or street? Why may it not require sheriffs to assign whites to one side of a court room, and blacks to the other? And why may it not also prohibit the commingling of the two races in the galleries of legislative halls or in public assemblages convened for the consideration of the political questions of the day? Further, if this statute of Louisiana is consistent with the personal liberty of citizens, why may not the state require the separation in railroad coaches of native and naturalized citizens of the United States, or of Protestants and Roman Catholics?[53]

Harlan considers the Louisiana law similar to ones that would require blacks to walk on one side of the street and whites on the other or that would segregate railway cars on the basis of citizenship status or on

---

[53] *Plessy* at 557–8, dissenting

the basis of being Protestant or Catholic. This is nothing other than the doctrine that that state exceeds its powers by acting on animus, animus that can take aim at any particular group or individual. Harlan does not imply that segregation laws are in some way rational, thereby requiring a heavy or overriding presumption of invalidity. Rather, he rightly suggests – more than one hundred fifteen years ago – that the law at issue in *Plessy* makes no sense. It discriminates against a group for no other or better reason than simply to discriminate against it.

Admittedly, Justice Harlan goes on to say in his dissent that there "is a race so different from our own that we do not permit those belonging to it to become citizens of the United States. . . . I allude to the Chinese race."[54] This anti-Asian sentiment is no doubt part of the racist system that we would now deem arbitrary. The fact that Harlan buys into it ought not to mitigate the significance of the framework he proposes, a framework that is more about powers than identity or higher scrutiny. At a minimum, he points to the arbitrary nature of Louisiana's segregation scheme. Tellingly, *Romer* invokes Harlan's dissent in striking down the antigay Colorado amendment.[55] Taken together, the dissent in *Plessy* and *Romer* inform an alternative way to strike down racist legislation under the Equal Protection Clause that does not require strict scrutiny.

Contrast Justice Harlan's dissent with Justice Warren's reasoning in *Brown*. Nowhere in *Brown* does the Court interrogate or question the justification behind segregation in public schools. It is as if Warren assumes that although the state has the power to segregate individuals in this way, it violates equal protection only when doing so harms blacks. Separate but equal, under this logic, is unconstitutional, because of its effect on the identity group not on account of its invoking a constitutionally inadmissible rationale.

Harlan, however, does not base his dissent on the way in which segregation harms blacks. His dissent is not grounded in the language of identity. Tellingly, he invokes other groups (Protestants and Catholics, or citizens and noncitizens) to draw out the simple fact that such a segregation scheme is based on animus. It is arbitrary because any

---

[54] *Plessy* at 561, dissenting; *see* Chin 1996
[55] *Romer* at 623

group could be subject to it. It makes the constitutional objection to segregation not about suspect classes or identity but solely about the arbitrary nature of state power, a logic that *Romer* draws on years later.

Perhaps *Plessy's* failure to strike down racial segregation explains the doctrinal need for heightened scrutiny. Scholars place the origins of strict scrutiny either with *Korematsu* and cases such as *McLaughlin* and *Bolling v. Sharpe* (1954), the companion case to *Brown* concerning segregation in the District of Columbia or earlier free speech cases.[56] None of this scholarly work, however, explains *why* the Court needed strict scrutiny to invalidate racist legislation – the motivating sting of this chapter. An appreciation of where *Plessy* went wrong provides one such explanation. Justice Brown's opinion in *Plessy* gutted the constitutional requirement – made clear in *Yick Wo* – that state power must be reasonable and nonarbitrary. It effectively held that this kind of racial segregation *was* reasonable. Rather than resuscitating this standard, one that I argue is sufficient to do the equality work, the Court has articulated a new one with the tiers-of-scrutiny approach. On this historical reading of constitutional jurisprudence, strict scrutiny arose precisely because a powers review failed in *Plessy*. This should be reason to reinstitute this review; to apply it correctly as Harlan did more than one hundred fifteen years ago.

In fact, it is imperative we do so. The Court's use of strict scrutiny for legislation that explicitly invokes racial classifications perversely affirms rather than undermines racist beliefs. In doing so, it needlessly stymies the constitutional argument for affirmative action. Affirmative action advocates would do well to reject the suspect class inquiry and the strict scrutiny standard that accompanies it. Otherwise, they create the very constitutional hurdle they seek to scale. Rather than fight against this scrutiny in the affirmative action context, we should reject it across the board turning to a powers analysis. Deploying a more stringent test of justification for legislation that explicitly discriminates against race runs the risk of rationalizing racism.

---

[56] *See, e.g.*, Robinson 2005, Siegel 2006, Simon 1978; for a critical assessment of both approaches, see Fallon 2007

4 WHY RACIAL PROFILING IS BASED ON ANIMUS

Strict scrutiny is not necessary to invalidate laws and policies that are based on animus. This means that the Court can strike down laws like the ones at issue in *Brown* or *McLaughlin* without invoking strict scrutiny. A powers review rightly reveals that such laws are based on nothing but hostility against blacks. Perhaps these are the "easy cases" in which an identity, strict scrutiny approach is not necessary. This chapter considers the harder case of racial profiling. Is racial profiling based on animus? What if individuals of a particular racial group are statistically more likely to commit a certain kind of crime than individuals of another race? In the last chapter, I noted that racial minorities are often disadvantaged economically and socially. Such disadvantage, in turn, explains why affirmative action policies are not based on animus.

If that is the case, why is it not rational for law enforcement to use race as a proxy to profile for crime? (assuming, of course, that law enforcement applies such a policy properly[1])? So, and this is the primary example this chapter discusses, if blacks are more likely to commit certain kinds of drug offenses than whites, is it rational for law enforcement to profile blacks on the highway?[2] Randall Kennedy concedes that the answer may be "yes":

> there are circumstances in which, as a statistical matter, a police
> officer would be correct in estimating that a man's blackness

---

[1] Even if a law is constitutional as written, it can be enforced in an unconstitutional manner. In *Yick Wo*, the animus arose in executing an otherwise constitutional policy. This chapter focuses on just whether a policy of racial profiling would itself be constitutional leaving to one side the possibility that law enforcement would act on animus in enforcing it

[2] For a good discussion of the difference between the irrationality and immorality of racial profiling, see Boonin 2011: 300–50

identifies him as more likely than a similarly situated white person to be involved in criminal wrongdoing. Just as race can signal a heightened risk that a black person will die younger, earn less money, reside farther away from employment opportunities, experience more unpleasant encounters with police, and possess less education than a white person, so, too can race signal a heightened risk that a black person will commit or has committed certain criminal offenses.[3]

And if this is indeed true, racial profiling seems to pass a powers review. It is not based on mere animus against blacks. To be sure, racial profiling may well (and indeed does) have the effect of stigmatizing racial minorities.[4] Among other things, it contributes to a jail population in which a disproportionate number of inmates are individuals of color. This undoubtedly makes us more likely to view racial minorities as deviant members of society. But a powers review does not hinge simply on the possible effects of a law or policy. Keep in mind that Justice Thomas provocatively argues in *Grutter* that affirmative action policies also stigmatize blacks, especially those who do gain admission to elite universities without preferential treatment. This may rightly invite discussion of the policy merits of such programs, discussion that is beyond the scope of this book. Again, this book is about the constitutionality of laws and policies, not whether they are wise. A powers review only asks whether the law invokes a constitutionally inadmissible rationale. As long as a policy, even one that discriminates on the basis of race, is not based on mere hostility, it passes a powers review. Such a review will uphold it.

After all, this kind of review eschews a focus on identity. It holds that a court should not invalidate a law simply because it discriminates against a particular group. This is why Randall Kennedy goes on to argue that even if such profiling is rational, such policies are still unconstitutional. This is because *"Race is different."*[5] Invoking the tiers-of-scrutiny approach, Kennedy says that when "officials discriminate on racial grounds, judges have typically demanded 'strict scrutiny' – the

---

[3] Kennedy 1997: 145
[4] *See generally* Cole 1999: Ch. 1
[5] Kennedy 1997: 146

most intense level of judicial review."[6] So the only way a court could strike down such laws is to reintroduce the identity approach I seek to reject. If race is a constitutional "red flag," as the strict scrutiny logic suggests, this will invariably doom any policy of racial profiling even on the assumption that a particular racial group is more likely to offend or commit a certain kind of crime than another. The constitutionality of racial profiling, then, stands as an important test for a powers review. Is a focus on animus sufficient to invalidate policies that profile on the basis of race? Or do we need the constitutional "red flag" of race to strike down such policies?

I argue that racial profiling is often indeed based on animus, because such profiling cannot be rational. Even if individuals of a particular racial group are more likely to offend than individuals of another (premise 1), this does not make such profiling rational. Simply put, for profiling to be rational, it must actually seek to reduce crime (premise 2). Drawing from Bernard Harcourt's insightful and novel analysis of the irrationality of racial profiling[7] this chapter argues, these two premises cannot both be valid. That is, the more the first premise is true, the more the second is false. Socioeconomic disadvantage faced by racial minorities explains why premise 1 may be true. And because racial profiling will not alter this disadvantage (in fact, it will most likely make a bad situation worse), it does not stand to reduce crime, thereby undermining premise 2. If this argument already strikes the reader as obvious, my point is made. If it does not, I spend the rest of the chapter making clear why premises 1 and 2 cannot both be true. I make clear that a court does not need to invoke the "red flag" of race to arrive at this conclusion.

Current sociological scholarly work shows that unlike their white counterparts, racial minorities often live in communities that suffer from severe poverty, joblessness, and family disruption.[8] These structural disadvantages at the community level make individuals who live there more likely to commit certain kinds of crime.[9] Such conditions

[6] Kennedy 1997: 147
[7] Harcourt 2007
[8] *See e.g.*, Peterson and Krivo 2005, Sampson and Bean 2006, Sampson and Wilson 1995
[9] Ibid.

delimit and constrain an individual's range of choices or opportunities. Because profiling people of color will not change these structural limitations, it will not appreciably reduce their likelihood to commit crime.

In fact, profiling these racial minorities stands to increase crime among the racial group *not* being profiled – namely, whites. This means that a policy of racial profiling cannot seek to reduce crime. If it cannot seek to reduce crime, why is law enforcement deploying it? This means its actual purpose must therefore be based on some kind of animus or hostility against the profiled racial group. Harcourt concludes that "the problem with racial profiling is about the profiling, not about race."[10] He does not conclude that profiling is wrong or that its costs outweigh its benefits. After all, these may well be the kinds of policy considerations that are best left to a legislature and not a court. Harcourt makes clear that profiling is irrational. Even on its own terms, profiling cannot seek to reduce crime.

That means any decision to profile racial minorities must be based on hostility. Although Harcourt does not connect this conclusion to the Equal Protection Clause or the constitutional ban on laws and policies that are based on animus, his argument informs the powers review I propose here, or so this chapter suggests. Harcourt does not object to racial profiling by arguing that it fails to serve a compelling purpose or that it is not narrowly tailored in some particular way. His language is more fundamental, pointing to the fact that profiling is simply irrational. We do not need to treat race as a "red flag" triggering strict scrutiny, once we realize that racial profiling cannot seek to reduce crime.

Crucial to this argument, then, is realizing the purpose of such profiling. Too often we assume that this purpose is just to apprehend more rather than fewer criminals. But this chapter argues that profiling must actually seek to reduce crime if it is not to be based on animus. After all, if profiling individuals of a certain race actually increases crime over a policy of random stops or searches; this cannot be a rational law enforcement strategy. It means that such profiling is based on something else: hostility against the profiled group. This goes

---

[10] Harcourt 2007: 215

unnoticed precisely because the language of identity has hijacked the racial profiling debate. Those who object to such profiling do better *not* to invoke the "red flag" of race. For a powers review rightly homes in on the actual purpose of such a policy. Doing so, as this chapter argues, reveals that racial profiling cannot be about reducing crime.

This chapter is in three parts. First, I briefly define "racial profiling" distinguishing it from law enforcement's use of race to apprehend a previously identified suspect. Second, I outline the two premises that are necessary for racial profiling to pass a powers review. Third, I suggest why these two premises cannot both be true, drawing from sociological work on structural disadvantage to inform Harcourt's argument. This means that law enforcement's decision to profile on racial grounds must be based on racial animus or hostility.

DEFINITION OF RACIAL PROFILING

I define "racial profiling" as a prospective law enforcement strategy that explicitly selects or profiles individuals of a particular race to uncover criminal activity. The crucial part of this definition is the prospective nature of a policy. Race may also be used in a retrospective manner. In fact, this may be the more common use of race by law enforcement. For instance, if a victim or eyewitness identifies an assailant as a white, tall, middle-aged man with a beard, authorities will be on the lookout for someone who fits that description. This may mean they will stop or focus their attention on individuals who are members of a particular race – in this case, those who are white. This is not an instance of racial profiling. Here the authorities are not profiling individuals of a particular racial group to reduce crime. Rather, they are focusing on such individuals to see if these individuals fit the description of a previously identified criminal. The first is prospective; the second is retrospective. It would not make sense if law enforcement could not use race in a retrospective manner. Here race is being deployed like any other characteristic that would be relevant to apprehend a suspect.

Although there is no Supreme Court case that directly speaks to this distinction, the Second Circuit Court of Appeals upheld the constitutionality of deploying race in a retrospective manner in *Brown v.*

City of Oneonta (2nd Cir. 2000). The town of Oneonta in upstate New York is a predominantly white community with, at that time, approximately 10,000 full-time residents of whom fewer than 300 are black. Additionally, the State University of New York College at Oneonta had a student population of 7,500 students of which just 2 percent were black. In 1992, just outside of the town, someone attacked an elderly woman in her house. She identified the assailant as a young black man with a cut on his hand. Consequently, police immediately contacted the university for a list of all black male students. The police then questioned each of these students also searching black young males on the streets for a cut on their hand. In total, law enforcement had questioned more than two hundred people, ultimately making no arrest.

Those who had been searched filed a lawsuit against the city raising various constitutional and statutory claims. Relevant here is their equal protection claim. The question is whether law enforcement violated the Constitution by using "an express racial classification by stopping and questioning plaintiffs solely on the basis of their race."[11] The court held that these actions did not violate the Constitution. In fact, the court refused to subject the city's decision to search to strict scrutiny. The court made clear that race was not the only factor used by law enforcement. The suspect "description contained not only race, but also gender and age, as well as the possibility of a cut on the hand."[12]

I suggest that crucial to the court's reasoning is not that the police deployed other criteria besides race but that that the police used the racial description not to profile but to apprehend a previously identified suspect. In *United States v. Avery* (6th Cir. 1997), the Sixth Circuit Court of Appeals held that law enforcement did not violate the Constitution in stopping Cortez Avery, a young black man who, as it turned out, was in possession of illegal narcotics. The court reasoned that because police stopped Avery for reasons that had nothing to do with his race (e.g., Avery appeared to be in a hurry, he had suspicious clothing), the police did not violate the Equal Protection Clause.[13] The court made clear that if law enforcement initiated "an

[11] *Oneonta* at 337
[12] *Oneonta* at 337
[13] *Avery* at 358

investigation of a citizen based solely on that citizen's race, without more, then a violation of the Equal Protection Clause has occurred."[14] The court in *Oneonta* focuses on the language of "without more" to hold that law enforcement's decision to search black residents and students was indeed based on something more: it was based on a victim's description of her assailant.

It may seem that, taken together, *Avery* and *Oneonta* stand for the proposition that law enforcement may search individuals as long as they do not exclusively rely on race. Suppose, police had stopped Avery precisely because he was a young black male operating on the assumption that individuals fitting that description are more likely to possess certain kinds of illegal narcotics than individuals who do not fit that description. Here the police are also operating on factors besides race. But this kind of search is categorically distinct from the search in *Oneonta*. In a genuine case of profiling, the police are not operating on a victim's description of the assailant but on some kind of statistical belief that certain individuals are more likely to offend than others. *Oneonta* captures this difference when it goes on to say that the "description [of a young black man with a cut on his hand] . . . originated not with the state but with the victim."[15] This is the crucial difference. The retrospective use of race is based on a victim's description, a description that could include any race. It all depends on whom the victim identifies as the assailant.

Contrastingly, the prospective use of race entails operating on what the state believes is a statistical probability about the likelihood to commit crime. This chapter does not analyze the retrospective use of race, a kind of policy that *Oneonta* deems constitutional. By "racial profiling," I mean a more controversial policy, one in which law enforcement singles out individuals of a particular race to reduce crime. The issue is not about whether law enforcement may use race along with other characteristics. That is largely irrelevant. Rather, the issue is *how* they use these criteria. If they deploy race along with other factors to locate a previously identified suspect, this seems rational. If they deploy race along with other factors to reduce crime (a prospective endeavor), we

[14] *Avery* at 355
[15] *Oneonta* at 338

have a more difficult case, one that is a genuine case of racial profiling. Policies such as stopping black male motorists more often than white ones with regard to drug crimes or searching Muslim-appearing men at airports with regards to terrorism are genuine instances of racial profiling. The rest of the chapter interrogates whether such policies are indeed rational or whether they are based on animus, violating a powers review.

THE ARGUMENT FOR RACIAL PROFILING

Consider a relatively uncontroversial case in which profiling would be irrational. In line with the example of the previous chapter, consider a policy of "letter profiling." If law enforcement began profiling individuals whose last names begin with S to Z for certain kinds of criminal activity, such a policy would make little sense. The Court would strike it down under a powers review for being based on animus or hostility against S–Zs. It seeks to "stick it" to those with last names beginning with a particular letter. So what does it take for a policy of profiling not to be based on animus? I submit that the following must be true:

> Premise 1: An individual who is a member of a particular group is more likely to commit a crime than an individual who is not part of that group.
> Premise 2: Explicitly targeting individuals of that particular group will reduce the incidence of crime more than not targeting them.
> Conclusion: Such profiling is not based on animus.

This argument works for any kind of profiling, not just racial profiling. Obviously, the focus of this chapter is on the constitutionality of racial profiling and, in particular, the question of whether law enforcement may profile blacks for certain kinds of criminal activity. For a policy of racial profiling not to be based on animus, each of the premises must be true with regard to the racial group being profiled. I consider each premise in turn. Ultimately, I argue that premises 1 and 2 cannot both be true. That is, if blacks are more likely to commit a crime, this means that profiling them will not reduce the incidence of crime.

Premise 1: Race as a Proxy for Likelihood to Commit a Crime

Most scholarly action and debate is on the validity of premise 1. On one hand, scholars argue that race may well be a legitimate proxy for likelihood to commit certain crimes. And we can specify this proxy as one that involves gender and age as well (e.g., being a young black male). Heather Mac Donald of the Manhattan Institute argues that certain racial minorities do offend at higher rates than whites and that we too often turn a blind eye to these kinds of facts.[16] It is also undeniable that "black non-Hispanic men" were, at least in 2010, incarcerated at a rate "that was nearly 7 times higher than white non-Hispanic males."[17] Economists have also put forth models that demonstrate that when it comes to certain kinds of drug offenses, blacks and other racial minorities are more likely to offend than their white counterparts.[18] These studies do not suggest that blacks are statistically more likely to commit any drug crime than their white counterparts. Rather, the studies suggest that at least with regard to certain more serious drug crimes, blacks are more likely to offend than whites. For instance, John Knowles, Nicola Persico, and Petra Todd, whose article is often cited to substantiate premise 1, conclude that blacks are more likely to carry "large quantities" of drugs than their white counterparts.[19] This means that for certain kinds of offenses, race is indeed a proxy for likelihood to commit crime.

But even if premise 1 is true, this may still reveal that racial animus is afoot. Frederick Schauer makes this kind of argument by focusing on whether the relevant democratic body deploys other kinds of "non-spurious proxies." Schauer suggests that "to pick out only one from a large array of non-spurious proxies" means that the relevant policy "has a goal other than that of using efficient proxies . . . for if that were the case than some of the other proxies would have been employed as well."[20] This informs the good-faith requirement of a powers review.

---

[16] Mac Donald 2001
[17] *See* http://bjs.ojp.usdoj.gov/index.cfm?ty=pbdetail&iid=2230
[18] *See, e.g.*, Borooah 2001, Knowles, Persico, and Todd 2001, Persico 2002
[19] Knowles, Persico, and Todd 2001: 228
[20] Schauer 2003: 148

If law enforcement profiles racial minorities for certain drug-related offenses, are they also deploying other proxies?

White-collar crime is highly correlated with race and gender: white males are far more likely to commit federal securities fraud than any other group. In fact, nearly every person that commits this kind of fraud is a white male.[21] A policy of racial profiling that merely stopped black drivers more frequently but did not also include some kind of additional screening or investigation of white males occupying or pursuing such business positions would suggest a racist purpose rather than a benign one. Obviously, there is a problem if law enforcement is profiling one racial group but giving a "pass" to another. It will not suffice to say that white-collar crime is insignificant or less important than drug-related offenses. Recent statistics by the Federal Bureau of Investigation reveal that this kind of fraud is hardly inconsequential.[22] But as Richard Delgado states, "nobody suggests racially profiling whites or requiring every corporate executive, design engineer, or accountant at a major firm to have his or her briefcase checked every day."[23] Tellingly, the debate over racial profiling invariably is about racial minorities, not the racial majority.

Even if we accept the idea that drug-related crime is worse than its white-collar counterpart, consider how harshly we treat convicted pedophiles. For instance, unlike convicted thieves or even murderers, pedophiles must register where they live with the local police. Even after serving their sentence, pedophiles are subject to a range of conditions that are not imposed on others. Statistically, three out of every four pedophiles is a white male.[24] This suggests that a legislature bent on curbing pedophilia ought to profile white males. For instance, consider a policy of imposing additional screening for white males seeking a career in elementary school teaching.

Certainly, a legislature may address a problem "one step at a time." It need not deploy all relevant proxies. But a law that only profiles racial minorities, not any white individuals, may suggest that the purpose is

---

[21] *See* Weisburd, Wheeler, Waring, and Bode 1999: 50–1
[22] *See* http://www.fbi.gov/stats-services/publications/financial-crimes-report-2010–2011
[23] Delgado 2003: 74
[24] *See, e.g.*, Jones, Pelissier and Klein-Saffran 2006: 90, Meloy 2005: 10

not efficiency but "animus" against a group.[25] The law's actual purpose is tainted or corrupted by racism. By invoking higher scrutiny in the case of racial profiling and cursorily dismissing its legitimacy, we fail to realize the severely unbalanced nature of the profiling debate, one that is invariably about people of color and not other groups.

To be clear, under this reasoning, the problem is not that the state deploys the use of race as proxy for various attributes (this may in of itself be rational, although I challenge this conclusion later in the chapter). Rather, the specter of racism arises because the state immediately and only considers membership in a racial minority group as a proxy. And the state does so to hurt that group. This explains the difference between a policy that searches or stops blacks because they are statistically more likely to be carrying drugs, and a policy such as affirmative action. Although the latter also homes in on being a member of a racial minority, it does so to help minorities. Policies like racial profiling, on the other hand, use minority group status to harm individuals of that group by subjecting them to a search. This is why the failure to use or even to discuss other proxies in the profiling debate, but not necessarily in the affirmative action one, points to a racist purpose. So even if premise 1 is valid, this may still reveal a racist purpose given that law enforcement only profiles racial minorities rather than individuals in the racial majority.

On the other hand, scholars simply argue that premise 1 is false. The idea that race is a proxy for likelihood to commit crime is fallacious. Evidence seeking to prove the premise is merely a self-fulfilling prophecy. More blacks are arrested simply because law enforcement has acted on racist beliefs, not because blacks are more likely than their white counterparts to commit crime. A higher likelihood of imprisonment does not necessarily mean a higher likelihood of engaging in criminal behavior. Racial profiling "results from a self-fulfilling statistical prophecy: racial stereotypes influence police to arrest minorities more frequently than non-minorities, thereby generating statistically disparate arrest patterns that in turn form the basis for further selectivity."[26] This criticism trades on the idea that racial profiling arises precisely because

---

[25] *See generally* Schauer 2003
[26] "Developments in the Law" 1998: 1508; *see also* Harris 2002

those in the criminal justice system believe that blacks compared with whites (or the poor compared with the rich) are intrinsically more likely to commit crimes. Because more blacks or more poor individuals are arrested, more are in prison, thereby perpetuating and legitimizing the belief that they are more likely to engage in criminal activity.

Reconsider the case of letter-ism. As a result of letter-ist policies, S–Zs suffer from structural disparities in wealth, education, and social status. Suppose further that law enforcement started concentrating their energies on individuals with last names beginning with S to Z. This means that the police begin aggressively monitoring and searching S–Zs. In turn, because police arrest more S–Zs than A–Rs, jails are full of individuals with last names beginning with these letters. The state, then, contends that letter profiling is rational: after all, look at how many S–Zs are in the criminal justice system. Economists even proffer models and statistics to show that such profiling is efficient. I am confident that we would quickly reject these arguments. After all, law enforcement's initial decision to look more closely at S to Zs was entirely arbitrary. There is no reason to think that these individuals are more likely to commit a crime. Similarly, we should reject the alleged rationality of racial profiling. Again, unless we believe that blacks are intrinsically more likely to commit crime (a racist belief on par with its letter-ist counterpart), racial profiling is not rational.

For the remainder of this chapter, however, I assume that premise 1 is valid and that authorities are indeed deploying other nonspurious racial proxies where appropriate. I do so fully conceding that this assumption may be controversial. But this chapter seeks to show that a court does not need to construct its own models engaging in the kind of statistical analysis that is characteristic of the literature in this area to strike down policies of racial profiling. If I am to suggest the superiority of a powers review, I must show how even in the face of the truth of premise 1, this kind of review is sufficient to do the equality work. Justice Harlan concluded that "[e]veryone knows" that the actual purpose of Louisiana's segregation scheme was to keep blacks away from whites. Similarly, I aim to show why a court must conclude that the actual purpose of racial profiling is also about animus against blacks. For even if premise 1 is true, such profiling cannot be rational.

Premise 2: Profiling Seeks to Reduce Crime

If premise 1 is true, it may seem that the debate over racial profiling is over. After all, this is often where scholarly work ends. Those who favor racial profiling policies seek only to show that race is a reliable proxy. Once this is established, law enforcement's decision to profile blacks for certain kinds of crimes must be rational. It is no surprise, then, that those who object to such profiling invoke the language of identity and the "red flag" of race to invalidate it on constitutional grounds. But, and this is the crucial point of this chapter, premise 1 is not sufficient to establish the rationality of racial profiling. The following argument is incomplete:

> Premise 1: An individual who is a member of a particular racial group
>   is more likely to commit a crime than an individual who is not part
>   of that group.
> Conclusion: Racial profiling is not based on animus.

Just because race is a reliable proxy for likelihood to commit crime does not mean that it is rational for police to profile individuals of that racial group. It must also be the case that singling out such individuals will lower the incidence of crime than not singling them out. This is a core argument of Bernard Harcourt's book *Against Prediction: Profiling, Policing, and Punishing in an Actuarial Age*, perhaps the most insightful contribution to the debate over racial profiling. Harcourt argues that even if a policy of racial profiling apprehends more criminals than a policy of random searches, it may still be irrational. This is because the goal of such profiling is to reduce crime not to catch more criminals. I cannot do justice to the thoroughness, nuance, and complexity of his argument in this chapter. I encourage the reader to read the book in its entirety. The following paragraph captures the core of his argument:

> Ironically, the detection of criminal activity is not necessarily the primary goal of law enforcement. To be sure, high search success rates . . . are good, but they are not a good in themselves. The primary goal of law enforcement is to decrease the rate of crime – not to detect crime. And unfortunately – somewhat paradoxically – these two goals may conflict. When members of the profiled group are

less responsive to changes in policing . . . but members of the non-
profiled group are very much more responsive to decreased policing . . . then profiling on a nonspurious trait may actually increase
the rate of the targeted crime.[27]

To exemplify the conceptual nature of this problem, Harcourt's
example is the Internal Revenue Service (IRS) profiling tax returns to
reduce tax evasion. Harcourt considers a hypothetical case in which
the IRS profiles tax returns by drywall contractors to reduce such evasion.[28] The agency does so operating on the valid premise (Harcourt
assumes this) that drywall contractors are more likely to engage in tax
evasion given their "poor cash flow situation."[29] Once this profiling is
known, those who are not drywall contractors – other subcontractors
such as "painters, roofers, electricians" and the like – consider skim-
ming on their taxes.[30] After all, although members of the nonprofiled
group may well be audited, they know that the IRS is focusing more
resources on drywall contractors than on them. This, in turn, will lead
to more tax evasion. And it will also likely not bring down the rate of
tax evasion by drywall contractors who, because of cash flow problems, are still forced to engage in such evasion. This suggests that it is
irrational for the IRS to profile drywall contractors. Doing so will not
reduce the incidence of tax evasion.

So for racial profiling to be rational, it must seek to reduce the
crime rate. Consider the example of racial profiling in airport security.
Assume that individuals who appear to be Muslim are more likely to
bomb or hijack a plane than those who do not appear to be Muslim.
That is, assume that religious affiliation is a reliable proxy. Because religion is not an obvious observable trait, authorities profile individuals
who appear to be of Middle Eastern descent. Obviously, there would
be no issue of profiling if authorities had enough resources and there
were enough time to thoroughly search each prospective passenger.
The issue is how to search with limited resources. One option would
be to search individuals randomly, which is what authorities often do.

[27] Harcourt 2007: 124
[28] Harcourt 2007: 136
[29] Harcourt 2007: 136
[30] Harcourt 2007: 136

Another option would be to focus resources on certain individuals instead of others. This is what a policy of racial profiling does, searching more thoroughly individuals who appear to be of Middle Eastern descent than those who do not.

The crucial point is why authorities are profiling individuals of a particular race. Why don't authorities just randomly search prospective passengers? Why focus on this particular group? Is it because authorities dislike those who appear Middle Eastern? If this is the case, such a policy of profiling is unconstitutional. It is based on some kind of hatred for the profiled group. Our inquiry would be over. Such a policy would be like the ones struck down in *Brown* or *McLaughlin*, based, in this case, only on dislike for individuals who appear Middle Eastern.

So if the actual purpose is not hostility, why profile? Simply put, such profiling must seek to reduce more crime than a policy of random searches or stops. In profiling, the authorities seek to reduce the number of terrorist attacks. Whatever else may be true about those who appear to be of Middle Eastern descent, racial profiling would be irrational if it did not stand to reduce the chances of such an attack. Otherwise, racial profiling would be irrational. But, and this is the crucial move of Harcourt's book, profiling Middle Eastern–appearing individuals will not be a more efficient strategy of reducing the number of terrorist attacks. For once would-be terrorists realize that authorities are profiling those who appear Middle Eastern, they will make sure that the next terrorist does *not* appear Middle Eastern. Simple as that. That is, they will seek to avoid being in the profiled group. According to Harcourt, while a racial profiling policy may catch more Middle Eastern–appearing individuals in the "*immediate* aftermath of implementing [it]," it will in the long term increase the incidence of attacks.[31] Again, once those who seek to engage in terrorist attacks learn about the profile, they will seek to avoid it. And if that's the case, a policy of profiling cannot be rational.

This is why Harcourt concludes that law enforcement is always better off engaging in a policy of random searches or stops: "What randomization achieves, in essence, is to neutralize the perverse effects

---

[31] Harcourt 207: 231

of prediction, both in terms of the possible effects on overall crime and of the other social costs."[32] Similarly, the IRS would do better to engage in a policy of randomization, auditing taxpayers randomly. Randomization does not focus attention on any single racial group. Anyone seeking to engage in a terrorist attack could be subject to a search just as any one could be subject to a tax audit. Because law enforcement's resources are not focused on any particular group, all groups are equally deterred from committing an attack. So if authorities *still* insist on profiling Middle Eastern–appearing individuals, they cannot care about reducing the number of terrorist attacks. Their actual reason must be based on something else. They may dislike Middle Eastern–appearing individuals so much that they are willing to compromise any goal of reducing the chance of a future attack. A powers review invalidates laws and policies that are based on this kind of dislike or mere hostility.

To be clear, this conclusion is independent from the fact that Middle Eastern–appearing individuals may be more likely (at least initially) to commit terrorist attacks. The point is that this profile will become irrelevant, even counterproductive, once authorities start acting on it. Insisting on a policy of racial profiling in the face of this fact cannot be rational. This is why premise 2 is crucial. It is not sufficient that a race is a reliable proxy. It must also be the case that *acting* on that proxy will, in fact, reduce crime.

In their philosophical defense of racial profiling, Mathias Risse and Richard Zeckhauser begin their article by assuming that "police can curb crime if they stop, search, or investigate members of such groups differentially. That is, we assume that such measures eliminate more crime than do other measures for equivalent disruption and expenditures of resources."[33] For, if this assumption fails, the philosophical question "addressed in this article no longer arises. The moral problem posed by profiling arises only if [it] contribute[s] to the provision of a public good as basic as security. Otherwise, racial profiling would be *obviously* illegitimate."[34] As Risse and Zeckhauser make

[32] Harcourt 2007: 238
[33] Risse and Zeckhauser 2004: 132
[34] Risse and Zeckhauser 2004: 132

clear, if racial profiling does not "eliminate more crime" than a policy of randomization, such profiling is illegitimate. There is no need to engage in a philosophical defense, as their argument goes on to do, if such a policy is, from the get-go, irrational.

Similarly, the doctrine of strict scrutiny is also unnecessary if racial profiling does not even make sense on its own terms. I illuminate the "obvious illegitimacy" of racial profiling by considering a policy of profiling blacks for certain kinds of drug offenses, a policy that is often at the center of this debate. For if profiling does not seek to reduce crime, a government's insistence on still deploying it reveals that racial animus is afoot.

INELASTICITY AND STRUCTURAL DISADVANTAGE

Both premises must be true for racial profiling *not* to be based on animus. To pass a powers review, it must be the case that blacks are indeed more likely to commit certain kinds of crime (premise 1) and that profiling them will reduce crime more than a policy of randomization (premise 2). Otherwise, why is law enforcement engaging in racial profiling? I argue that if premise 1 is true, premise 2 must be false. I assume that premise 1 is true. Again, that means a policy of racial profiling will result in law enforcement apprehending more criminals than a policy of randomization. Because blacks offend at a higher rate than whites, focusing on them will result in more arrests. But this does not automatically make such profiling rational. Profiling must seek to reduce drug-related crimes It must seek to lower the overall crime rate just as profiling Middle Eastern–appearing individuals must seek to lower the incidence of terrorist attacks. Harcourt argues that we "have every reason to believe" that the overall crime rate will in fact increase.[35] This is because (1) the group not being profiled (i.e., whites) will (now) be more likely to offend and (2) the group being profiled (i.e., blacks) will not be less likely to offend. Central to this argument is what Harcourt calls the "elasticity" of each group. He defines elasticity as "the degree to which changes in policing affect

[35] Harcourt 2007: 123

changes in offending."[36] Whites will be elastic to law enforcement's decision not to focus on them. Simultaneously, blacks will be inelastic to law enforcement's decision to focus on them. I want to consider each of these in turn.

First, the very reason law enforcement searches individuals in airports or stops them on the highway is to deter criminal activity. If the would-be terrorist knows he may be searched and thereby arrested, he will be less likely to engage in a terrorist attack. Similarly, if the would-be drug carrier knows he will be stopped and thereby arrested for carrying drugs, he will be less likely to carry drugs. This is a basic assumption of rational behavior in light of this kind of law enforcement policy. After all, if individuals were not deterred by the possibility of arrest pursuant to a search, there would be no need to search or stop them. So if law enforcement does not focus on searching or stopping a particular group, that group will have more incentive to offend. Members of the group will change their behavior and increase their likelihood of committing crime. If authorities move from a policy of randomization to one in which they racially profile blacks, whites will be elastic to this change. Whereas whites and blacks had an equal chance of being searched or stopped, whites are now less likely to be stopped. That means that whites will have more of an incentive to offend, under a policy of racially profiling blacks, thereby increasing the crime rate.

Second, and more important, blacks will not decrease their likelihood to commit crime. They will be inelastic to being profiled for drug-related crimes. Why? Harcourt says:

> If [minorities] do in fact offend more, there is every reason to believe that they may also be *less* elastic to policing. . . . If they are, for instance, offending more because they are socioeconomically more disadvantaged, then it would follow logically that they may also have less elasticity of offending to policing because they have fewer alternative job opportunities.[37]

Precisely because blacks will be inelastic to being profiled, racial profiling will not reduce the overall crime rate. Unfortunately, outside of

---

[36] Harcourt 2007: 23
[37] Harcourt 2007: 123

a few sentences regarding disadvantage such as the ones just noted, Harcourt does not do enough in buttressing these claims. After all, the contention that profiling does not stand to reduce the crime rate among blacks is the lynchpin of his argument. That is, Harcourt does not fully explain why on one hand, blacks may be more likely to commit certain kinds of crime but on the other hand, they would be inelastic to being profiled. Fully explaining this point better illuminates why premises 1 and 2 cannot both be true.

Consider again premise 1 which I assume is true. If it is true, why is it true? That is, why is race a proxy for likelihood to commit certain kinds of drug crimes? The economic models that seek to show that individuals of one racial group are more likely to offend than another do not ask this follow-up question. But it is precisely this explanation that I argue reveals the irrationality of racial profiling. For if such profiling seeks to reduce crime, it matters why race is indeed a proxy.

There are two possible answers, one of which we can dismiss as racist. This explanation maintains that blacks or any racial group simply have a taste for violent crime. This explanation suggests that by virtue of being black, blacks are more likely to commit violence. This would mean that race is not so much a proxy for likelihood to commit crime but is *itself* an indication of criminality. Although this is certainly an explanation for why premise 1 is true, it is a patently racist one. The idea that that individuals of a particular racial group *qua* racial group are more likely to offend is nothing other than the idea that one race is intrinsically inferior to another. This kind of explanation explicitly trades on notions of racial animus or hostility, hostility that the Court rules out as unconstitutional. Such explanations are just as arbitrary as ones that contend that the first letter of one's last name is itself an indication of criminality. This cannot be an explanation as to why premise 1 would be true. A court can rule it out automatically.

So if premise 1 is true, it must be so because race is a *proxy* for likelihood to commit crime. It is not race *qua* race that is doing the explanatory work. Race is standing in for something else, hence the language of "proxy." What is this "something else?" Harcourt remarks that it is conditions such as socioeconomic disadvantage and fewer job alternatives. Again, it is precisely such disadvantage that explains why remedial policies like affirmative action are not based on mere animus. While this explanation about socioeconomic status is intuitive, there is a robust sociological literature that informs this explanation. Robert J. Sampson and William Julius Wilson, the leading figures in this line of scholarly work, show that

> [u]nlike the dominant tradition in criminology that seeks to distinguish offenders from nonoffenders, the macrosocial or community level of explanation asks what is it about community structures and cultures that produces differential rates of crime [citations omitted]. As such, the goal of macrolevel research is not to explain individual involvement in criminal behavior but to isolate characteristics of communities, cities, or even societies that lead to high rates of criminality. From this viewpoint the "ecological fallacy" – inferring individual-level relations based on aggregate data – is not at issue because the unit of explanation and analysis is the community.[38]

The central insight here is that likelihood to commit to crime is based on a community-level analysis. Subsequent studies have confirmed that there is a wide variability among crime rates across black and white communities due in large part to socioeconomic disadvantage.[39] What are these community disadvantages that produce differential crime rates? Scholarly work looks to "differing combinations of poverty, income, family disruption, and joblessness/ unemployment."[40] Race is a proxy for likelihood to commit crime, because race is a proxy for where individuals are likely to live.

This suggests that such "structural variables predict violent crime in the same way for all racial and ethnic groups."[41] This "racial invariance hypothesis" has been confirmed by other studies looking at data from both black and white communities.[42] Put differently, one's likelihood to commit crime is based on one's community environment, not one's race. And as a statistical matter, blacks live in worse communities than whites. After all, "whereas less than 10 percent of poor Whites typically

---

[38] Sampson and Wilson 1995: 38–9
[39] *See generally* Peterson and Krivo 2005, Pratt and Cullen 2005
[40] Peterson and Krivo 2005: 337
[41] Peterson and Krivo 2005: 338
[42] *See, e.g.*, McNulty 2001, Shihadeh and Shrum 2004, Wooldredge and Thistlethwaite 2003; *see generally* Peterson and Krivo 2005: 338–43

live in extreme poverty areas, almost half of poor Blacks live in such areas."[43] This means that it is hard to find white communities that share the same debilitating poverty, joblessness, and family disruption that is often found in certain black communities. This disparity is so severe that in an article titled "Urban Black Violence: The Effect of Male Joblessness and Family Disruption," Sampson concludes that data "show . . . racial differences are so strong that the worst urban contexts in which whites reside with respect to poverty and family disruption are considerably better off than the *mean* levels for black communities."[44] So race is a proxy for likelihood to commit crime, precisely because it is a reliable proxy for likelihood to live in these poor, disadvantaged neighborhoods. This also informs the grim reality that blacks, as compared to whites, are more likely to be poorer, less educated, and in worse health.

Importantly, this explanation of why premise 1 is true illuminates why premise 2 must be false. Law enforcement policies that profile racial minorities do not at all stand to decrease the crime rate among these groups. This is because such policies do not seek to alter the structural disadvantage that makes individuals living in those communities more likely to resort to crime than those who are living in more advantaged neighborhoods. After all, profiling blacks for drug-related crimes will not alter the poverty, joblessness, and lack of opportunities that contribute to differential crime rates in the first place. If police profile individuals of that group, the group's range of options does not change. The disadvantage does not miraculously disappear. Individuals may be more likely to be apprehended by the police, but this does not stand to change their behavior. The more one thinks that such profiling will deter criminal behavior; the more one must deny the structural disadvantage explanation for why premise 1 may be true. And the more one denies that explanation, the more credible the racist explanation that blacks simply have a taste for crime becomes.

Profiling operates on the assumption that the profiled group will indeed be less likely to offend. That is, a policy of profiling (if it is to be rational) must seek to reduce the crime rate. But if crime rates among

---

[43] Sampson and Bean 2006: 12
[44] Sampson 1987: 353–4

racial groups differ due to differences in structural deprivation at the community level, profiling the higher offending group will not change their likelihood to commit crime. Again, such differential rates are due to structural features – features that rest at the level of the community, not at the level of the individual. "Everyone knows" that racial profiling does not seek to address the problem of racial inequality. But it is this very inequality that contributes to a higher crime rate among blacks.

If anything, profiling blacks stands to exacerbate the structural disadvantage that contributes to these differential rates. Harcourt devotes an entire chapter to what he calls the "ratchet effect."[45] This effect occurs because racial profiling apprehends more criminals who are black than a policy of randomization. This, in turn, means that more blacks will be arrested, and as more are arrested, more are imprisoned. The carceral population now has a higher proportion of blacks. Law enforcement looks to this population and devotes even more resources to profiling blacks. This leads to even more arrests and an even higher percentage of inmates who are racial minorities. What began as only a small difference in the percentage of inmates who are individuals of color (due to differing offending rates) ratchets up to an even larger difference. And this larger difference means that even more resources will be devoted to focusing on racial minorities. This, in turn, will only increase the percentage of individuals of color in the carceral population.

Harcourt treats this effect as a social cost to racial profiling. This is no doubt true. Such a ratchet effect amplifies the idea that blacks are the face of criminality. But even more important, this drive to arrest even more racial minorities reinforces the structural disadvantage that leads to a higher offending rate in the first place. These arrests lead to even more family disruptions at the community level, disruptions that stand to reinforce and exacerbate existing structural disadvantage. Again, premise 1 is true (race is a proxy for likelihood to commit crime) because blacks are more likely to live in communities with these debilitating conditions. Far from decreasing the crime rate in these areas, racial profiling and the ratchet effect stand to increase it.

[45] Harcourt 2007: 145–71

Well-established theory and a solid body of evidence indicate that high levels of incarceration concentrated in impoverished communities has a destabilizing effect on community life, so that the most basic underpinnings of informal social control are damaged. This, in turn, reproduces the very dynamics that sustain crime.[46]

This informs the conclusion that racial profiling is "obviously illegitimate." Premise 1 is true in virtue of the fact that certain racial minorities live in communities with extreme poverty, joblessness, and family disruption. These factors are so severe that profiling that group will not change their offending rates. This informs the inelastic nature of the profiled group. If anything, such a policy makes the situation worse. By further disrupting networks and families (the very structures that lead to the validity of premise 1), law enforcement makes a bad situation worse. This suggests that profiling not only fails to reduce crime but also may even intensify it. Not to mention the fact that the non-profiled group will increase its crime rate. After all, law enforcement is focusing fewer resources on searching or stopping whites. Premise 2, then, must be false for the very reason premise 1 is true. Both cannot be true.

This means racially profiling blacks for drug-related crime is irrational. Thus, any decision to engage in it must be based on hostility against the profiled group. Its actual purpose cannot be the reduction of crime but rather animus against blacks. Invoking the constitutional "red flag" of race and the strict scrutiny doctrine that accompanies it misses this important point. It conveniently permits a court to strike down racial profiling without revealing that a state that seeks to institute it must be doing so on the basis of animus. By short-circuiting this analysis, we fail to realize that racial profiling is not about reducing crime but about "sticking it" to those racial minorities who offend at higher rates. Like its Jim Crow counterparts, laws that seek to profile blacks for drug-related offenses are therefore unconstitutional.

A constitutional decision that does not focus on race but rather the profiling part of racial profiling reveals one way the state can in fact reduce crime. Profiling blacks is irrational, but investing in their communities, dismantling structural barriers they face, is not. This

---

[46] Clear 2002: 193

kind of policy stands to decrease crime rather than increase it. This means that the rational strategy is not to profile blacks but rather fix the structural conditions in those communities that contribute to a higher crime rate. The constitutional language of identity and the "red flag" of race obscure this important point. If a court quickly invalidates racial profiling because it discriminates on the basis of race, it sweeps under the constitutional rug the real problem relating to race and crime. In this regard, strict scrutiny perversely masks the debilitating poverty, joblessness, and family disruption that are regrettably present in many communities of color. Only by revealing the way in which racial profiling is based on animus does a powers review highlight this problem.

This argument is significant because it permits us to reject racial profiling without making the rejection hinge on an identity-centered framework. After all, Harcourt often uses examples that employ profiles that do not concern race, such as the IRS focusing their resources on tax returns by drywall contractors. This is why Harcourt makes clear that "the problem with racial profiling is about the profiling, not about race."[47] This is the crucial move that suggests that a powers approach is sufficient to do the equal protection work. A court can invalidate such policies without making the argument hinge on race and the identity-centered framework that accompanies it. A court can simply conclude that racial profiling cannot be rational because its two premises cannot both be true.

[47] Harcourt 2007: 215

Part III   **SEX AND SEXUAL ORIENTATION**

5   THE PUZZLE OF INTERMEDIATE SCRUTINY

The tiers-of-scrutiny framework does not approach sex discriminatory laws in the same way as it does their racial counterparts. Although race-segregated bathrooms or black-only military platoons are patently unconstitutional, sex-segregated bathrooms or male-only combat platoons are not. Laws mandating the former are subject to strict scrutiny, whereas laws mandating the latter are not. Laws and policies that explicitly invoke sex receive intermediate scrutiny, a level of scrutiny that is higher than rational review but lower than strict scrutiny. Under intermediate scrutiny, the Court asks whether the law has an important purpose and whether the law's means are substantially related to that purpose. Like "compelling" and "narrowly tailored," words such as "important" or "substantially related" provide little constitutional guidance, inviting justices to decide cases on ideological groups.

Drawing from feminist theory, this chapter criticizes the intermediate scrutiny standard, elaborating on how a powers review more clearly captures the Court's underlying logic in this area. I argue that this middling level of scrutiny for laws that discriminate on the basis of sex problematically adopts the difference approach of feminism. Because this approach assumes that females and males are importantly different, it does not go far enough in challenging laws and policies that rest on the idea that there is an appropriate relationship between sex and gender. This chapter argues that we ought to question the constitutionality of sex segregation and male-only military conscription/combat troops, precisely because such legislation is based on the idea that males must act or be a certain way (aggressive or warlike) and females must act or be another way (passive or sheltered).

Generally, "sex" refers to the biological category: male or female. Females can get pregnant and bear young; males cannot. Females

menstruate; males do not. "Gender," on the other hand, refers to
the attributes that are often associated with the biological category,
attributes that include femininity, masculinity, or aggressiveness, or
social roles such as caregiver or breadwinner. These attributes fall
under the description of "man" or "woman." This distinction between
gender and sex is a familiar one in feminist theory. It stands at the center
of the argument in this chapter. Simone de Beauvoir's classic statement
that "One is not born, but rather becomes, woman" speaks to it.[1] The
crucial implication of this distinction, one I assume in this chapter, is
that there is no necessary or natural connection between gender and
sex. Just because someone is of a particular sex does not necessarily
mean he or she has to be a particular gender. A person may be female
but exhibit none of the social or behavioral characteristics associated
with women as a gender. Similarly, a person may be male but exhibit
only feminine qualities, betraying the description that comes with the
term "man." After all, individuals ought to be free to revise, adopt, or
reject any gendered attributes. This informs the antiessentialist critique
of identity outlined in Chapter 1. Throughout the chapter, I try to stay
with the terms "male" and "female" rather than "man" and "woman"
to denote the biological rather than social distinction.

Although this distinction between sex and gender is a familiar
one in feminist legal theory,[2] its relationship to liberal neutrality has
gone largely unnoticed. The idea that there is a necessary connection
between sex and gender is nothing other than a particular perfectionist
belief about what it means to be male or female. This is exactly the
kind of conception of the good life that the liberal commitment to public reason rules out. And, as it turns out, the Court's equal protection
jurisprudence on sex tracks this very argument, deeming constitutionally inadmissible laws and policies that are based on the idea that males
must be breadwinners and females must be caregivers. The thrust of
this chapter is that, properly understood, the Equal Protection Clause
invalidates laws and policies that are based on the idea that there *is an
appropriate relationship between sex and gender*. I define "sexism," then,
as the belief that males or females ought to act or be a certain way. For

[1] Beauvoir 2009 [1949]: 283; *see also* Butler 1990
[2] *See, e.g.*, Case 1995, Cohen 2010, Valdes 1995

instance, I consider the following to be sexist beliefs: females ought to be passive, performing the role of caregiver; males must be warlike and aggressive. Once we realize that such sexist beliefs are conceptions of the good, it becomes apparent that a powers review rules them out.

This chapter is in four parts. First, to frame my constitutional argument, I suggest that properly understood, public reason informs feminism rather than undermining it drawing from *Miss. Univ. for Women v. Hogan* (1982), a case that invalidated a female-only, state-supported professional nursing school. Second, and this is the main focus of this chapter, I argue that both the intermediate and strict scrutiny standards fall short of properly enforcing equality under the law. The Court's current doctrinal test of intermediate scrutiny problematically adopts the difference approach of feminism, suggesting that males and females are different in a way that blacks and whites are not. Adopting strict scrutiny, however, problematically endorses the sameness approach of feminism. It suggests that laws and policies ought to be sex-blind, that males and females – like blacks and whites – are always similarly situated. Third, I argue that a powers review analysis in line with the overall argument of this book better captures equality under the law, fulfilling the goals of feminist theory. This framework rightly calls into question all types of legislation that are based on conceptions of masculinity (e.g., males must be aggressive) or femininity (e.g., females must be passive). Simultaneously, this framework importantly permits the relevant democratic polity to pass a wide range of laws that seek to combat sexism. I argue that a powers review eschews both sameness and difference feminism. This chapter suggests that a powers framework may, as a result, inform Catharine MacKinnon's account of dominance. Finally, I revisit the abortion debate through the lens of a powers review.

PUBLIC REASON AND FEMINISM

Liberalism is often seen as opposed to feminism.[3] Much of this criticism arises because of liberalism's commitment to a private sphere, a

---

[3] *See generally* Nussbaum 1999: 55–80

commitment I criticize in my previous work.[4] With regard to public reason, feminist theory criticizes John Rawls for failing to exclude sexist views as a possible basis for justifying laws and policies.[5] Framed in this way, public reason is indeed at odds with feminism. But, as Christie Hartley and Lori Watson argue, this tension arises only with a view of public reason that permits any and all kinds of reasons to count as "public."[6] Again, this book draws from an exclusionary interpretation of public reason embodied in a commitment to liberal neutrality, a commitment that excludes conceptions of the good. Liberal neutrality, then, according to Hartley and Watson, rules out "nonpublic conceptions of the person or nonpublic conceptions of value."[7]

This chapter explains that a belief in the appropriate relationship between sex and gender is nothing other than a conception of the good, a conception of what it means to live or act a certain way. Such beliefs are "nonpublic" ones and ought not to count as a basis for lawmaking. Again, Rawls defines a conception of the good as what "we regard as a worthwhile human life."[8] This includes what we regard as a worthwhile *female* or *male* life for its own sake. The belief that females should be feminine or males ought to be aggressive is a belief in the appropriate relationship between gender and sex. Although certain religious doctrines may endorse such a relationship, secular accounts reject it. Because reasonable individuals may disagree as to what a desirable female or male life must be for its own sake, the state ought to be neutral with regard to such conceptions of the good.

In line with a powers review I work out in this chapter, such ideas do not count as a constitutional basis for laws and policies. This affinity between feminism and liberal neutrality importantly places the emphasis not on the identity category at stake (once again, this book asks us to look beyond the language of identity in doing the legal equality work) but the reason or rationale underlying the legislation. Understood in this way, liberal neutrality represents a powerful tool for feminism.

---

[4] *See* Bedi 2009
[5] *See, e.g.,* Abbey 2007, Okin 1994, 2004, 2005
[6] *See* Hartley and Watson 2009, 2010; *cf.* Brake 2004
[7] Hartley and Watson 2009: 518
[8] Rawls 1999 [1971]: 302

Consider *Miss. Univ. for Women v. Hogan* (1982) in which the
Court invalidated a female-only, state-supported professional nursing school. A male student, Joe Hogan, who was denied admission
to the Mississippi University of Women School of Nursing (MUW)
solely because of his sex, challenged the constitutionality of the school.
The crux of this kind of discrimination, as with the other cases in
this chapter, is about sex, not gender. It did not matter whether
Hogan was effeminate or that the students at MUW were not. MUW
denied him admission irrespective of whether he was womanly or
manly.

Mississippi argued that the school was created to remedy the effects
of sexism. It was a type of educational affirmative action. The Court
rejected that rationale, contending that females did not lack "opportunities to obtain training in the field of nursing."[9] As the Court
made clear, "in 1970, the year before the School of Nursing's first
class enrolled, women earned 94 percent of the nursing baccalaureate
degrees conferred in Mississippi and 98.6 percent of the degrees earned
nationwide."[10] Even though the law discriminated against males, not
females, even creating an additional educational option for females, the
Court struck it down on justificatory grounds:

> By assuring that Mississippi allots more openings in its state-
> supported nursing schools to women than it does to men, MUW's
> admissions policy lends credibility to the old view that women,
> not men, should become nurses, and makes the assumption that
> nursing is a field for women a self-fulfilling prophecy.[11]

According to the Court, Mississippi's rationale for MUW rests on the
idea that females make better nurses than males. Because the state's
justification for MUW entails assigning gendered attributes – being
caring or empathetic – to females, it is sexist. It violates a powers
review. According to the Department of Labor, as of 2009, 92 percent
of all registered nurses were females.[12] The "old view" that females
are better suited to the nursing profession, then, is undeniably widely

---

[9] *Hogan* at 729
[10] *Hogan* at 729
[11] *Hogan* at 729–30
[12] *See* http://www.dol.gov/wb/stats/main.htm

accepted. It is precisely because of the existence of this belief – one that still informs and influences the lives of those who choose the nursing profession – that renders MUW unconstitutional. A state-mandated policy that encourages this belief, making this kind of statistic a "self-fulfilling prophecy," invokes a constitutionally inadmissible rationale. MUW is based on a particular view of what females ought to do or be. It is telling that MUW is not a male-only nursing school. Males ought to be medical doctors, solving problems and treating patients, not caring for them in a secondary fashion like their nursing counterparts – or so this kind of sexist belief system maintains. To contend that a particular profession is more suited to one sex than the other, then, is a conception of the good. It is a system or set of beliefs that places a particular meaning on what it means to be male or female.

So whereas a law like the one in *Hogan* violates a powers review, legislation that seeks to address the effects of sexism does not. Consider a law that established a female-only school for medical doctors. According to the American Medical Association, as of 2006, 72 percent of all medical doctors are male.[13] The "old view" of gender/sex suggests that whereas females are better suited to be nurses, males are better suited to be doctors. The statistics bear out the success of this idea or belief. The state could decide to challenge it by creating a female-only medical school. The justification for such a school would not be a particular conception of gender/sex but rather an attempt to decouple sex from a gendered view of the medical profession. Such a policy would be neutral with regard to the appropriate relationship between sex and gender. Given the sex divide in the medical professional, a female-only medical school is *not* based on the idea that females make better medical doctors. Quite the contrary, such a school seeks to challenge the existing belief that there is an appropriate profession for a particular sex. It aims to remedy sexism rather than be based on it. Like its racial affirmative action counterpart, such laws and policies do not invoke a constitutionally inadmissible rationale.

---

[13] *See* http://www.ama-assn.org/ama/pub/about-ama/our-people/member-groups-sections/women-physicians-congress/statistics-history/table-1-physicians-gender-excludes-students.page

DIFFERENCE (INTERMEDIATE SCRUTINY) VERSUS SAMENESS (STRICT SCRUTINY)

Doctrinally, how do we ensure that the Court invalidates laws and policies that are sexist while upholding legislation that seeks to remedy sexism? I argue that the Court's current doctrinal test of intermediate scrutiny falls short. I then argue that a turn to strict scrutiny goes too far, threatening laws that rightly aim to decouple gender from sex. Central to my analysis is the distinction between difference and sameness feminism, a distinction that maps onto the intermediate and strict scrutiny approaches.

The Court did not immediately settle on intermediate scrutiny. In *Reed v. Reed* (1971), one of the first sex discriminatory cases to come before the Court, the Court invalidated an Idaho law that automatically favored males over females to be executors of an estate. In *Reed*, a minor, who was adopted by the parties to the case, died. Both adoptive parents, who had separated by the time of their son's death, petitioned to be the executor of their son's estate. Both individuals met the eligibility requirements set by Idaho law (e.g., "neither of the applicants was under any legal disability" that affected their fitness to be an executor).[14] But the Idaho probate law explicitly required that in the case of "several persons claiming and equally entitled [to administer the estate], males must be preferred to females."[15] The Court invalidated the sex preference scheme reasoning that a "classification 'must be reasonable, not arbitrary, and must rest upon some ground of difference having a fair and substantial relation to the object of the legislation, so that all persons similarly circumstanced shall be treated alike.'"[16] Suggesting that females and males are "similarly circumstanced," the Court held that the law was the "very kind of arbitrary legislative choice forbidden by the Equal Protection Clause."[17] Like *Romer* or Justice Harlan's dissent in *Plessy*, the Court in *Reed* enforced

[14] *Reed* at 73
[15] *Reed* at 73
[16] *Reed* at 73
[17] *Reed* at 76

the Equal Protection Clause without the language of higher or height-ened scrutiny.

Yet, just two years later, the Court began treating sex discrimination in line with its race counterpart. In *Frontiero v. Richardson* (1973) (invalidating a federal statute that treated the spouses of servicewomen differently from the spouses of servicemen), the Court held that women count as a suspect class. The Court reasoned that sex is an immutable characteristic "determined solely by the accident of birth" and on the basis of it, women have suffered a history of discrimination.[18] Because women constitute a "discrete and insular group," sex is a suspect classification. This is another instance of the identity approach the Court deploys to enforce equality under the law. After all, once the Court identifies the relevant suspect class, laws and policies that invoke it receive heightened scrutiny. In *Frontiero*, the Court concludes as follows:

> With these considerations in mind, we can only conclude that clas-sifications based upon sex, like classifications based upon race, alienage, or national origin, are inherently suspect, and must there-fore be subjected to strict judicial scrutiny. Applying the analysis mandated by that stricter standard of review, it is clear that the statutory scheme now before us is constitutionally invalid.[19]

So the Court here treats sex as it does race: laws and policies invoking either receive strict scrutiny. And, as noted in Chapter 3, strict scrutiny requires that the law serve a compelling purpose and be narrowly tailored to serve that purpose.

Three years later, however, the Court moved away from impos-ing this level of scrutiny ultimately settling on an intermediate scrutiny standard. In *Craig v. Boren* (1976), the Court invalidated an Oklahoma law that made sale of a kind of beer dependent on one's sex. Under the law, males must be at least twenty-one years old to purchase beer, but females must be at least eighteen years old. The question was whether the law's "denial to males 18–20 years of age"[20] violated the Equal

[18] *Frontiero* at 686
[19] *Frontiero* at 688
[20] *Craig* at 192

Protection Clause. The Court reasoned that to "withstand constitutional challenge, previous cases establish that classifications by gender must serve important governmental objectives and must be substantially related to achievement of those objectives."[21] The language of "important" and "substantially related" is not as stringent as the language of "compelling" and "narrowly tailored." The Court imposes higher scrutiny for sex discriminatory laws but falls short of imposing strict scrutiny.

So whereas the Court acknowledges that women count as a suspect class, making sex a suspect classification, the Court does not explain why it subjects sex discriminatory laws to intermediate scrutiny. What is the underlying theory that explains this lower level of review? Surprisingly, the Court does not provide an answer. Even scholarly work fails to do so. It will not suffice to say that the Equal Protection Clause is only about banning racial discrimination, because the clause's original meaning had nothing to do with sex. This historical explanation for the varying treatment of sex does not explain the Court's acceptance of intermediate scrutiny. If the Equal Protection Clause is only about race, the Court ought not to subject laws that discriminate on the basis of sex – or, for that matter, the first letter of one's last name – to heightened scrutiny. Sex discriminatory laws ought to receive only rational review, if we take seriously the historical argument, one that this book admittedly does not explicitly engage. So the fact that the Court imposes some kind of higher scrutiny for sex discrimination but falls short of imposing strict scrutiny cannot be explained simply by appeal to original meaning.

I suggest that the Court seems to accept the difference theory of feminism as grounds for deploying intermediate scrutiny. This may explain its varying treatment of sex. This explanation may also shed light on why political theory often treats sex differently from race.[22] Put simply, although individuals of different racial groups are really the "same," the intermediate scrutiny standard suggests that males and females are not. There is no denying that females and males are biologically different: females can get pregnant and bear young, and

---

[21] *Craig* at 197
[22] For a discussion of this dissimilar treatment, *see generally* Okin 2002: 207–16

males cannot. Crudely put, from this singular fact come two domi-
nant approaches in feminism: sameness and difference. The sameness
approach contends that females and males are essentially the same.[23]
They are no more different than blacks and whites or A–Rs and S–Zs.
Laws and policies, then, ought to treat males and females the same.
The difference approach, on the other hand, argues that females and
males are essentially different.[24] It means that the law ought, in certain
circumstances, to treat males and females differently.

So although strict scrutiny underlies the sameness approach, intermediate scrutiny underlies the difference approach. If distinctions
based on sex are just like distinctions based on race, sex discriminatory laws and policies ought to receive the same scrutiny as their
race counterparts – namely, strict scrutiny. If females and males are
always similarly situated (like blacks and whites), the Court (under the
current tiers-of-scrutiny approach) ought to impose the highest level
of scrutiny on legislation invoking sex. But if males and females are not
always similarly situated (distinctions based on sex are not the same as
distinctions based on race), the Court ought to impose a less vigorous,
intermediate level of review.

Justice Potter Stewart's concurrence in *Michael M. v. Superior Court*
(1981) provides some explanation for constitutional law's varying
treatment of sex. In that case, the Court upheld California's statutory rape law that made it illegal for males but not females under the
age of eighteen to engage in sexual intercourse:

> [D]etrimental racial classifications by government always violate
> the Constitution, for the simple reason that, so far as the Consti-
> tution is concerned, people of different races are always similarly
> situated [citations omitted]. By contrast, while detrimental gender
> classifications by government often violate the Constitution, they
> do not always do so, for the reason that there *are differences between
> males and females that the Constitution necessarily recognizes.* In this
> case, we deal with the most basic of these differences: females can
> become pregnant as the result of sexual intercourse; males can-
> not.[25]

23 *See, e.g.*, Epstein 1993 [1981], Williams 1989
24 *See, e.g.*, Gilligan 1982, West 1988
25 *Michael M.* at 478, concurring (emphasis added)

It is precisely because people of difference races are "always similarly situated" that the Court imposes strict scrutiny for laws that discriminate on the basis of race. But, according to the Court, males and females are not "always" similarly situated. This is an endorsement of the difference approach. Consider that although there are no longer any race-segregated bathrooms, almost all bathrooms are sex segregated. If the Court imposes strict scrutiny on all sex discriminatory laws and policies, it threatens to invalidate these kinds of policies, including the one upheld in *Michael M*. To avoid this, the Court imposes the less vigorous intermediate standard of review. This middling level of review gives the Court flexibility in invalidating *some* but not all legislation that invokes sex. It informs the difference approach to feminism.

What are the laws and policies that this level of scrutiny invalidates? In practice, the Court has deployed intermediate scrutiny to deem unconstitutional legislation that is based on a caregiver/breadwinner idea of the family.[26] For instance, in *Stanton v. Stanton* (1975), the Court struck down a Utah law under which males attained majority at twenty-one but females at eighteen. The case arose as a result of a divorce proceeding where the defendant was required to pay child support payments for his two minor children – a male and a female. When the female child reached the age of eighteen, the law no longer required child support payments. Child support for the male child, however, did not end until he reached twenty-one. The Court invalidated this kind of sex discriminatory legislation reasoning that:

> If a specified age of minority is required for the boy in order to assure him parental support while he attains his education and training, so, too, is it for the girl. To distinguish between the two on educational grounds is to be self-serving: if the female is not to be supported so long as the male, she hardly can be expected to attend school as long as he does, and bringing her education to an end earlier coincides with the role-typing society has long imposed.[27]

By extinguishing child support at age eighteen for only females, the law effectively makes sure that females stay caregivers, denying them the resources to gain an education like their male counterparts. Even

---

[26] *See generally* Brest et al. 2006: 1213–19
[27] *Stanton* at 15

if one concedes that in the 1970s, females married at an earlier age than males, this would not render the law's rationale benign. After all, the Utah law specifically stated that "all minors obtain their majority by marriage."[28] So even if females do marry at an earlier age, the law already extinguishes their child support if they do so. This means the actual reason for the law must be a belief that females ought to be caregivers. They ought to be supported by a male by the time they turn eighteen and that males must be supporting females by the time they turn twenty-one. This is a sexist rationale precisely because it rests on the idea that with a particular sex comes a gendered attribute.

Likewise, in *Frontiero v. Richardson* (1973), *Weinberger v. Wiesenfeld* (1975), and *Califano v. Goldfarb* (1977), the Court struck down policies that rested on the idea that females must be caregivers and males breadwinners. In each case, the law provided benefits on the basis of sex. In *Wiesenfeld* and *Goldfarb*, the law favored widows over widowers in providing Social Security benefits. In both cases, the wife worked paying into Social Security. After her death, her husband – a widower – applied for benefits. In each instance, federal law rejected his application. The rejection was based simply on sex, had he been female, he would have received the survivorship benefits. In *Frontiero*, the law favored males over females in providing fringe benefits for military service personnel. The program automatically provided benefits such as medical and dental care to the spouses of service men. That is, service men could simply declare their wives as dependents under the Congressional scheme. However, service women could not automatically enroll in the program. Service women had to prove via affidavit that their husbands were indeed dependent on them.

The Court rightly invalidated these schemes, because they were based on a caregiver/breadwinner conception of the family. There is no denying that when these cases were decided (and this may have certainly changed in the past thirty-five years), a wife was more likely to be at home taking care of the household or children and her husband at work providing for the family. In each of these policies, Congress sought to justify its sex discriminatory treatment on administrative convenience grounds. Because females are more likely to be caregivers

[28] *Stanton* at 14

and males the breadwinners, it is economically more efficient to assume that reality rather than conduct an individualized inquiry into each family's situation. Although the Court does not deploy the language of "bad faith," it effectively concludes that this efficiency rationale is not proffered in good faith. First, Congress failed to show that these sex discriminatory policies actually save money. For instance, the Court reasons in *Frontiero*:

> The Government offers no concrete evidence, however, tending to support its view that such differential treatment in fact saves the Government any money ... [T]here is substantial evidence that, if put to the test, many of the wives of male members would fail to qualify for benefits. And in light of the fact that the dependency determination with respect to the husbands of female members is presently made solely on the basis of affidavits rather than through the more costly hearing process, the Government's explanation of the statutory scheme is, to say the least, questionable.[29]

Second, and more important, in each of these cases, the wife was a presumptive breadwinner in the family. As the Court reasons in *Goldfarb*,

> [while] the notion that men are more likely than women to be the primary supporters of their spouses and children is not entirely without empirical support ... such a gender-based generalization cannot suffice to justify the denigration of the efforts of women who do work and whose earnings contribute significantly to their families' support.[30]

In this and the other cases, the wife was not simply or only a caregiver. In *Goldfarb* and *Wiesenfeld*, the deceased wife contributed to Social Security through her employment. If she had been the caregiver, her widower would not be seeking benefits. He would have no presumptive claim to them. His wife would not have contributed to the federal program. Similarly, in *Frontiero*, the wife was employed by the military. It is her employment, her role as a breadwinner not a caregiver, that triggers eligibility in the military's fringe benefits program. In *Frontiero*,

[29] *Frontiero* at 689–90
[30] *Goldfarb* at 205–6

Wiesenfeld, and *Goldfarb*, the family was not an empirically typical one: the female being the sole caregiver and the male the sole breadwinner. These are not cases in which benefits are being doled out to everyone but being rationed on various nonspurious distinctions or categories. It is only in those cases in which the female is a presumptive breadwinner – in which the wife contributes to Social Security or works for the military – that the law becomes relevant. Because these laws categorically assume that a *wife who is working* is not the primary breadwinner, the justification cannot be about mere efficiency. Rather, these policies "denigrate" females by effectively punishing those who are not caregivers. So far from reflecting reality, these policies seek to alter it by punishing wives and their possibly caregiving husbands. By not automatically providing benefits, these laws punish families for failing to adhere to the conventional idea that females must stay to care for the children, and the male must work to support them. This is a conception of the good, a conception of what counts as the appropriate or best type of arrangement between males and females. These cases are not about saving administrative costs but the appropriate relationship between sex and gender.

But intermediate scrutiny does not invalidate all laws and policies that are sexist, that are based on conceptions of what it means to be a good female or male. For instance, by adopting the difference approach of feminism, the Court has upheld the federal policy of male-only military conscription as well as a range of other kinds of sex segregation. In *Rostker v. Goldberg* (1981), the Court upheld the Military Selective Service Act that requires all resident males eighteen to twenty-six years of age to register for the draft. Congress' purpose in conducting such a registration is to prepare for combat by drafting troops. At that time, females were legally barred from combat roles. In January 2013, the Department of Defense lifted all such formal barriers paving the way for full integration of combat troops.[31] Subjecting the law to intermediate scrutiny, the Court upholds it. The Court reasons that because "women are excluded from combat, Congress concluded that they would not be needed in the event of a draft, and therefore

[31] http://www.defense.gov/releases/release.aspx?releaseid=15784

decided not to register them."[32] The Court deems the Selective Service Act constitutional by assuming the constitutionality of the policy on female combat exclusion.

But, as the dissent points out, this reasoning does not justify the categorical exclusion of females. For even assuming the constitutionality of combat exclusion, male-only registration is unjustifiable. After all, females could be drafted for noncombat roles:

> [T]he Government makes no claim that preparing for a draft of combat troops cannot be accomplished just as effectively by *registering* both men and women by *drafting* only men if only men turn out to be needed.[33]

By failing to register females, according to the dissent, the Court "places its imprimatur on one of the most potent remaining public expressions of 'ancient canards about the proper role of women.'"[34] In doing so, the Court excludes "women from a fundamental civic obligation."[35]

The Court specifically concedes that an "all-black or all-white, or an all-Catholic or all-Lutheran, or an all-Republican or all-Democratic registration" would be unconstitutional.[36] After all, those of different racial groups or political parties or even those with different letters in their last names are always similarly situated. They are the "same" for purposes of the law. But females and males "are simply not similarly situated for purposes of a draft or registration for the draft."[37] This informs the difference approach to feminism. Because males and females are not similarly situated in every respect, male-only registration or male-only combat platoons are constitutional.

Now *Rostker* did not explicitly consider the constitutionality of female combat exclusion. In fact, no court has done so. In 2003, a federal district court in Massachusetts dismissed a constitutional objection

---

[32] *Rostker* at 77
[33] *Rostker* at 95, dissenting
[34] *Rostker* at 86, dissenting
[35] *Rostker* at 86, dissenting
[36] *Rostker* at 78
[37] *Rostker* at 78

to male-only registration citing the fact the some version of the female combat exclusion policy was still in place.[38] With the recent lifting of this policy, any constitutional challenge to such exclusion is moot. But in light of the argument of this chapter it is useful to consider why such a policy is unconstitutional. Importantly, combat exclusion did stand at the core of Congress' refusal to register females for the draft. The *Rostker* Court cites the relevant Congressional report that the "principle that women should not intentionally and routinely engage in combat is fundamental, and enjoys wide support among our people. It is universally supported by military leaders who have testified before Congress."[39]

The policy's universal support at that time does not necessarily mean it is not sexist. Consider that the SEALS, the U.S. Navy's elite sea, air, and land unit, are self-described as a "special breed of warrior."[40] Unsurprisingly, this unit is one of the combat roles that females were formally excluded from joining. It is worth pointing out that even with the lifting of the ban, various military branches will have an opportunity to petition for exceptions to full integration.[41] Importantly, the combat exclusion informs the difference approach to feminism, precisely because it rests on the idea that males ought to be aggressive and warlike. After all, it does not matter whether a female meets the physical or strength requirements set by the military for these combat roles. She would still be excluded from them. The combat exclusion policy like the registration requirement is based simply on sex. Males who are effeminate must still register, yet females who are not may not register. This kind of categorical exclusion rests on a conception of the appropriate relationship between sex and gender.

Consider that other kinds of mandatory sex segregation have gone largely unchallenged under the Equal Protection Clause. Various laws and policies require sex segregation in such places as governmental prisons, military barracks, and bathrooms in public buildings. Sex-segregated bathrooms may be the most familiar example of the seeming

---

[38] *Schwartz v. Brodsky* (D. Mass. 2003)
[39] *Rostker* at 77
[40] *See* http://www.sealswcc.com/seal-default.aspx
[41] http://www.defense.gov/releases/release.aspx?releaseid=15784

legitimacy of the difference approach. David Cohen's provides one of the most robust critiques of segregation on the basis of sex.[42] He argues that such segregation reinforces "hegemonic masculinity." These policies, including combat exclusion, rest on the idea that males are "heterosexual," "physically aggressive," "not feminine."[43] One of the primary reasons Cohen articulates for such segregation is the commitment to heterosexuality:

> [A]ssumed heterosexuality is one of the basic reasons behind the sex segregation of prisons, as men must be kept from women because men are heterosexual and will seek out sex with women, either consensually or non-consensually. . . .
>
> A similar dynamic is at work in restroom segregation. Although, like the prison . . . fear of violence is certainly part of the reason for sex segregation restrooms, fear of heterosexual sexual interaction is another one of the reasons. . . . Society assumes heterosexuality; thus men and women cannot be together in a setting involving the exposure of their genitalia . . . [T]o preserve heterosexuality, men must be prohibited from being exposed to women in private moments. The norm is heterosexuality; the aberration is homosexuality.[44]

Obviously, "fear of violence" may be part of the reason for sex segregation, but it is hard to see how this fear is doing all the explanatory work. Most sex-segregated bathrooms in public buildings are next to each other. If the worry is that males may be likely to assault a female, this worry ought to extend to the placement of the respective bathrooms. If anything, the actual act of segregating the bathrooms on the basis of sex informs this fear. This fear, in turn, serves to justify sex segregation. This is the kind of "self-fulfilling prophecy" that Mississippi's all-female nursing school creates: more females will pursue nursing, which will in turn validate the idea that they are better suited to that profession than their male counterparts. Similarly, mandatory sex segregation reinforces not only the value of heterosexuality but also the belief that males are aggressive and females passive.

---

[42] Cohen 2010, 2011
[43] Cohen 2010: 522
[44] Cohen 2010: 529–30

The fact that such segregation rests on a particular relationship between sex and gender is evident in the recently repealed Don't Ask, Don't Tell (DADT) policy, a policy that barred service members from being openly gay or lesbian.[45] DADT makes clear that homosexuality is unsuitable for military service. The policy's explicit justification was to ensure that "the high standards of morale, good order and discipline, and unit cohesion that are the essence of military capability" are not jeopardized.[46] Tellingly, the presence of "out" gays and lesbians threatens unit cohesion for exactly the same reason that mandatory sex segregation is so widespread: the valuing of heterosexuality over homosexuality. Such antigay policies inform sex segregation, resting on the same kind of conception of the good: males must be aggressive, masculine, and heterosexual.[47] If they are feminine, "sissies," or gay, they undermine a heterosexual conception of sex and gender.

Taken to its logical conclusion, a powers review deems unconstitutional laws and policies that are based on this kind of moral vision of the good life. Again, according to *Lawrence*, simply because the majority "has traditionally viewed a particular practice as immoral is not a sufficient reason for upholding a law prohibiting it."[48] Basing laws and policies on the belief that males ought to be attracted to females and vice versa violates equality under the law. The difference approach – embodied by intermediate scrutiny – stands to keep such segregation in place. We would not tolerate racially segregated bathrooms or racially segregated military barracks and platoons. But under difference feminism, females and males are not always similarly situated, so segregation on the basis of sex is constitutional.

Adopting the sameness approach – imposing strict scrutiny – may well call into question male-only military conscription and sex segregation. At a minimum, a turn to sameness contends that males and females be treated exactly like. So as long as females can fulfill the responsibility and requirements of combat (I revisit this argument later in the chapter), they ought to be permitted to do so. If males and

[45] U.S.C. § 654; policy concerning homosexuality in the armed forces
[46] U.S.C. § 654 at 340
[47] For the connection between sex and sexuality discrimination, *see generally* Koppelman 1994
[48] *Lawrence* at 577

females are always similarly situated, like blacks and whites, mandatory sex segregation turns out just as unconstitutional as black-only
registration or separate black/white bathrooms.

But strict scrutiny would invariably turn out to be too strict. Again, it
is precisely the presence of strict scrutiny in cases concerning race discrimination that jeopardizes remedial legislation, legislation that aims
to undo the effects of racism. If males and females are always similarly
situated, legislation that treats them differently is presumptively unconstitutional. This is the formal equality approach analyzed in Chapter 3.
Just as the law ought not to invoke race, it ought not to invoke sex. This
sex-blind approach turns out to invalidate laws and policies that seek
to remedy sexism. In *Kahn v. Shevin* (1974), *Schlesinger v. Ballard*
(1975), and *Califano v. Webster* (1977), the Court upheld policies that
sought to do just that, providing some kind of benefit for females
instead of males. In each case, the Court subjected the law to intermediate scrutiny. In *Kahn*, the Court upheld a Florida law that gave
widows but not widowers $500 in property tax exemption reasoning
that there "can be no dispute that the financial difficulties confronting
the lone woman in Florida or in any other State exceed those facing the
man."[49] These financial difficulties arise "from overt discrimination
or from the socialization process of a male-dominated culture."[50] The
"job market is inhospitable to the woman seeking any but the low-
est paid jobs."[51] In *Schelsinger*, the Court upheld a naval policy that
granted females more time toward tenure to the rank of officer than
their male counterparts. The Court acknowledged the reality that males
and females are "not similarly situated with respect to opportunities
for professional service."[52] Because females may not participate in
"combat and in most sea duty," they will not have complied the same
kind of record for promotion as their male counterparts.[53] And in
Webster, the Court upheld a Social Security policy that gave a retired
female wage earner a slightly higher average monthly wage than her
male counterpart.

[49] *Kahn* at 353
[50] *Kahn* at 353
[51] *Kahn* at 353
[52] *Schelsinger* at 508
[53] *Schelsinger* at 508

The Court distinguished these cases from the benefit provisions struck down in *Frontiero, Wiesenfeld,* and *Goldfarb*:

> The more favorable treatment of the female wage earner enacted here was not a result of "archaic and overbroad generalizations" about women, or "the role-typing society has long imposed" upon women, such assumptions that women are "the weaker sex" or are more likely to be child-rearers or dependents.[54]

Here the law sought to challenge sexism by acknowledging the unfortunate fact that females are at a societal disadvantage. Imposing strict scrutiny threatens the constitutionality of such laws. Although it calls into question mandatory sex segregation, it also calls into question laws like the ones in *Kahn*. The sameness approach rejects policies that discriminate on the basis of sex. Sameness feminism, like colorblindness, fails to realize that even if sex does not intrinsically track gendered attributes, many individuals certainly believe it does. A commitment to sex-blindness fails to realize that precisely because of sexism, legislation may have to invoke sex. In the same way, policies may have to invoke race to remedy or combat the effects of racism. So although intermediate scrutiny does not go far enough, strict scrutiny goes too far. We must move beyond the options of difference and sameness.

POWERS REVIEW (DOMINANCE)

A powers review is sufficient to do the feminist work. By avoiding the tiers-of-scrutiny framework, it rightly invalidates laws and policies that are based on sexism while permitting the polity to combat it. This means it is simply outside the power of the state to pass legislation that aims to assign gendered attributes to a particular sex. The Court already engages in this kind inquiry by invalidating laws that rest on idea that females out to be caregivers and males breadwinners. This framework would, of course, invalidate laws like the ones in *Frontiero, Wiesenfeld,* and *Goldfarb*, but the Court would not need the conventional

---

[54] *Webster* at 317

heightened scrutiny to do so. It is telling that before the Court even settled on any kind of higher scrutiny, it invalidated sexist laws like the one in *Reed* on the basis of rational review alone. Again, the Court in *Reed* appealed to the language of "arbitrary," directly implicating the powers review I work out in this book. In the end, making clear what counts as a constitutionally inadmissible rationale – in this case, a belief that with a certain sex comes certain gendered attributes – the Court does not need higher scrutiny, intermediate or otherwise.

A powers review goes farther than intermediate scrutiny by also calling into question male-only registration and a wide range of mandatory sex segregation, including the now defunct female combat exclusion. If these laws and policies also rest on the belief that males ought to be aggressive and masculine, just as females must be caregivers, they are unconstitutional. If sex segregation is based on valuing heterosexuality over homosexuality, this is a blatant privileging of one conception of the good over another. This kind of reason or rationale violates a powers review.

Simultaneously, a powers review permits the relevant democratic polity to pass policies that seek to decouple gender from sex. Without any kind of heightened scrutiny to stand in its way, the polity may easily pass laws like the ones in *Kahn*, *Schelsinger*, and *Webster*. In line with much feminist theory, such review would permit the polity to pass legislation that would, for instance, subsidize day care, provide health care for children and caregivers, require paid leave, and create job flexibility.[55] These kinds of laws would combat sexism by making it less relevant in the workplace.

I suggest that a powers framework may inform Catharine MacKinnon's account of dominance.[56] MacKinnon criticizes difference and sameness feminism for making the standard a male-dominated one. For the sameness approach, females are told to meet this male standard, a standard that masquerades as impartial. For the difference approach, females are told to deviate from it. In both cases, the male-centered standard is anchoring the approach. Although she does not connect her critique to the language of identity, I suggest that the problem is

---

[55] *See generally* Crittenden 2001, Fraser 1997, Heymann 2000, Okin 1989
[56] MacKinnon 1987

that both perspectives invoke the language of identity. If we seek the equality of women, the question is equal to whom? Presumably, the answer is that women ought to be equal to men. But framing it in this way invites MacKinnon's critique: it makes man the standard by which a woman is judged. MacKinnon's positive method treats the "equality question" as a "question of the distribution of power . . . specifically of male supremacy and female subordination."[57]

It will not suffice to treat MacKinnon's dominance approach as a simple commitment to antisubordination. First, it invites the contentious question of whether women are indeed a political minority, whether they are a suspect class requiring extra protection in the democratic process. Ely himself reasons that precisely because women are half the electorate, there is no need to treat them as a subordinated minority. If they choose to enact "overdrawn stereotype[s]" through legislation,[58] the Court ought not to second-guess their democratic choice. This is the problem with the suspect class inquiry, which requires we decide which groups are "in" and which are "out."

Second, even assuming that females are a political minority needing additional protection in the democratic process, laws that discriminate against *males* would not violate antisubordination. If this represents the dominance approach, it turns out inadequate. It means that laws such as the one in *Hogan* do not count as an instance of dominance. In that case, the all-female nursing school discriminated against males, not females. Yet the school is based on a gendered conception of the nursing profession. This kind of school reinforces sexism by making the belief that nursing is a female, not a male, profession a "self-fulfilling prophecy." MUW dominates females even though it does not legally discriminate against them.

We avoid both these problems by taking seriously the Court's commitment to a powers review, one that rules out conceptions of the appropriate relationship between gender and sex. I suggest that dominance occurs precisely because laws and policies are based on an idea that males and females must act or be a certain way. Although MacKinnon does not make an argument in constitutional jurisprudence,

[57] MacKinnon 1987: 40
[58] Ely 1980: 165; *but see* Wasserstrom 1977

there is an interesting affinity between a powers review and her account of dominance.

In fact, a powers review may also call into question laws and policies that are based exclusively on the experiences of males instead of females. MacKinnon criticizes the difference and sameness approaches for failing to realize that allegedly sex-neutral requirements and policies are, in fact, gendered. This is because the experiences of men define, *inter alia*, "most sports," "auto and health insurance coverage," "workplace expectations and successful career patterns," and military citizenship.[59] With the repeal of the combat exclusion policy for women, the military may also have to reconsider the physical and strength requirements attached to combat roles. Maia Goodell, a lawyer and former naval officer, argues that

> it is by no means apparent [these requirements are] the only, or even the best, way to design military equipment and procedures. Both the measures and the tasks are designed to fit men. Critics often respond to suggestions that tasks and equipment be modified by claiming that inserting women into a man's world is an unnecessary expense taken only to further social engineering instead of military readiness. This argument ignores the constant redesign needed to maintain the United States military's technological advantage.[60]

Goodell goes on to argue that the "chief difficulty with this cost argument is that the military is, and must be, constantly in the process of upgrading its equipment. Technological advancement is one of the major ways that the United States remains a world military leader."[61]

If these conditions are not the best or only way to structure "military equipment and procedures" and the military is always constantly updating equipment/technology, what justifies maintaining these physical/strength standards? If the standards are based on a male's body rather than an average human being's body, they are sexist. They must rest on the idea that males are better suited to engage in military combat than females. Otherwise, the military would have used a female's body

---

[59] MacKinnon 1987: 36
[60] Goodell 2010: 44
[61] Goodell 2010: 45

or even some kind of hybrid average to determine these requirements. The assumption that the male body/experience is the "standard" by which to generate working conditions, successful career paths, or military strength requirements is sexist. It rests on the idea that there is an appropriate relationship between sex and the work place or the military. This is a conception of the good that a powers review, taken seriously, may rule out. Laws based on such assumptions, then, are unconstitutional. This may rightly be the fate of a wide variety of laws that are based on the experiences of only males, unconstitutionally privileging a certain view of sex/gender over another.

REVISITING THE ABORTION DEBATE

Under a powers review, the equal protection question is not about whether abortion laws invoke a prohibited identity category or class. Rather, it is about whether the reasons underlying abortion legislation are constitutionally inadmissible. I realize that under current constitutional doctrine, such legislation violates a right to privacy. I leave that particular line of reasoning to one side. Again, this book is not about individual rights but about equality under the law. I argue that a powers review has the potential to invalidate abortion laws precisely because such laws are based on the idea that females must be mothers. Crucial to this inquiry is realizing that the *actual* purpose of laws and policies prohibiting abortion is constitutionally inadmissible. Suppose the state decides that failing to carry the fetus to term – deciding to terminate the pregnancy by removing the fetus – ought to be a crime. No matter how the woman got pregnant (be it by rape, incest, or consensual sex), the innocent life in her must be saved. As a result, the majority passes a law outlawing abortion similar to a law struck down in *Roe v. Wade* (1973). Even though the pregnant woman has no desire to carry the fetus to term (presume she can do so without herself dying), the state has decided that she must do so. The presumptive justification is to preserve fetal life, to prevent harm to the fetus. For many pro-life advocates, the fetus is a person. Although saving the life of the fetus does not seem to invoke a particular conception of the good, this justification must be proffered in good faith.

Here it is relatively easy to realize that the something other than preserving life is afoot, even if one concedes that the fetus is a life that ought not to be destroyed. First, if the state has decided to compel the pregnant female to carry the fetus to term based on the justification of preserving life, it ought to compel others in similar situations to help as well. Forcing her to carry a child to term exposes her to great physical burdens, burdens that the law is reluctant to impose on others.[62] She must, for example, eat properly, avoiding many kinds of activities that could endanger the fetus.

If the justification behind passing a law against abortion is to ensure that someone sustain a life even against her will, why is this obligation only visited on pregnant females? Consider a trivial but illustrative example. Suppose I happen to come across a drowning child in a lake who through no fault of her own finds herself in this predicament. Imagine someone else threw her in. Imagine further that to save her, I need only get my pants wet. If the democratic majority cares about preventing harm to the fetus by forcing the mother to carry it to term, it must *a fortiori* care about the harm to the child, a child who can only be saved by forcing the bystander to help. If cutting the umbilical cord allowing the fetus to die in the mother's womb is "murder," why is failing to help the child not a crime?

This incongruity is all the more illuminating because American law does not generally require any kind of compelled Samaritanism.[63] The current state of American law repudiates such forced Good Samaritan duties. It flatly rejects such conscription. For instance, the Restatement of Torts says: "The fact that the actor realizes that action on his part is necessary for another's aid or protection does not itself impose upon him a duty to take such action."[64] Moreover, only two states in the United States – Minnesota and Vermont – legally compel this kind of aid.[65] In other words, failing to help the drowning child – "killing" her – is not a crime in most places. Said differently, the law does not generally *require* that I help others in critical need.

---

[62] *See* Regan 1979: 1579–91
[63] *See* Regan 1979; *cf.* Thomson 1971: 64
[64] Restatement 1965 § 314
[65] Eisenberg 2002: 654, fn. 25

202 Beyond Race, Sex, and Sexual Orientation

Because the democratic majority does not seek to pass forced Good Samaritan laws, it cannot justify prohibiting abortion on grounds of preserving life.

The passerby who sees the drowning child in the lake, unlike the pregnant woman, then, suffers minimal hardship in being forced to save the child's life. Vermont's forced Good Samaritan law, one of only a few such statutes in the United States, only compels help if it can be done "without danger or peril to" oneself or "interference with" other important duties.[66] It requires far less than what an abortion statute requires of women. The Texas abortion statute at issue in *Roe* only permitted an exception for "saving the life of the mother."[67] The comparison is stark and telling. Under the Vermont statute, you *need not* help if doing so will expose you to some non-life-threatening danger or interfere with other "important" duties.[68] The abortion statute, though, requires the pregnant woman to carry the fetus to term for nine months unless doing so threatens her very life. Although there may even be disagreement over whether the fetus is a person, there is no doubt that the innocent drowning child is one. In fact, the penalty for violating the Vermont statute – for failing to help – is a fine of no more than $100. Contrastingly, the statute overturned in *Roe* doled out a prison sentence of two to five years for anyone helping a woman procure an abortion.[69]

Second, even if the law may constitutionally impose this burden on pregnant females but not others, it is even more telling that the state does not seek to compensate them for carrying the fetus for nine months. Because the fetus cannot be removed without destroying it, the pregnant female is the only who can carry the fetus to term. But this does not mean she has to shoulder all the costs. This does not mean she is the only one who can help. Why can't the state assist her by compensating her for the pregnancy? Or why can't the male who impregnated her be liable for such damages in an effort at least to mitigate the woman's burden?

In his partial concurrence to *Planned Parenthood v. Casey* (1992) (invalidating a spousal notification requirement before procuring an

---

[66] 12 V.S.A.§ 519 (a) (1968)
[67] *Roe* at 118
[68] 12 V.S.A.§ 519 (a) (1968)
[69] *Roe* at 118

abortion), Justice Blackmun states that by "restricting the right to terminate pregnancies, the State conscripts women's bodies into its service, forcing women to continue their pregnancies, suffer pains of childbirth, and in most instances, provide years of maternal care."[70] Jed Rubenfeld puts it even more starkly:

> Laws that prohibit abortion differ categorically from virtually every other law on our books. They do not merely prohibit a particular act. They oblige an unwilling individual to carry out a specific, sustained, long-term, life-altering, and life-occupying course of conduct. A woman forbidden to abort an unwanted pregnancy is forced to bear a child. She is made to accept significant health risk. She will undergo radical bodily change. She may die.[71]

Realizing that only women bear this burden, Blackmun remarks that the "State does not compensate women for their services; instead it assumes that they owe this duty as a matter of course."[72] Laws prohibiting abortion do not contemplate any kind of compensation or cost spreading for the pregnant women. In fact, Andrew Koppelman argues that, as a result, laws against abortion amount to involuntary servitude, something that the Thirteenth Amendment categorically prohibits.[73] According to Koppelman:

> If citizens may not be forced to surrender control of their persons and services, then women's persons may not be invaded and their services may not be coerced for the benefit of fetuses. It is as simple as that. The injury inflicted on women by forced motherhood is lesser in degree than that inflicted on blacks by antebellum slavery, since it is temporary and involves less than total control over the body, but it is the same *kind* of injury.[74]

The fact that this kind of servitude is only placed on pregnant females means that the justification for laws like the one in *Roe* is about something besides preventing harm to the fetus.

The reason is sexism. I suggest that this is the justificatory implication of Blackmun's concurrence. Laws against abortion seek to impose

[70] *Casey* at 929, concurring in part
[71] Rubenfeld 2005: 110
[72] *Casey* at 929, concurring in part
[73] Koppelman 1990
[74] Koppelman 1990: 487

a particular conception of the good on pregnant females violating a powers review. Tellingly, whereas federal law only registers males for military conscription, abortion legislation only conscripts females. This contrast rests on the idea that females must act or be a certain way (mothers) and that males must act or be another way (warriors). And it is worth reiterating that whereas males are paid for their forced military service, women are not paid for their forced motherhood. Scholarly work even suggests that abortion legislation is about gender roles and motherhood.[75] Kristen Luker's classic work on the subject argues that this debate is really about substantive "attitudes toward children, sexuality, parenthood, the proper role of women, and the like."[76] Reva Siegel characterizes abortion legislation as a kind of sex-based regulation precisely because these laws compel women to become mothers.[77] In rewriting *Roe*, Jack Balkin similarly argues that

> restrictions on abortion require pregnant women to bear children and become mothers whether or not they wish to. They force women either to devote themselves to traditional roles and responsibilities of child care that lack both status and economic remuneration or else to suffer the stigma and shame of admitting their inability to care for their own children by placing them up for adoptions. Restrictions on abortion thus employ basic social expectations about the duties and responsibilities of motherhood as a lever to pressure women into traditional roles of child care.[78]

And such legislation seeks to place this burden only on females. After all, those who favor prohibiting abortion do not seek to compel others – namely, males – to help.

But this line of scholarly work fails to connect this analysis to the powers review I develop here. For instance, Balkin's insightful rewriting of *Roe* ultimately invalidates abortion legislation under the conventional identity approach to equal protection. He argues that criminal prohibitions on abortion violate equality under the law because they "create or maintain an inferior caste or class of citizens."[79] He focuses on

---

[75] *See, e.g.*, Balkin 2005, Luker 1984, Siegel 1992, 2005, West 2005
[76] Luker 1984: 10
[77] Siegel 1992, 2005
[78] Balkin 2005: 45
[79] Balkin 2005: 42

the fact that the law discriminates against a subordinated group, here women. But this familiar argument invites the problems of identity outlined in Chapter 1. It needlessly frames the argument in terms that affect only the interests of a particular group (here, women), rather than the interests of all. And it is worth pointing out that the Court has held that pregnancy discrimination is not sex discrimination under the Equal Protection Clause because not all women become pregnant.[80] This kind of formalism reveals the way in which identity categories can be rigid and constraining. Is there only one suspect class – namely, women? Or is the relevant class pregnant women? Similarly, is there only one suspect class, racial minorities? Or is the relevant class women of color? This raises the problem of intersectionality encountered in Chapter 1. A powers review avoids this pathology by hanging the constitutional objection on the reason underlying abortion legislation rather than the group or class affected. Even conceding that the fetus is a life that may not be destroyed, as currently written, abortion laws are based on a particular conception of the good life – in this case, the idea that females ought to be mothers. Such laws are a kind of morals legislation, legislation that the Court has held is unconstitutional.

In fact, a powers review stands to inform the debate over abortion funding. Too often, this debate is about the nature of a constitutional right. Although the state may not pass laws prohibiting abortion, it does not thereby need to fund such procedures. The latter entails a positive right (the state must under certain circumstances provide the means to procure an abortion); the second concerns a negative right (the state may not interfere with a woman's liberty to abort). In *Harris v. Mcrae* (1980), the Supreme Court upheld the Hyde Amendment, a federal law selectively withholding health care funds from abortions. Although this federal scheme provided funds for childbirth for indigent women, it refused to provide funds for an abortion. Informing the conventional view, the Court reasoned that a woman's right to choose did not carry with it "a constitutional entitlement to the financial resources to avail herself of the full range of protected choices."[81] Whereas the U.S.

---

[80] *See Geduldig v. Aiello* (1974)
[81] *Harris* at 316

Constitution enshrines negative rights, it does not contemplate positive
or affirmative ones.

A powers review has the potential to avoid affirming any kind of
positive right. The Court need only ask whether the Hyde Amendment, like laws that seek to prohibit abortion, invoke a constitutionally
inadmissible rationale. If the answer is "yes," this kind of amendment is
unconstitutional. Justice Brennan's dissent in *Harris* implicitly suggests
as much:

> By funding all of the expenses associated with childbirth and none
> of the expenses incurred in terminating pregnancy, the Govern-
> ment literally makes an offer that the indigent woman cannot afford
> to refuse. It matters not that in this instance the Government has
> used the carrot rather than the stick. What is critical is the realiza-
> tion that as a practical matter, many poverty-stricken woman will
> choose to carry their pregnancy to term simply because the Gov-
> ernment provides funds for the associated medical services, even
> though these same women would have chosen to have an abor-
> tion if the Government had also paid for that option, or indeed if
> the Government had stayed out of the picture altogether and had
> defrayed the costs of neither procedure.[82]

Although he does not deploy the language "morals legislation," Brennan's argument effectively argues that by selectively withholding funds
for abortion but not live births, the state compels a particular conception of the good. This, as Balkin states, "pressure[s] women into
traditional roles of child care."[83] It favors the idea that females must
be caregivers, that it is virtuous for them to bear children and become
mothers. The fact that the state does not go as far as outlawing abortion
does not make the Hyde Amendment constitutional. A powers review
is indifferent to whether a law is coercive. The question is whether the
law is based on a constitutionally inadmissible rationale. If the reason
for withholding federal funds for abortion is to encourage a particular
way of life for its own sake, this violates a powers review.

Michael McConnell criticizes this line of reasoning, suggesting that
it proves too much. If the state must fund abortions as long as it

---

[82] *Harris* at 333–4, dissenting
[83] Balkin 2005: 45

also funds life births, it ought to fund religious schools as long as it also funds secular ones. What is the difference? McConnell proclaims that while "Justice Brennan, of course, would reject the argument as it applies to school funding," he "has never explained why."[84] The explanation is simple. The opposite of a religious school is not a secular school but an antireligious school. Public or secular schools do not discourage students from pursuing a faith-based way of life. Rather, they seek to remain neutral, neither endorsing nor encouraging a religious conception of the good. This is why secular schools do not violate the Establishment Clause. To be sure, if the state funded schools that were antireligious, teaching that an atheistic lifestyle is best for its own sake, such institutions would violate the Establishment Clause, and in turn, the powers review I develop here. Again, the Establishment Clause requires religious neutrality. The state may not endorse religion or nonreligion.

The Hyde Amendment is inapposite, precisely because it does privilege a certain way of life – namely, one that says females must be mothers. The amendment does not, for instance, compensate those indigent women who are forced to carry a fetus to term. Neither does it require that the man who impregnated her bear any kind of cost to alleviate this burden. Of course, the federal government may refuse to fund both live births and abortions. The Equal Protection Clause does not require that the government do anything. But when it decides to act, deploying either its funding or coercive power, it must not invoke a particular conception of the good life.

A powers review relieves the need for the tiers-of-scrutiny approach. It relieves the need to ask whether a law discriminates on the basis of sex, triggering either intermediate or strict scrutiny. The question is not about identity but justification. The Court need simply proclaim that laws prohibiting abortion are outside the power of the state to enact. For once we realize that abortion legislation is based on a conception of what it means to be female, invoking a constitutionally inadmissible rationale, such legislation is unconstitutional.

---

[84] McConnell 1991: 990

6 SAME-SEX MARRIAGE AND THE DISESTABLISHMENT OF MARRIAGE

A powers review also stands to reframe the constitutional debate over same-sex marriage. We celebrate marriage in ceremonies and parties, in newspaper and magazine announcements, in television shows, movies, and books where the hero or heroine usually find "true love," and in our everyday "congratulations" to a newlywed couple. And gays and lesbians are slowly being able to partake in this celebration. By marrying individuals, the state encourages and sanctions this, in addition to providing the numerous legal benefits that come with the status of being married. But what about those who the law defines as single – those who are not married? These individuals may live alone, with their siblings, with their grandparents, or with an unmarried partner. In any case, they fall short of the marriage ideal. I argue that this is problematic. For once we acknowledge that the state invokes constitutionally inadmissible rationales in limiting marriage to opposite-sex couples, marriage itself begins to unravel. Being in the "marriage business," the state operates on the idea that a certain kind of relationship is special, that it is morally significant. The state does so by consecrating the union of two individuals with the label of marriage.

I interrogate the relationship between same-sex marriage and the disestablishment of marriage, arguing that there is indeed a constitutional slippery slope from the former to the latter. Consider that in his dissent in *Lawrence*, Justice Scalia argues if laws based on mere "moral choices" are unconstitutional, this calls into question "laws against bigamy, same-sex marriage, adult incest, prostitution, masturbation, adultery, fornication, bestiality, and obscenity."[1] He reasons that the "Court makes no effort to cabin the scope of its decision to exclude

---

[1] *Lawrence* at 590, dissenting

them from its holding."[2] This slippery slope argument is a powerful one. It means that if the Court bases its decision on a particular principle, that principle may suggest that other laws and policies are unconstitutional.[3] Or take Hadley Arkes testimony before the subcommittee considering the Defense of Marriage Act:

> [I]f marriage ... could mean just anything the positive law proclaimed it to mean, then the positive law could define just about anything as marriage ... [W]hy shouldn't it be possible to permit a mature woman, past child bearing, to marry her grown son? In fact, why would it not be possible to permit a man, much taken with himself, to marry himself? ... [w]hat is being posed here is a question of principle: [w]hat is the ground on which the law would turn back these challenges?[4]

This chapter takes seriously the force of this question. Ultimately, I argue the constitutional slope is even steeper than Arkes suggests: it leads to the very disestablishment of marriage. By "marriage," I mean only civil marriage, the state's conferral of the status of being married on two individuals. Religious groups may have their own rules, customs, and procedures for marrying individuals. The constitutional ban on denying individuals equal protection of the laws applics to the state, not to private associations. My concern then is not with why religious or other voluntary groups may be in the "marriage business" but rather why and how the state permits and limits this institution.

I argue that if we take seriously the powers approach I propose in this book, the slope toward the disestablishment of marriage is indeed slippery, more slippery than liberals may like to believe. Although the identity approach permits us to short circuit the slope, it invites the problems just outlined. My particular focus is on the relationship between the following two arguments: limitations on same-sex marriage are illegitimate, and marriage itself is illegitimate. Liberal scholarly work seems to consider either one or the other claim. Scholars argue that laws prohibiting same-sex marriage problematically violate

---

[2] *Lawrence* at 590, dissenting
[3] *See generally* Volokh 2003
[4] Defense of Marriage Act: Hearings on H.R. 3396, 104th Cong. 97–102 (1996)

the equal rights of gays and lesbians[5] and that the very idea of marriage is problematic.[6] But what is the connection between these two claims? Does the second conclusion inevitably follow from the first, as the slippage of the slope would suggest?

Elizabeth Brake, one of the few scholars who actually considers this question, answers in the affirmative.[7] She argues that liberal neutrality invalidates both prohibitions on same-sex marriage and marriage itself. According to Brake, "Same-sex marriage advocates have argued that it is unjust to define marriage legally on the basis of contested moral views regarding same-sex activity."[8] Brake agrees but argues that such advocates have "failed to follow the implications of such neutral or political liberal reasoning to the extreme conclusion" that we question marriage itself.[9] I analyze this slippery slope by considering its constitutional implications. If prohibitions on same-sex marriage are unconstitutional, does this mean marriage laws themselves are unconstitutional?

Ultimately, I argue that the answer depends on whether we adopt an identity-centered framework or a powers one. On one hand, if the Court adopts a framework of powers to invalidate laws against same-sex marriage, we quickly move down the slope to concluding that the state ought not to be in the "marriage business." Limitations on same-sex marriage violate the Equal Protection Clause, because they rest on the intrinsic moral superiority of one set of couplings (a heterosexual conception of an appropriate or good relationship) over another (a homosexual one). And in a similar fashion limitations on adult incestuous or plural marriage privilege one conception of the good – a two, non-blood related union – over another – a three person or a blood-related union. In fact, by conferring the status of marriage, the state takes sides in a very personal decision about what constitutes the good life. It thereby exceeds its powers in marrying individuals under a powers review.

---

[5] See, e.g., Ball 2003, Gerstmann 2008, Koppelman 2002, Richards 2005, Wolfson 2004
[6] See, e.g., Brake 2012, Card 1996, Estlund 1997, Fineman 1995, Metz 2010, 2007, Polikoff 2008
[7] Brake 2012
[8] Brake 2012: 133
[9] Brake 2012: 135

On the other hand, if the Court continues to deploy an identity approach, it can invalidate prohibitions on same-sex marriage while sustaining other limitations on marriage and even marriage itself. The language of identity stands to distinguish same-sex marriage from its plural or adult incestuous counterparts. Whereas a prohibition on same-sex marriage discriminates against gays and lesbians, improperly discriminating on a supposed suspect class, limitations on plural or adult incestuous marriage and even marriage itself do not.

This is what is at stake in adopting the powers approach I elaborate on and the identity one I criticize. It is only fitting that the final chapter brings this distinction to a head. This chapter lays out this fundamental tension between a focus on those reasons that are constitutionally inadmissible and a focus on suspect class. First, I argue that taking seriously a powers review leads to the disestablishment of marriage. Second, I explain how the identity approach short-circuits this slope. Third, I briefly consider another way the state may validate gay and lesbian relationships without violating a powers review.

A POWERS REVIEW: FROM SAME-SEX MARRIAGE TO PLURAL MARRIAGE TO THE DISESTABLISHMENT OF MARRIAGE

This book frames the same-sex marriage issue as the following: does the state have the power to limit marriage to opposite-sex couples? I argue that the answer is no, precisely because the state acts on a constitutionally inadmissible reason in doing so. It seeks to privilege heterosexual relationships over homosexual ones simply because they are heterosexual. It is the intrinsic moral privileging of a certain conception of intimacy or living over another that renders such a prohibition unconstitutional. But this reasoning, as I argue, also dooms prohibitions on plural marriage or adult incestuous ones. Here too the state seeks to privilege certain relationships – two, non-blood-related adults – over others for the simple reason that they are morally superior. Taking a powers review seriously means that the slope is even steeper. If the state may not privilege particular conceptions of the good life over others on purely moral grounds, it may not confer on individuals the morally special status of marriage. If only constitutionally inadmissible rationales underlie the state's decision to be in the "marriage business," we cannot avoid a run down the slope.

Same-Sex Marriage

Often, those against same-sex marriage invoke concerns involving pro-creation and the raising of children[10] or the preservation of "tradi-tional" marriage[11] in doing the justificatory work. But it is relatively easy to see that these reasons fail. First, consider the reason that the state limits marriage in this way to promote a stable environment for the procreation or the raising of children. If these concerns are indeed relevant to marriage, why does the state not at all regulate marriage licenses in light of them? After all, the state does not ascertain whether an opposite-sex couple is fit to raise a child before issuing a license. Those who profess no desire to raise a child or even to procreate are not denied a marriage license. Two elderly individuals past their child-rearing age may just as easily obtain such a license as two younger individuals ready to start a family. Marriage and the begetting and raising of children are distinct issues even for those who currently protest same-sex marriage.[12]

The California Supreme Court rejected this kind of justification when it invalidated that state's prohibition on same-sex marriage.[13] Although the court does not explicitly use the language of "bad faith," its reasoning informs this crucial part of a powers review. The court concludes that

> the right to marry never has been viewed as the sole preserve of individuals who are physically capable of having children. Men and women who desire to raise children with a loved one in a recognized family but who are physically unable to conceive a child with their loved one never have been excluded from the right to marry.[14]

. . .

---

[10] *See generally* Blankenhorn 2007
[11] *See generally* Wardle 2008
[12] *See generally* Joslin 2011
[13] *In re Marriages* (Cal. 2008). *See also Goodridge v. Dept. of Public Health* (Mass. 2003)
[14] *In re Marriages* at 825

A person who is physically incapable of bearing children still has the potential to become a parent and raise a child through adoption or through means of assisted reproduction, and the constitutional right to marry ensures the individual the opportunity to raise children in an officially recognized family with the person with whom the individual has chosen to share his or her life. Thus, although an important purpose underlying marriage may be to channel procreation into a stable family relationship, that purpose cannot be viewed as limiting the constitutional right to marry to couples who are capable of biologically producing a child together.[15]

The court also cites *Turner v. Safley* (1987), a Supreme Court decision that specifically considers the relationship of procreation and marriage. *Safley* points to the "bad faith" charge of the procreative objection to same-sex marriage. In *Safley*, the state of Missouri Department of Corrections promulgated various penal regulations. One of these regulations prohibited inmates from marrying unless they first received approval from the superintendent, approval that should be given only "when there are compelling reasons to do so."[16] The Department of Corrections stated that "only a pregnancy or the birth of an illegitimate child would be considered a compelling reason."[17] Why does pregnancy or birth, but not love, commitment, or the wide variety of benefits attached to marriage, constitute a compelling reason? Marriage is primarily about procreation, about the raising of children – or so the prison regulation here implies.

The Court invalidates this regulation concluding that "[m]any important attributes of marriage remain.... after taking into account the limitations imposed by prison life.... [including the] expressions of emotional support and public commitment [that] are an important and significant aspect of the marital relationship."[18] This language is cited approvingly by the California Supreme Court to establish the point that procreation is not a requirement for marriage. In fact, *Safley* rehearses the legal benefits that arise from marriage including "the receipt of government benefits" such as Social Security and "property

---

[15] *In re Marriages* at 826
[16] *Safley* at 82
[17] *Safley* at 96–7
[18] *Safley* at 95–6

rights."[19] An inmate may well seek to marry for these reasons, reasons that have nothing to do with procreation. Procreation is not necessary to avail oneself of the institution of marriage. Evan Gerstmann rightly points out that these attributes of emotional support and public commitment "are as applicable to same-sex couples as to heterosexual couples."[20] So as a constitutional matter, concerns of procreation and hence the raising of children cannot underlie a prohibition on same-sex marriage just as they could not underlie limiting an inmate's ability to marry. Those who make such an argument in the context of same-sex marriage do not do so in good faith. Something else must be going on.

Along with the argument from procreation and the raising of children is the concern about preserving traditional, opposite-sex marriages. This explains why those who defend prohibitions on same-sex marriage are sometimes willing to permit gays and lesbians to gain civil union status but not full-blown marriage. When the Vermont Supreme Court became one of the first courts to invalidate a state prohibition on same-sex marriage (*Baker v. Vermont* (Vt. 1999)), the court gave the legislature the option of granting same-sex couples the status of marriage or a civil union. At that time, the Vermont legislature chose the latter (it ultimately passed legislation to grant marriage in 2009). The civil union law said in part:

> While a system of civil unions does not bestow the status of civil marriage, it does satisfy the requirements of the Common Benefits Clause. Changes in the way significant legal relationships are established under the constitution should be approached carefully, combining respect for the community and cultural institutions most affected with a commitment to the constitutional rights involved.[21]

But what does this concern for the "respect for the community" and its "cultural institutions" amount to? There are two possible answers, one that is circular and another that is (like its procreative counterpart) proffered in bad faith. First, it seems circular to justify a prohibition on same-sex marriage on grounds of tradition or culture. This is exactly what is often done. For instance, the official website for Proposition

[19] *Safley* at 96
[20] Gerstmann 2008: 97
[21] V.S.A. Ch. 23, Sec. 1 (10) (2000)

8 says that "The [California] Supreme Court's decision to legalize same-sex marriage did not just overturn the will of California voters; it also redefined marriage for the rest of society. . . . This decision has far-reaching consequences." In explaining what these "far-reaching consequences" actually are, the Proposition 8 supporters go on to say that by "saying that a marriage is between 'any two persons' rather than between a man and a woman, the Court decision has opened the door to any kind of 'marriage.' This undermines the value of marriage altogether at a time when we should be restoring marriage, not undermining it."[22] Thus, the alleged bad consequence of redefining marriage is that marriage will now be undermined because the definition will have changed. This is patently circular. Of course, changing the definition of marriage will undoubtedly undermine the traditional meaning of marriage.

Because marriage has historically been limited to opposite-sex couples, we should keep it as is. This is the "that's how it's always been" reason for such a limitation. But just because we have done something one way in the past does not mean we should continue to do it to preserve "respect for the community." That kind of argument would allow the state to justify any practice, such as Jim Crow, on grounds that the state has always done it that way. Appeal to tradition stands to undo a powers review. After all, just because there is a tradition of homophobia or racism does not mean that laws like *Romer* or *Yick Wo* are constitutional. Again, this is why Sunstein argues that the Equal Protection Clause stands as a challenge to the appeal to tradition. The meaning of marriage no doubt changed with the invalidation of antimiscegenation laws: from same-race couplings to the possibility of interracial ones. If avoiding change were a constitutionally legitimate rationale, the Court would not be able to invalidate any law. Endorsing this kind of reason would gut a powers review.

Second, perhaps the concern for detractors is that same-sex marriage will destroy the institution of marriage for opposite-sex couples or lead to more divorces among them. There is an empirical and normative response to this kind of claim. As William Eskridge notes, in European countries such as Denmark and Sweden where same-sex

[22] Yes on Proposition 8 website, May 20, 2008. http://www.protectmarriage.com/about/why

unions have been legally recognized in some fashion since 1989, there has been no adverse effect on the institution of marriage for hetero-sexuals.[23] If anything, the effect has been positive.[24] This trend is borne out in recent numbers from the Division of Vital Statistics at the Centers for Disease Control.[25] Massachusetts began issuing same-sex marriage licenses in 2004. The divorce rate in 2007 for the state was 2.3 per 1,000 people, which was less than the average rate for the rest of the country. In fact, all the states that permit same-sex marriage have a lower rate of divorce than the average of the others.[26]

More important, this kind of justification for a prohibition on same-sex marriage cannot be made in good faith. Those who support such a prohibition on these grounds do not seek to prevent divorce or even the number of times an individual may marry. It is revealing that those who place referenda such as Proposition 8 on the ballot do not seek to place restrictions on divorce. Nothing is more detrimen-tal to the institution of marriage than the ability to obtain a divorce. James Q. Wilson suggests that the adoption by states of a regime of no fault divorce has undermined marriages.[27] No fault divorce laws mean that a spouse can procure a divorce for any reason or no reason at all.

All fifty states have incorporated some provision for no fault divorce.[28] So even states that prohibit same-sex marriage permit no fault divorce. How can these states simultaneously proffer the protec-tion of marriage as a justification for limiting marriage if they do not limit the number of times an individual may marry or restrict their abil-ity to procure a divorce? This is telling from a powers review. It means that reasons related to procreation, divorce, or preserving opposite-sex marriages are made in bad faith. If the concern is with undermining opposite-sex marriage or increasing the frequency of children born out of wedlock, states should aim to repeal no fault divorce or the num-ber of times an individual may marry. These policies straightforwardly

---

[23] Eskridge 2000: 659–62; *see also* Liu and Macedo 2005
[24] Eskridge 2000: 659–62
[25] *See* http://www.cdc.gov/nchs/data/nvsr/nvsr58/nvsr58_25.htm
[26] http://www.divorce.com/blog/cdc-report-shows-massachusetts-has-lowest-divorce-rate
[27] Wilson 2003
[28] Hackstaff 1999: 28

damage the institution of marriage, making it perhaps less likely that individuals will desire to marry.

Consider that the Catholic Church forbids divorce as an ecclesiastical matter: "divorce separates what God has joined together."[29] The Church specifically states that the "remarriage of persons divorced from a living, lawful spouse contravenes the plan and law of God."[30] Divorcees, according to the Catechism, cannot receive Communion.[31] So if the Catholic Church justified its refusal to marry same-sex couples within its church to prevent more divorce among heterosexual couples, their justification would (at least as an internal matter) be proffered in good faith. But those who seek to restrict marriage to heterosexuals on such grounds suffer the justificatory charge of bad faith. This is because states that ban same-sex marriage have not repealed their divorce laws or limited the number of marriages an individual may undertake in his or her lifetime.

Ultimately, the justification for limiting marriage to opposite-sex couples may be some particular religious view of the institution or a belief in the intrinsic goodness of certain relationships over others. Borrowing Justice Ginsburg's language in *Gonzales*, such limitations are "untethered to any ground genuinely serving the Government's interest in" procreation or the raising of children.[32] Rather, they seek to mandate a "moral code."[33] This is what is often going on in defending prohibitions on same-sex marriage. According to the Pew Forum on Religion and Public Life, many religious groups object to same-sex marriage on precisely such grounds.[34] For instance, the U.S. Conference of Catholic Bishops justifies their position on grounds that "marriage is a faithful, exclusive and lifelong union between one man and one woman.... Moreover, we believe the natural institution of marriage has been blessed and elevated by Christ Jesus to the dignity of a sacrament."[35]

---

[29] *See* http://www.vatican.va/archive/ccc_css/archive/catechism/p2s2c3a7.htm
[30] *See* http://www.vatican.va/archive/ccc_css/archive/catechism/p2s2c3a7.htm
[31] Ibid
[32] *Gonzales* at 182, dissenting
[33] Ibid
[34] Pew Forum on Religion and Public Life: http://pewforum.org/docs/?DocID=291
[35] United States Conference of Catholic Bishops, September 10, 2003: http://www.usccb.org/comm/archives/2003/03–179.shtml

But the Establishment Clause rules out these religious rationales. Stephen Macedo argues that there is "no reasoned, secular case" against same-sex marriage.[36] This is why Gordon Babst characterizes a prohibition on same-sex marriage as a "shadow establishment" drawing from the constitutional ban on establishing religion.[37] Legal scholars who challenge prohibitions on same-sex marriage rarely invoke the Establishment Clause. Gary J. Simson, one of few scholars who does invoke the constitutional principle of nonendorsement argues that laws "prohibiting same-sex marriage are extremely difficult to understand in secular terms and extremely easy to understand in religious terms."[38] The problem, of course, is that those states that do ban same-sex marriage will not candidly admit that religious reasons are doing the underlying work.[39] In fact, this is why the proponents of Proposition 8 in *Schwarzenegger* specifically refused to invoke such reasons in justifying California's ban on same-sex marriage. Rather, proponents have unsurprisingly sought to justify such bans by appealing to arguments of responsible procreation, tradition, and preserving the current institution of marriage. But, as already demonstrated here, these arguments are either circular or proffered in bad faith. Once we realize that these justifications are inapplicable, the Establishment Clause carriers serious constitutional weight as an important way to invalidate such limitations on marriage.

It is worth pointing out that even those who invoke God or religion to limit marriage do not seek to prevent atheists from marrying. If marriage is a God-given institution and our laws and policies regulating the institution ought to reflect that, those who do not believe in God stand to undermine it. They are by definition unable to appreciate the sanctity of marriage. But it is telling that detractors are not seeking to keep atheists out. Even religious objections to same-sex marriage, then, may be proffered in bad faith, revealing that mere hostility to gays and lesbians is doing the actual work.

---

[36] Macedo 1995a: 261
[37] Babst 2002, *see also* Den Otter 2009: 245–261 (describing the public unjustifiability of a prohibition on same-sex marriage as an "easier case")
[38] Simson 2012: 147–8
[39] *See generally* Stone 2009

To be sure, those who defend prohibitions on same-sex marriage do not only invoke religious arguments, arguments about God and faith.[40] They may simply find same-sex relationships disgusting or gross.[41] Or they may find them morally inferior. This is precisely the view of certain natural law theorists who self-consciously argue for a perfectionist conception of the good in terms of intimacy and marriage where gay intimacy is morally inferior to its opposite-sex, marriage counterpart.[42] This does not strike me as a strictly religious justification. It is not simply about faith or God but about the idea that certain ways of living are simply gross, inferior, or just plain wrong. But such perfectionist views also violate a powers review.

Others may object to same-sex marriage on sexist grounds. The belief that males must act or be a certain way – masculine and heterosexual – often justifies limiting marriage to opposite-sex couples. Monte Neil Stewart, president of the Marriage Law Foundation, argues that marriage is "[s]ociety's primary and most effective means of bridging the male-female divide."[43] In fact, Stewart describes a same-sex marriage as a "gender-less" marriage pointing to the importance of the gendered aspect of the institution.[44] She argues that marriage is

> the only institution that can confer the status of husband and wife, that can transform a male into a husband or female into a wife (a social identity quite different from "partner"), and thus can transform males into husbands/fathers (a category of males particularly beneficial to society) and females into wives/mothers (likewise a socially beneficial category).[45]

This is not a religious argument grounded in faith but rather one grounded in a belief about the appropriate relationship between gender and sex. In fact, often the argument is that marriage has a civilizing influence on men[46] (an argument that is sometimes made in the context

---

[40] *Contra* Macedo 1995b: 335
[41] *See generally* Nussbaum 2009: 695, 2004
[42] *See, e.g.*, Finnis 1993, George 2004
[43] Stewart 2008: 322
[44] Stewart 2006
[45] Stewart 2006: 19
[46] Stewart 2008: 332

of same-sex marriage as well[47]). But as the previous chapter makes
clear, such sexist rationales fail a powers review. Such justifications
trade on the idea that males are sexually aggressive – in need of a
mollifying influence. If the rationale for marriage is that males ought
to be husbands, fathers, or breadwinners and that females ought to be
wives, mothers, or caregivers (this is a "particularly beneficial" social
category), this suggests that gendered attributes attach to a certain
sex. Two males or two females could not create a husband and wife
pair. Males cannot be wives and females cannot be husbands. This
justification for limiting marriage to opposite-sex couples violates a
powers review by sustaining the sexist belief that only with a particular
sex can there be certain gendered qualities. This means the actual
reason for prohibiting same-sex marriage is about a conception of
the good or even simple dislike or hostility against gays and lesbians.
Either kind of reason is constitutionally inadmissible under a powers
review. Again, in *Schwarzenegger,* Judge Walker finds that the "evidence
at trial . . . uncloaks the most likely explanation for [a prohibition on
same-sex marriage]: a desire to advance the belief that opposite-sex
couples are morally superior to same-sex couples."[48]

Plural or Adult Incestuous Marriages

But if limiting marriage on the basis of sex invokes constitutionally
inadmissible reasons, what about limiting marriage only to two individuals or only to those adults who are not related by blood? In fact,
recent work in liberal political theory argues that restrictions on plural
or adult incestuous marriages are difficult to justify from a commitment to antiperfectionism.[49] Andrew March makes a persuasive case
for the illegitimacy of these limitations, even characterizing his argument as "The Slippery Slope and the Slide from Same-Sex Marriage
to Polygamy."[50] My purpose is not to rehearse his arguments or others
but rather stress the implications of taking seriously the powers review

---

[47] *See* Sullivan 2003: 76, 1989: 20; *see also* Eskridge 1996
[48] *Schwarzenegger* at 1002–3
[49] *See, e.g.,* March 2011, 2010, Den Otter 2009
[50] March 2011

I propose in this book. Although March does not deploy the language of "bad faith," I argue the requirement of public sincerity underlies his analysis.

At the outset, as in the case of same-sex marriage, we cannot look to concerns of tradition or preserving current heterosexual marriages to short-circuit the slope. Again, this type of reason turns out to be either circular or proffered in bad faith. Simply suggesting that marriage has always been about *two, non-blood-related* individuals instead of three or four blood-related individuals is circular. Just because that specification has been the "positive law's" definition of marriage in the past does not mean it is constitutional for the definition to remain that way.

A prohibition on adult incestuous marriages (take as an example the possible marriage of two same-sex adult siblings) easily *fails* a powers review. Although the lack of procreation was important to justify a prohibition on same-sex marriage, here it is the possible presence of procreation that may justify a prohibition on adult incestuous marriage. The concern is that we want to avoid, borrowing March's language, "the creation of bad lives"[51] – namely, children with severe birth defects. Interestingly, March argues that this concern may turn out to be too weak to justify such a limitation.[52] But even more telling is that this kind of reason cannot be offered in good faith. It would only prohibit two blood-related opposite-sex siblings from marrying. Two adult brothers (or two sisters) who seek to marry do not trigger any possible concerns of procreation or the "creation of bad lives."

So a state's *categorical* ban on consanguinity cannot be based on concerns about procreation. The means deployed by such a ban reveal that such concerns are proffered in bad faith; otherwise a state would permit two sisters or two brothers to marry. This kind of ban, then, must be based on the idea that adult incest is a taboo or that certain ways of living are intrinsically inferior. Or, even worse, this kind of limitation on marriage is based on animus or hostility against those who would seek to marry their adult brother or sister. These rationales are constitutionally inadmissible failing a powers review.

[51] March 2010: 49
[52] March 2010: 49–54

The case of plural marriage is more complex. Here, March considers and rejects two primary justifications for prohibiting such marriages: preventing harm to women and children and ensuring that wealthy men do not monopolize women in the marriage market. I concede there may be additional related justifications for limiting marriage to only two individuals. Again, I will not analyze these justifications in detail, something March does well. Rather, my purpose is only to flag the nature of how a powers review would approach these issues from a requirement of good faith. As a threshold matter, a court can realize that both concerns assume polygynous marriage (one man and two or more women) rather than polyandrous ones (one women and two or more men) or marriages composed of individuals of the same sex. One man and many women may be the more popular instance of plural marriage but certainly not the only kind. This is why I adopt the neutral language of "plural marriage."

For instance, a marriage of three gay men does not raise the concerns of preventing harm to women and children that come with the more familiar one man/more than one woman union. Obviously, in a marriage of three men, there is no issue of gender inequality. And a state could permit such a marriage and simultaneously prohibit such a union from adopting or raising children. After all, the issue of adoption is distinct from the issue of marriage. This is sufficient to establish that a powers review sends us down the slope to invalidating at least *some* limitations on these kinds of marriages. Here too the means deployed by the law reveal that concerns about preventing harm cannot be doing the actual justificatory work.

But even on their merits, these concerns may well be proffered in bad faith.[53] First, March argues that if the concern is genuinely about inequality, harm to children, or a women's ability to exit, the state can regulate "multiple-member" unions just as the state regulates two-person ones, "with special concern for the autonomy, property rights, and freedom of exit for vulnerable women."[54] Interestingly in *Reynolds v. United States* (1878), the Court upheld a federal law

[53] March 2011: 262–8
[54] March 2011: 260

prohibiting bigamy, citing concerns of patriarchy.[55] I leave to one side the religious and cultural arguments that may be relevant in the case of plural marriage and, in particular, polygyny.[56] It is telling that women could not vote at that time (the Nineteenth Amendment was not passed until 1920). In fact, until recently, the common law of many states saw husband and wife as one person. Spouses "could not be on opposite sides of any lawsuit for either personal injury or property damage."[57] Consequently, a husband could physically abuse his wife with no threat of legal sanction.[58] At that time, even two-person couplings posed concerns of exit and domination for women. This strains the credulity of claiming that harm to women is doing the justificatory work.

Second, a concern that permitting plural marriage will lead to wealthy men monopolizing the market for eligible women also cannot be doing the actual justificatory work. If this were a genuine justification, why does the law fail to limit the influence of wealth on dating or the intimacy market in general? As March argues: "Who is to say what one's 'fair share' of intimacy is, and who is going to impose this fair share at the expense of unwilling persons?"[59]

But I concede that a ban on plural marriage may well reduce the influence of wealth in the marriage market. Richard Posner suggests this as a possible economic rationale for prohibiting certain kinds of plural marriage[60] – again, marriages involving just women or just men do not seem to trigger such concerns. However, a powers review does not ask whether there *could be a reason* for the law that is not inadmissible. This type of *ex post facto* argument – is there an argument from efficiency that could justify the law? – may be important to economists, but it is at odds with a powers review. The constitutional question ought to be whether the *actual* reason or rationale for such a limitation is constitutionally inadmissible. That is, those who seek to justify restrictions on plural marriage often do so retrospectively. We now

---

[55] *Reynolds* at 166
[56] For such an analysis, *see, e.g.,* Gutmann 1993, Okin 1999, Song 2007
[57] Epstein 1995: 944
[58] Ibid.: 944
[59] March 2011: 266
[60] Posner 1992: 253–60; www.becker-posner-blog.com/archives/2006/10/should_polygamy .html

have such restrictions, so what are the reasons for continuing to apply them. But this after-the-fact inquiry invites the kind of bad faith arguments a powers review rejects. The constitutional question is whether the state's actual reason for prohibiting marriages between two or more individuals is constitutionally inadmissible.

Ultimately, the actual reason for a categorical ban on *all* types of plural marriage, even those involving members of the same sex, must be about the intrinsic moral superiority of two-person couplings over couplings of three or more. This is what underlies extant prohibitions on plural marriage. Justice Scalia's dissent in *Lawrence* makes clear that current laws against bigamy are based on nothing other than "mere moral" considerations. Limitations on plural marriage fail for the same reason as limitations on same-sex marriage. If a law values a certain a way of life simply or only because the state considers it morally superior, this fails a powers review.

Marriage as a Morally Special Status: The Case for Disestablishment

This is telling. If prohibitions on same-sex marriage, certain adult incestuous marriages, and perhaps even plural marriages (or at least some of them) invoke constitutionally inadmissible rationales, what about the very institution of marriage itself? If we take the moral superiority argument seriously – that is, the state ought not to privilege certain relationships over others – then the entire idea of marriage (and again, I mean here only civil marriage) seems to unravel. In fact, scholarly work has argued that liberal neutrality may rule out marriage.[61]

Tamara Metz makes a persuasive case for the disestablishment of marriage on liberal grounds. Although she does not speak in the language of powers, her argument informs the powers review I defend here. She conceptualizes the liberal state as one that may not do any and everything it chooses. This limitation on state power is meant to enhance the freedom of individuals to live as they choose:

---

[61] *See, e.g.*, Brake 2012, Card 1996, Estlund 1997: 162–4, Fineman 1995, Metz 2010, 2007, Polikoff 2008, Raz 1986: 110

Traditionally, liberals have treated the commands of the state as limiting action (not belief) for the narrow purpose of ensuring social order, protecting citizens from harm, and guaranteeing political fairness [citation omitted]. Generally, the state confers legal status for instrumental convenience, not to alter self-understanding in any deep and enduring way. The familiar idea behind the limited state is that freedom consists, in large part, in individuals being free from interference to live according to their own design.[62]

Given this view of the liberal state, conferring the status of marriage seems to confound it. Central to Metz's argument is the distinction between civil unions and marriage. The former entail all the instrumental legal benefits, burdens, and responsibilities that come with the status of marriage. But the label of marriage does something more than just provide these benefits. This is why the Vermont legislature first decided to grant gays and lesbians a civil union status but not full-blown marriage. This was seen as a less controversial move, precisely because it withheld the all-important status of marriage. Even though gay couples would receive all the same benefits, burdens, and responsibilities that come with marriage, they would not receive the label of "marriage." As noted earlier, Vermont granted all couples the status of marriage in 2009. The label of "marriage" is important, because it adds something to the relevant union, something that goes above and beyond the tangible benefits and burdens that accompany civil unions. In *Goodridge v. Dep't of Public Health* (Mass. 2003), the Massachusetts Supreme Judicial Court invalidated Massachusetts' prohibition on same-sex marriage, making clear that "[t]angible as well as intangible benefits flow from marriage."[63]

In *Maynard v. Hill* (1888), the Court held that a state legislature may dissolve the bonds of marriage. Justice Stephen Field, writing for the Court, famously reasoned that marriage is a kind of status. Marriage is

declared a civil contract for certain purposes, but it is not thereby made synonymous with the word "contract" employed in the common law or statutes.... The relation is always regulated by

---

[62] Metz 2010: 115
[63] *Goodridge* at 322

government. It is more than a contract. It requires certain acts of the parties to constitute marriage independent of and beyond the contract. It partakes more of the character of an institution regulated and controlled by public authority, upon principles of public policy, for the benefit of the community.[64]

Alongside this view of marriage as a status is a conflicting one that considers it like any other contract, a view that was also present in the nineteenth century.[65] This distinction between status and contract is crucial in the debate over same-sex marriage. As Janet Halley points out, "advocates and opponents [of same-sex marriage have] converge[d] on an image of marriage as status."[66] On one hand, gays and lesbians seek that status to affirm their relationships. On the other hand, detractors seek to protect it from alteration. Joseph Singer, writing positively in light of the decision in *Goodridge*, makes clear that

> [a]fter all, marriage is not just an ordinary contract; it is a status conferred by state officials who issue a license and conduct a ceremony in which they state: "By the authority invested in me by the Commonwealth of Massachusetts, I hereby declare you to be married."[67]

This is why those who seek to invalidate bans on same-sex marriage do not simply advocate for civil unions. Civil unions may entail all the contractual or tangible rights that accompany marriage. But they do not have the intangible quality that comes with the status of being married. One scholar of marriage law even characterizes the Vermont's Civil Union Statute as a "secular alternative to marriage for same-sex couples."[68] This implies that unlike a civil union, marriage is based on something besides a secular purpose. In fact, Perry Dane argues that the "'secular' and 'religious' meanings. . . . of marriage are so intermeshed in our history, legal and religious imagination" that we cannot "wall off" marriage from its "religious considerations."[69] Civil unions,

---

[64] *Maynard* at 212–13
[65] *See generally* Grossberg 1988
[66] Halley 2010: 4
[67] Singer 2005: 5
[68] Katz 2003: 21
[69] Dane 2009: 1129

then, do not capture the status that comes with marriage. Marriage is more than just its attendant secular contractual parts. Because marriage and civil unions are different, as the same-sex marriage debate makes clear, marriage must be a kind of status. It provides a good that civil unions do not.

What is this intangible good? What is the special symbolism of marriage? According to Metz, marriage "functions as a special symbolic resource that individuals can use to say something about who they are to themselves, their partners, and their communities."[70] It functions as an affirmation of the moral worthiness of this kind of union. This is why gays and lesbians do not merely seek to be civilly unionized. They seek the morally special status that comes with saying that they are married.

The perspective of recent natural law theory is instructive in elucidating this special status. Robert George, one of key figures in this tradition, argues that marriage is an "intrinsic," not merely "instrumental good."[71] It is the "one flesh union" that arises from procreative sex within marriage that constitutes this good:

> The central and justifying point of sex is not pleasure (or even the sharing of pleasure) per se, however much sexual pleasure is sought – rightly sought – as an aspect of the perfection of marital union; the point of sex, rather, is marriage itself, considered as an essentially and irreducibly (though not merely) bodily union of persons – a union effectuated and renewed by acts of sexual congress–conjugal acts.[72]

Under this view, the sex act within an opposite-sex marriage is morally superior to sex acts that occur outside of it. George explicitly privileges this conception of the good, this way of living. He does not argue that this way of life is superior because it provides benefits to others. Marriage is an intrinsic good. It is worthwhile for its own sake, providing a kind of good that other ways of living including being unmarried, having "flings" or multiple partners, or being with platonic friends cannot. So if the meaning expressed by marriage is the belief that a

[70] Metz 2010: 89
[71] George 2004
[72] George 2004: 73

certain of way of living is intrinsically superior to another, this violates liberal neutrality.

Civil unions may simply provide instrumental benefits to those who undertake it. The status of "being married," as George makes clear, does something more. It provides an intrinsic good, expressing the belief that these kinds of relationships are morally special. Marriage, as Metz says, is "a unique kind of expressive good, the value of which exceeds the sum of the delineable benefits and burdens that attach to it."[73] In declaring individuals married, the state alters "self-understanding."[74] Metz calls this the "expressive" or "constitutive" part of marriage.[75] The state goes beyond its "limited" role of providing mere instrumental benefits. This is why, according to Metz, the state "assumes [through marriage laws] the role of *ethical authority.* . . . violating the type of neutrality necessary for the state to secure liberty and equality in a diverse polity such as ours."[76] This amounts to the conclusion that the state does not have the power to enact this kind of constitutive or expressive institution.

Now George's argument for marriage explicitly excludes same-sex couples. He would no doubt withhold the state's conferral of marriage to gays and lesbians. Gays and lesbians do not fulfill the procreative part of his definition of marriage. But again, this procreative requirement cannot be the basis of current marriage laws. After all, the state issues marriage licenses without at all taking into account a couple's ability or desire to procreate. This leaves the "companionate" justification or model of marriage.[77] Richard Posner defines it as

> between at least approximate equals, based on mutual respect and affection, and involving close and continuous association in child rearing, household management, and other activities, rather than merely the occasional copulation [of the procreative model].[78]

Goodridge also adopts the companionate model of marriage:

[73] Metz 2010: 36
[74] Metz 2010: 93
[75] Metz 2010: 89–94
[76] Metz 2010: 115
[77] Khalsa 2005
[78] Posner 1992: 45

While it is certainly true that many, perhaps most, married couples have children together (assisted or unassisted), it is the
exclusive and permanent commitment of the marriage partners
to one another, not the begetting of children, that is the sine qua
non of civil marriage.[79]

Or as Evan Wolfson puts it, "marriage is first and foremost about a
loving union between two people who enter into a relationship of emotional and financial commitment and interdependence."[80] Marriage
expresses their commitment to this kind of union. Marriage is about
enjoying one's life with another. This model of marriage is, as William
Eskridge suggests, "most similar to those that are typically valorized
by most modern Western perspectives."[81]

Marriage is a morally special status. By conferring it, the state takes
a side in what ought to be each individual's personal decision about
how to live. Brake, in line with Metz, argues that marriage laws are
based on the "belief that marriage and companionate romantic love
have special value."[82] It consists

in the assumption that a central, exclusive, amorous relationship
is normal for humans, in that it is a universally shared goal, and
that such a relationship is normative, in that it should be aimed
at in preference of other relationship types. The assumption that
valuable relationships must be marital or amorous devalues friend-
ships and other caring relationships, as recent manifestos by urban
tribalists, quirkyalones, polyamorists, and asexuals have insisted.[83]

This kind of belief about the morally special status of marriage fails liberal neutrality. In fact, David Estlund also argues that a "more neutral,
more liberal, liberalism" must reject marriage laws.[84]

Perhaps this conclusion is too quick. Stephen Macedo thoughtfully suggests that marriage promotes "public welfare."[85] For instance,
"[m]arried men (much evidence suggests) live longer, have lower rates

[79] *Goodridge* at 332
[80] Wolfson 1994: 579
[81] Eskridge 1993: 1436
[82] Brake 2012: 88
[83] Brake 2012: 88–9
[84] Estlund 1997: 164
[85] Macedo 1997: 94

of homicide, suicide, accidents, and mental illness than unmarried ones."[86] But even if we assume the accuracy of the public welfare claim (and this itself may be a controversial empirical assumption),[87] it hardly proves that the state should stay in the marriage business. This is for two reasons. First, the state could accomplish such public welfare goals by simply making available a civil union status to everyone. For instance, if the purpose were to facilitate economic stability, facilitating issues such as inheritance or child support, civil unions would be sufficient to accomplish this. Why deploy the label of "marriage"? It is not at all clear that downgrading marriage in this way would undermine any such benefits, assuming such benefits exist.

Second, it is entirely possible – even likely – that the reason unmarried individuals may have higher rates of mental illness, suicide, and the like is because their way of living is not privileged by the state. The state stigmatizes unmarried individuals by conferring the status of marriage only to those who choose this as a their conception of the good. This is a self-fulfilling prophecy. By valuing one way of living for its own sake, the state marks another as socially undesirable. This, in turn, makes it more likely that those who undertake the "socially undesirable" option will suffer more than those who do not.

Similarly, it seems equally likely that fifty years ago, gays and lesbians had higher rates of suicide and mental distress than their straight counterparts (and this is probably true even today). Gays were (and, of course, still are) forced to hide their sexuality. But we would reject the conclusion that "being straight" somehow promotes the "public welfare" even if it is true that gays are individually worse off in society. The conclusion to draw from these facts is not that heterosexuality is the answer but that the state ought to stop privileging that kind of lifestyle. And in the same way, it ought to stop conferring the morally special status of marriage. Doing so stands to stigmatize those who are not married just as the myriad laws and policies that ban gay sex and privilege heterosexuality stigmatize individuals for being gay.

---

[86] Macedo 1997: 94 (citing Wilson 1995: 178)

[87] For an argument that unmarried individuals live happy and healthy lives, see DePaulo 2006

If a powers review deems inadmissible laws and policies based on the idea that a certain kind of orthodoxy or way of life is intrinsically good, this stands to call into question the constitutionality of marriage itself. By conferring the status of marriage, the state deems this kind of life, as opposed to an unmarried one, morally special. Again, under a powers review, the question is what is the actual reason for the law or policy. The state cannot simply argue that marriage is based on the legal benefits, burdens, and responsibilities that accompany it. It cannot simply point to certain economic justifications to explain marriage. Although this may justify civil unions, it does *not* explain the intangible good that comes with the label of marriage. If the justifications were the same, the label would be irrelevant. States cannot justify marriage laws as if they were civil unions. This would point to an unconstitutional mismatch between alleged secular ends (e.g., regulating inheritance) and the means used to effectuate them, deploying the crucial label of marriage.

As the debate over same-sex marriage makes clear, marriage and civil unions are not the same. One journalist covering the Vermont decision in 2000 summed up the reaction of an unnamed minister as follows: "'I don't care what people do,' [the minister] insisted. 'Just don't call it marriage. It can't be marriage.'"[88] This is because there is something special about marriage. Same-sex marriage proponents see this morally special status as necessary to validate gay and lesbian relationships. Opponents see this status as reason to "protect" it from same-sex relationships. In either case, marriage provides a good that civil unions do not. This good is about the morally special status of being married, a status that straightforwardly privileges a conception of the good life that involves romantic companionship. Marriage is not just about instrumental benefits. It is about something more, something that speaks to living a more perfect life. Once we realize this, marriage laws themselves violate a powers review.

Now, the Court has asserted on numerous occasions that marriage is "the most important relation in life,"[89] that it is "fundamental to the

---

[88] Walker 2000
[89] *Maynard* at 205

very existence and survival of the race."[90] But we ought to be wary of the constitutionality of these kinds of arguments, ones that invariably look to tradition simply asserting that a particular practice is allegedly crucial to the maintenance of society. And this language is inconsistent with more recent cases such as *Lawrence* that proclaim that "neither history nor tradition" can save a law from "constitutional attack."[91] Again, it will not suffice to point out that the state has always married individuals, so it ought to continue to do so. This kind of appeal to tradition would easily justify any kind of practice. After all, those who defend prohibitions on same-sex marriage often make appeals to these very arguments. For instance, those who defend prohibitions on same-sex marriage often invoke the argument from tradition, contending that marriage is indeed the foundation of society. Redefining it will therefore undermine society. But same-sex marriage is already a reality in nine American states with no signs of societal decay or crumbling. These appeals to public welfare are just convenient canards that mask justifications that rest on controversial moral or even religious premises. The logic of this canard, then, is evident in the justification of marriage itself. Here too appeals to tradition or some idea of public welfare mask a belief that marriage confers a morally special status, a status that is unavailable to other relationships; that it provides, as much natural law suggests, certain intrinsic goods that benefit those individuals who undertake the marriage contract.

There is no reason to believe that the sky will fall with the disestablishment of marriage just as there is no reason to believe that it will fall by permitting gays and lesbians to marry. And, to be clear, even if the state gets out of the marriage business (as I am suggesting a powers review requires), this does not mean religious groups and other organizations will stop marrying individuals. Why wouldn't marriages rightfully undertaken by private, voluntary groups provide the allegedly favorable moral status? Metz considers the case of baptism or a bar mitzvah.[92] These ceremonies may well have important benefits for those who undertake them. Suggesting that we permit the state to

---

[90] *Skinner v. Oklahoma* (1942) at 541
[91] *Lawrence* at 577–8
[92] Metz 2010: 114–15

establish or confer such practices (imagine a state-sanctioned "coming of age" ceremony) would violate a powers review, not to mention the Establishment Clause. This is because such a ceremony represents a deep moral and personal decision, one that is often central to an individual's conception of the good life.

Consider that recent work suggests religious individuals are less likely than their nonreligious counterparts to abuse drugs and alcohol, to be stressed, and to suffer from low self-esteem.[93] Even if this may be evidence that individuals ought to consider becoming religious, it would be unconstitutional for the state to establish a religion. Because religion, like marriage, is such a personal decision, so central to a conception of the good life, the state ought to remain neutral toward it in line with the principle of nonestablishment.

This reveals a powerful tension between the constitutional objection to prohibitions on same-sex marriage and a constitutional defense of the institution of marriage itself. The dissenting opinion in *Goodridge* upheld Massachusetts' prohibition on same-sex marriage reasoning that

> the institution of marriage has systematically provided for the regulation of heterosexual behavior, brought order to the resulting procreation, and ensured a stable family structure in which children will be reared, educated, and socialized.[94]

But the Supreme Judicial Court of Massachusetts rejects this line of reasoning, as does *Schwarzenegger*. The justifications from tradition, begetting and raising children, and preserving an allegedly crucial institution of civil society all fail in rendering prohibitions on same-sex marriage constitutional. These rationales are constitutionally inadmissible or simply proffered in bad faith. But to now invoke them to defend marriage itself is hypocritical. It stands to validate those reasons that the state routinely invokes to limit marriage to opposite-sex couples. We cannot have it both ways. Either prohibitions on same-sex

---

[93] Ellison, Boardman, Williams, and Jackson 2001, http://www.heritage.org/research/reports/2006/12/why-religion-matters-even-more-the-impact-of-religious-practice-on-social-stability

[94] *Goodridge* at 381, dissenting

marriage are unconstitutional along with marriage itself, or marriage
is constitutional along with prohibitions on same-sex marriage.

Michael Sandel points out this very tension in his analysis of
Goodridge:

> As if to avoid entering into the moral and religious controversy
> over homosexuality, [*Goodridge*] describes the moral issue before
> the court in liberal terms – as a matter of autonomy and freedom
> of choice. The exclusion of same-sex couples from marriage is
> incompatible with "respect for individual autonomy and equality
> under law," [*Goodridge* proclaims]. . . . But autonomy and freedom
> of choice are insufficient to justify a right to same-sex marriage. If
> government were truly neutral on the moral worth of all voluntary
> intimate relationships, then the state would have no grounds for
> limiting marriage to two persons; consensual polygamous partner-
> ships would also qualify. In fact, if the state really wanted to be
> neutral, and respect whatever choices individuals wished to make,
> it would have to . . . get out of the business of conferring recognition
> on any marriages.[95]

He suggests that on one hand, the decision invokes the principle of
liberal neutrality, that in deciding the constitutionality of bans on same-
sex marriage, the court must not invoke contested religious or moral
premises. But on the other hand, if these premises are constitutionally
inadmissible, how may the state still deploy the label of marriage.

So if we disestablish marriage (as this chapter suggests), what (if
anything) do we put in its place? We could downgrade marriage to a
civil union status for everyone, attempting to avoid the morally special
status that comes with the label of "marriage." Or we could leave
individuals to enter into contracts for themselves just as individuals
are able to do so for any other kind of service or arrangement. Or we
could find another kind of state-sanctioned union that does not violate
a powers review. For example, after making the case for disestablishing
marriage, Metz seeks to put in its place what she calls an intimate caregiving union (ICGU).[96] Her justification for this kind of union is to
promote, protect, and regulate intimate care giving. It would be open

---

[95] Sandel 2010: 257
[96] Metz 2010, *see also* Brake 2012

to "sexually intimate unions" and "nonsexuallly intimate" ones.[97] It would not necessarily invoke the morally special status that comes with the label of marriage. Someone who has no romantic partner could still form an ICGU with an elderly loved one whom he or she is caring for.

Ultimately, I leave the question of what to replace marriage with to one side: whether it be civil unions for all, private contract, ICGUs, or some other system. My purpose is only to show that, taken to its logical constitutional conclusion, a powers review calls into question marriage statutes. It leads to the disestablishment of marriage. It suggests that the state exceeds its power under the Equal Protection Clause in conferring the morally special status of marriage.

We cannot avoid this conclusion by simply invoking a constitutional right to marry. In *Loving v. Virginia* (1967) (invalidating antimiscegenation laws), the Court held that the "freedom to marry has long been recognized as one of the vital personal rights essential to the orderly pursuit of happiness by free men."[98] In these and other cases, the Court makes clear that there is a fundamental right to marry under the Constitution.[99] But in all these cases, the constitutional question concerned state action that limited or regulated the marriage contract (e.g., limited it to those of the same race or those who are not in prison). That is, in these cases, the state treated individuals unequally in granting marriage licenses. None of these cases concerned an instance in which the state simply failed to issue marriage licenses altogether. As Cass Sunstein rightly points out: a right to marry is "an individual right of access to the official institution of marriage *so long as the state provides that institution*."[100] In *Perry*, the Ninth Circuit Court of Appeals reiterates this point saying that "the Constitution [does] not compel the state to confer [marriage] in the first place."[101]

With no state action, with no such "official institution," there is no presumptive constitutional infraction. This is because constitutional rights are negative in character. Rights like the rights to privacy, free

---

[97] Metz 2010: 135
[98] *Loving* at 12
[99] *See, e.g., Griswold v. Connecticut* (1965), *Zablocki v. Redhail* (1978)
[100] Sunstein 2005: 2096 (emphasis added)
[101] *Perry* at 1081

speech, religion, or to bear arms all constrain state action.[102] That is, a state violates them when it acts in a particular way, when it passes certain laws and policies. The right to privacy, for instance, does not require that the state do anything. It only limits the kinds of laws the state may pass, laws that, for instance, ban the use of contraception[103] or restrict a woman's liberty to procure an abortion.[104] The Equal Protection Clause requires that "No State shall....,"[105] and the due process clause of the Fourteenth Amendment begins with the words "nor shall any State...."[106] The Constitution does not contain positive rights, rights that require the state to provide a certain good or benefit. Only when the state acts do constitutional rights become relevant. So if a state banned marriages, passing a law that no private group could "marry" its members, this may well violate a fundamental right to marry. But in simply disestablishing marriage, there are no marriage laws. Hence, there is no state action. With no state action, the Constitution in this regard does not even apply.

Under a powers review, the disestablishment of marriage may be constitutionally inevitable. Because the basis of marriage laws is the idea that certain kinds of intimate relationship have morally special status, they invoke reasons that are constitutionally inadmissible. And because a constitutional right to marry does not require that the state pass marriage laws, there are no subsequent grounds on which to challenge this disestablishment.

THE IDENTITY APPROACH: SHORT-CIRCUITING THE SLOPE

The language of identity stands to short-circuit this slope, to prevent the unraveling of the institution of marriage. Again, the Court's current interpretation of the Equal Protection Clause employs three conceptual steps, steps that are irrelevant under a powers review. First,

---

[102] For purposes of this analysis, I treat enumerated and nonenumerated rights the same way
[103] *Griswold v. Connecticut* (1965)
[104] *Roe v. Wade* (1973)
[105] Amendment XIV, U.S. Constitution
[106] Amendment XIV, U.S. Constitution; *see also* Amendment V, U. S. Constitution

the law at issue must discriminate against a class or group. If the law regulates behavior, it does not meet this threshold doctrinal requirement. A law that prohibits possession of a handgun, for example, does not discriminate against a class. It only regulates behavior. Thus, the Equal Protection Clause cannot be invoked, at least under the identity approach. Second, the class must be suspect; it must, for instance, exhibit some combination of immutability, history of discrimination, and discreteness and insularity. Not all groups or classes count as suspect. A law that discriminates against those with last names beginning with a particular letter does not pass this second step. Third, once a law discriminates against a suspect class, the Court imposes heightened scrutiny where the law will most likely be struck down. This is the familiar suspect class and its accompanying tiers-of-scrutiny approach to equal protection, an approach this book has criticized. Relevant here are the first two steps of the identity approach. Both steps stand to distinguish same-sex marriage from plural or adult incestuous marriage, avoiding the constitutional slope to the disestablishment of marriage.

I argue that although these arguments may well short-circuit the slope at each step, they come at the cost of deploying the identity approach. From the political left, the difficulty is that a court must deem that the desire to marry someone is fundamental, an essential component of a good sexual (gay) life. This may pass the first step but invariably essentializes a certain view of being gay, a view that marginalizes those who do not ascribe to it. From the political right, the Court must strike down a prohibition on same-sex marriage on grounds that although gay and lesbians count as a suspect class, plural marriage enthusiasts do not. This may pass the second step but at the cost of inviting the "special rights" retort.

The First Step: Class versus Behavior

The threshold requirement of the identity approach is that a law must discriminate against a class. If the law merely regulates behavior, the identity approach is inapplicable. Prohibitions on same-sex marriage as well as their plural or adult incestuous counterparts do seem to regulate behavior. They prohibit individuals from doing something, in one case marrying individuals of the same sex, and in the other marrying one's adult sibling or two or more individuals. So how can we constitutionally distinguish a prohibition on same-sex marriage from limitations on consanguinity and numerosity under the identity approach? This would be an easy task if the relevant prohibition were written in such a way that it explicitly barred a gay individual from marrying someone (e.g., marriage will be a union between two heterosexual individuals of the opposite sex). This kind of law would be easy to distinguish from a ban on plural marriage, because it facially discriminates against a status – namely, homosexuality. It would be similar to a ban on interracial marriage, the amendment struck down in *Romer*, or the recently repealed Don't Ask, Don't Tell policy on military exclusion of homosexuals.[107]

But a prohibition on same-sex marriage, as written, does not explicitly discriminate against homosexuals as a class. After all, a gay man may marry a lesbian. The law tracks sex, not sexuality. Certainly, as scholarly work suggests, we could make an argument about sex or gender to argue that this kind of law discriminates against a suspect classification.[108] But as a constitutional matter, this invites the problem of what level of scrutiny to impose, intermediate or strict. As I argued in the previous chapter, whereas intermediate scrutiny would not go far enough in certain sex discriminatory cases, strict scrutiny would go too far. More important, there is a sense that, as Edward Stein puts it, sexism does not capture the harm these laws inflict: "[The argument from sexism] mischaracterizes the nature of laws that discriminate against lesbians and gay men to see them as primarily harming women (or even as harming women as much as they harm gay men, lesbians, and bisexuals)."[109]

Leaving the sex or gender argument to one side, prohibitions on same-sex marriage seem to regulate behavior or desire: here, a desire to marry someone of the same sex. Similarly, plural or adult incestuous marriages regulate the desire to marry more than one person or the desire to marry one's sibling, respectively. And if this is the case, how

---

[107] For a survey of the different kinds of antigay legislation, see Eskridge 1999
[108] *See, e.g.*, Appleton 2005, Farrell 2004, Koppelman 2002, 1994, Law 1988, Widiss, Rosenblatt, and NeJaime 2007
[109] Stein 2001b: 500

does the Court bring in the conventional suspect class framework under this first step? The problem is how to distinguish the same-sex marriage ban from other limitations on marriage. Andrew Sullivan seeks to solve it in the following way:

> Almost everyone seems to accept, even if they find homosexuality morally troublesome, that it occupies a deeper level of human consciousness than a polygamous impulse, Even the Catholic Church, which believes that homosexuality is an "objective disorder," concedes that it is a profound element of human identity. It speaks of "homosexual persons," for example, in a way it would never speak of "polygamous persons." And almost all of us tacitly assume this, even in the very use of the term "homosexuals." We accept also that multiple partners can be desired by gays and straights alike: that polygamy is an activity, whereas both homosexuality and heterosexuality are states.[110]

Even if a prohibition on same-sex marriage does not explicitly invoke sexuality, it regulates desire that is, according to Sullivan, fundamental to who gays and lesbians are. Bans on plural marriage (and by implication, adult incestuous marriage) do not regulate behavior or desire that is central to who someone is. As Jonathan Rauch argues:

> Do homosexuals actually exist? I think so. . . . By contrast, no serious person claims there are people constitutively attracted only to relatives, or only to groups rather than individuals.[111]

Whereas the desire for someone of the same sex is constitutive of gay identity, the desire for more than one person or one's brother is not.

This means that prohibitions on same-sex marriage strike at who gays and lesbians are. These prohibitions therefore discriminate against a class. Limitations on consanguinity or numerosity do not strike at who adult incestuous or plural marriage enthusiasts are. These limitations only regulate behavior. This may suggest that the former meet the threshold requirement of the identity approach but the latter do not.

But this argument comes at a cost. It turns out to privilege certain kinds of gay lives over others. Sullivan and Rauch imply that the desire

---

[110] Sullivan 1997: 278
[111] Rauch 1997: 286

to marry someone of the same sex is crucial to being gay just as marrying someone of the opposite sex may be crucial to being straight. It is not enough to say that desiring someone of the same sex is central to gay identity. If that were the case, limiting marriage to opposite-sex couples would clearly not frustrate it. After all, as long as individuals may choose to have sex with and live with individuals of the same sex, even setting up domestic partnerships or civil unions to that effect, current marriage laws would not strike at the core of gay desire. Although a law criminalizing sodomy (like the one in *Lawrence*) strikes at who gays and lesbians are, preventing them from acting on their desire or love for someone of the same sex, prohibitions on same-sex marriage do not. Such a prohibition does not frustrate gay people's ability to love someone of the same sex. It merely frustrates their desire to *marry* the person they desire or love. For such a prohibition to discriminate against a class rather than behavior, this desire must be constitutive of what it means to be gay or lesbian. Only then do limitations on same-sex *marriage* discriminate against gays and lesbians rather than simply a desire or behavior.

But, of course, and this is the rub, there are many gays and lesbians (as well as many heterosexuals to be sure) who do not desire to marry, who may even despise the idea. They may prefer nonmonogamous, anonymous, or multipartner sex or choose to remain unmarried. To suggest that the desire to marry is fundamental essentializes the notion of gay identity. It foists, in Appiah's language, an identity script onto individuals who may be gay and lesbian. In particular, this kind of argument advocates a heteronormative depiction of human desire – one that privileges monogamy and commitment over being unmarried and sexually active with multiple partners. Those who choose to be unmarried are, under the terms of this argument, defective. They are failing to live up to their essential nature as human beings to marry someone they love. Making the desire to marry fundamental straightforwardly marginalizes those who choose to remain unmarried. This strategy to distinguish same-sex marriage from its plural or adult incestuous counterpart brazenly views being unmarried as inferior. It treats marriage as an intrinsic good. This is natural law but with a gay spin.

This irony has not gone unnoticed. Self-described "queer theory" criticizes the mainstream gay and lesbian identity for reaffirming these values.[112] Darren Rosenblum argues that many self-proclaimed "queers" explore and celebrate other kinds of sexuality: "public sex (parks, tearooms, 'adult bookstores,' backrooms), anonymous sex, group sex, promiscuity, sadomasochism, and role-playing."[113] Rendering marriage constitutive of gay identity essentializes it, stigmatizing these non-heteronormative desires and behaviors. Ultimately, this argument (surprise, surprise) privileges marriage over being unmarried. In conceptualizing gay identity in terms of marriage, we reinforce the idea that a life with a committed partner is superior to a life without one.

There is a dilemma, then, in distinguishing plural and same-sex marriage on the basis of behavior versus class. If the desire to marry someone of the same sex is fundamental to gay identity, a prohibition on same-sex marriage discriminates against a class. It prohibits gays and lesbians from actualizing a central longing to commit themselves to another person. Whereas a limitation on plural marriage does not frustrate such a fundamental desire, a prohibition on same-sex marriage does. But this argument invariably essentializes and excludes those desires, behaviors, and lifestyle choices that do not fit the mold of marriage. However, if this desire is not fundamental (acknowledging the plurality of sexuality within the gay community), there is no difference between a restriction on same-sex marriage and one on plural marriage. Neither invokes a class or group, because both kinds of law regulate a behavior, a desire to marry someone of the same sex or a desire to marry more than one person. So for current prohibitions on same-sex marriage to discriminate against an identity class, triggering the identity approach, we must privilege certain conceptions of the good over others.

Second Step: Suspect Class

The second step of equal protection doctrine requires that the group being discriminated against be a suspect class. Let's concede that laws against same-sex marriage as well their plural/adult incestuous

---

[112] *See generally* Jagose 1997, Sullivan 2003, Warner 1999
[113] Rosenblum 1994: 108

counterparts discriminate against a class or group – that is, assume that such laws pass the first step. Another way to short-circuit the slope is to argue that only in the former case does the law discriminate against a *suspect* class. Although gays and lesbians meet the criteria for suspect status, passing this second step, those who partake of plural marriage or adult incestuous ones do not. And to be sure, those who are unmarried also do not count as a suspect class. Although the desire for more than one person or one's sibling or to remain unmarried is a preference (a voluntary choice one can make), sexuality is not. Sexuality is an immutable trait for which individuals have suffered a history of discrimination, desiring to be in a plural/incestuous marriage or to remain unmarried is not.

Jonathan Rauch reasons that "[h]eterosexuals can now marry any of millions of people; even if they can't marry their parents or siblings, they have plenty of choice. Homosexuals want the same freedom, subject to the same restrictions." Currently, they have "zero marital choice" to marry someone they love.[114] Gays may certainly marry someone of the opposite sex, but why does that choice not count? Why does that choice still leave them with "zero marital" options? Simply put, gays cannot choose to be attracted to or love, in this way, someone of the opposite sex. This is not a preference but an orientation. Whereas plural marriage enthusiasts may *prefer* to love two or more individuals, gays and lesbians do not *prefer* to love someone of the same sex. Someone gay may desire to remain unmarried, or to marry his or her sibling, or to marry more than one person. But being gay is more fundamental. Individuals are not born with the desire to love more than one person or desire their sibling or to remain unmarried. This requires that gays indeed view their desire for someone of the same sex as immutable. And, of course, it is undeniable that homosexuals have suffered discrimination in a way that these other "groups" have not.

Only limitations on same-sex marriage, then, invoke a suspect class. So, whereas gays are "in" for suspect class purposes (or at least ought to be), plural marriage or adult incestuous enthusiasts and those who are unmarried are "out." This means that a prohibition on same-sex marriage will receive higher scrutiny, scrutiny that will invariably

[114] Rauch 1997: 286

doom it. This short-circuits the slope by invalidating a prohibition on same-sex marriage but upholding limitations on consanguinity or numerosity, limitations that would only get rational review under the tiers-of-scrutiny framework.

But this perversely stigmatizes the gay condition, fueling the nature/nurture debate[115] and the problems outlined in Chapter 1. It requires that gays see themselves as victims of their desires, desires that nature has foisted on them, rather than desires gays have "voluntarily" undertaken. Otherwise, there is no way they can constitutionally elevate or distinguish themselves as a class from plural marriage enthusiasts or those who seek to marry their adult sibling. Making this all-too-familiar suspect class argument requires that gays and lesbians highlight how they are different, how they are constitutionally "special" from these other groups.

The desire to be with more than one person is not immutable, not constitutionally special triggering the criteria of suspect class status, but the desire to be with someone of the same sex is. Yet if the Court makes this argument in striking down prohibitions on same-sex marriage but not their plural marriage or adult incestuous counterparts, it privileges certain individuals over others. It favors gays and lesbians but not plural marriage enthusiasts or those who are unmarried. This suggests that the Court is not taking into account the interests of everyone just the interests of a particular class. The Court would have to invalidate a prohibition on same-sex marriage by upholding the equal rights of gays but not the equal rights of plural marriage enthusiasts or those who are unmarried. This raises the specter that gays and lesbians are being treated as constitutionally special.

Nancy D. Polikoff rightly points out that "the marriage-equality movement is a movement for gay civil rights, not for valuing *all* families."[116] If the movement cared about all families, it would care about at least some plural marriages or even some adult incestuous ones. This suggests that although the option of marrying someone of the same sex is constitutionally significant, the option of marrying two or more people is not. The former is special, the latter is not. This makes it all

---

[115] *See* Stein 2001a
[116] Polikoff 2008: 7

too easy for detractors to balk contending that the Court is favoring the interests of certain groups (gays and lesbians) over others (plural marriage enthusiasts).

Here too there is a dilemma, then, in attempting to distinguish gays and lesbians from these other groups. If the Court deems all of them suspect classes, it stands to invalidate bans on plural and adult incestuous marriage along with their same-sex counterparts. This would constitutionally lump gays and lesbians with plural marriage enthusiasts. If the Court constitutionally elevates the former above the latter, treating them as a suspect class, it exacerbates the sting of the counter-majoritarian difficulty. This, in turn, stands to invite the "special rights" retort.

THE STATE'S EXPRESSIVE CAPACITY AS A POSSIBLE ALTERNATIVE

The fate of gay and lesbians are at the crosshairs of the argument of this chapter. After all, it is undeniable that as a sexual minority, they have suffered from the lack of recognition that comes with the state's stamp of marriage. Heterosexual relationships are not seen as inferior. Straight individuals are not routinely harassed, beaten, bullied, or even killed for being straight. But gay relationships are seen as inferior; gay individuals are beaten and bullied for desiring someone of the same sex. It is precisely the morally special status of marriage that seeks to challenge this inferiority. The very reason that marriage is constitutionally problematic explains why it is so important to gays and lesbians. The label of marriage provides the necessary moral legitimacy to gay relationships.

Imagine that same-sex marriage were legal today in all fifty states and recognized by the federal government. If this discussion of dis-establishment took place one hundred years from now, the concern about leaving gay relationships in the lurch would be far less relevant. Perhaps in that case, gays and lesbians themselves would largely favor disestablishment, advocating for a civil union status for everyone. They would have had one hundred years of seeing their relationships vali-dated as morally special by the state via the institution of marriage.

To unwind the institution of marriage now – to equalize down to civil union or some other system – seems unfair. This may be the underlying concern for those who seek to invalidate prohibitions on same-sex marriage while maintaining the institution of marriage. That is, the problem is not with abolishing marriage per se but doing so at a time when gays and lesbians have been unable to avail themselves of it. There is some appeal to this claim, even though two constitutional wrongs do not necessarily make a constitutional right.

Perhaps there is another way to challenge homophobia, if marriage is not an option consistent with a powers review. Again, this book is about how the Court invalidates laws and policies under the Equal Protection Clause. The clause does not require the state to pass any particular law or policy, only that when the state acts, it must not invoke a constitutionally inadmissible rationale. My primary focus, then, is not on what kinds of legislation (if any) the state ought to pass.

Nevertheless, I conclude this chapter by suggesting a possible way the state may challenge homophobia without maintaining marriage. In discussing the issue of abortion funding, I discussed the state's spending or expressive power, a kind of power that, like its coercive counterpart, is subject to a powers review. Corey Brettschneider deploys it in the problem over hate speech. Brettschneider's concern is that liberals seem to have only two options with regard to hate speech (speech that explicitly contradicts liberal values): either deploy the coercive power of the state to censor this kind of speech or tolerate this speech leaving victimized groups vulnerable to such verbal attacks. Brettschneider provides a provocative third alternative that draws not from the state's coercive power but rather from its "expressive power," "its ability to influence beliefs and behavior by 'speaking.'"[117] The state does not need to censor hate speech but may well have an obligation to "speak" in favor of liberal values. It can do this "in a variety of ways, ranging from the direct statements of politicians to the establishment of monuments and public holidays."[118] Also, the state can express and promote the value of equality "through [its] action as educator."[119]

[117] Brettschneider 2012: 3
[118] Brettschneider 2012: 95
[119] Brettschneider 2012: 95

Brettschneider includes as part of this expressive capacity the state's use of public "funds for [such] democratic persuasion."[120]

What is important here is that this framework provides another avenue besides marriage to challenge homophobia. The state's conferral of the status of marriage violates a powers review. This is because current marriage laws rest on the idea that there is something intrinsically special about this status. Yet, as educator, the state could make sure that students recognize the equality of gay and lesbian relationships. Gays and lesbian could be included in textbooks that discuss the struggle for equality in this country. Specifically, in sex education classes, the state could ensure that gay relationships are considered as another acceptable option for individuals. The state could even fund a print and media campaign that celebrates same-sex desires. In doing so, and this is the crucial point, the state would not be saying that being gay is intrinsically special. These kinds of law and policies do not seek to privilege one way of living over another. In fact, they seek to counter the idea that straight relationships are intrinsically better than their gay counterparts. Such a law would be like a female medical school that seeks to challenge the idea that males ought to be medical doctors and females should be nurses. Here the justification is to challenge the idea that straight relationships are superior to their gay ones.

Now, in deploying its expressive capacity, the state may well run afoul of the Equal Protection Clause if it moves from simply challenging homophobia to advocating a particular way of life for its own sake. When that happens, the Court ought to step in and invalidate such expressive laws. This was the case with Hyde Amendment discussed in the previous chapter. The state violated a powers review by privileging childbirth over abortion. By specifically withholding funds for indigent women to procure an abortion, this federal policy favors a particular role for females, one that involves motherhood. So although the expressive capacity of the state is a possible alternative to challenging homophobia (in lieu of marriage), it is also subject to the same justificatory constraint.

[120] Brettschneider 2012: 110

In line with a powers review, the institution of marriage may seem to unravel. The slope from same-sex marriage to the disestablishment of marriage is indeed slippery. Once we turn our focus away from the language of identity and suspect class asking whether the state has the power to privilege certain ways of living over others, there is no principled stopping point. This is the strength of a powers review, one that stands to question the constitutionality of marriage itself.

This brings the constitutional debate over same-sex marriage into sharper focus. If the debate is about suspect class, it may avoid a run down the slope, but at the cost of inviting the problems that come with invoking identity. The identity approach will invariably be beset by the retort of "special rights" and the problem of immutability. If the debate is about those reasons that are constitutionally inadmissible, it is hard not to avoid the disestablishment of marriage. After all, if prohibitions on same-sex marriage are unconstitutional, because they are based on some religious or moral meaning of marriage, marriage itself suffers the same constitutional fate.

CONCLUSION

At its core, this book is about the reasoning the Court deploys to strike down laws and policies. Even if the Court arrives at the "correct" result, it matters *how* the Court gets there. Political scientists often focus simply on the result, neglecting the crucial reasoning that underlies it. Constitution legal scholars focus on this reasoning but pay little attention to its effect on framing the larger political debate. The underlying impulse of this book betrays both mindsets. It suggests that we ought to care about the Court's reasoning (not just its result) precisely because this sets the terms of the debate.

Stephen Macedo highlights two distinct strands of liberalism that are relevant to the argument of this book: one, "a commitment to broad guarantees of liberty and equality" that specify "our basic liberties" (an equal-rights-based approach) and two, "a commitment to a practice of public reasonableness."[1] The equal-rights-based approach calls into question those laws that discriminate on the basis of certain identity affiliations, and the "public reasonableness" or justificatory approach calls into question those laws that invoke certain kinds of reasons that may be widely viewed as unacceptable. This book is about reframing equality under the law as a commitment to "public reasonableness" instead of a commitment to equal rights.

Consider that the debate over same-sex marriage is invariably about gay or lesbian rights. It is about spotlighting the way prohibitions on same-sex marriage fail to treat gays and lesbians as equals. The conventional constitutional argument of suspect class or identity has drowned out the value of a focus on "public reasonableness." The 2012 Republican Platform defends "the traditional concept of marriage" as the

---

[1] Macedo 1997: 1

"union between a man and a woman" making clear that judicial efforts to change it constitute an "activist judiciary."[2] If such efforts entail recognizing gays and lesbians as a suspect class, we all too easily invite this charge of judicial activism. Gays were not a constitutionally suspect class, but now they are (or ought to be). This conventional constitutional logic needlessly invites the charge that judges are seeking to redefine marriage for ideological reasons.

But a powers review stands to squash this charge. Prohibitions on same-sex marriage are not about gays and lesbians but about those reasons that are already constitutionally inadmissible. A law that limited marriage to those who are religious under the theory that atheists cannot appreciate the sanctity of the obligation would not require that the Court deem atheists a suspect class. Such a limitation, like a prohibition on same-sex marriage, is based on religious rationales, rationales that are already constitutionally inadmissible. A judge who then strikes down such a prohibition is not redefining marriage but rather making clear the implications of a constitutional commitment to the nonestablishment of religion. It is telling that the 2012 Republican Platform does not mention the Establishment Clause or the idea that the state may not base laws and policies on religious rationales. If anything, same-sex marriage detractors invoke religion to defend limitations on marriage. But in doing so, they invoke reasons that are already constitutionally illegitimate. Consider again that even the proponents of Proposition 8 did not appeal to such reasons to defend the California amendment in court. We do better to emphasize this justificatory approach, calling out detractors as religious partisans, rather than constantly emphasizing the language of identity and the equal rights of gays and lesbians.

Carlos A. Ball argues that this language of "public reasonableness" is often anemic. It does not capture the lived experiences of gays and lesbians. It does not capture, as he puts it, "their real-life concerns."[3] "What remains . . . is a rather sterile account of a debate over policy and rights that has no correspondence to what people on both sides of the debate consider to be most important."[4] I readily concede that

---

[2] Republican Platform 2012: 10; www.gop.com/2012-republican-platform_home
[3] Ball 2003: 27
[4] Ball 2003: 27

a powers review does not capture the joy, fulfillment, or love that comes with being gay or lesbian. But it is precisely because of this, that a powers review stands as a more salutary strategy for invalidating prohibitions on same-sex marriage. We ought not to place justices in a position to decide the constitutionality of such prohibitions on their familiarity with some set of experiences. Doing so only stands to invite the sting of the counter-majoritarian difficulty. It may well be that a powers review is the more "sterile" way of invalidating limitations on marriage. But for this reason, it represents a more principled and less subjective method of doing so. As a result, we ought to prefer it.

This is not to suggest that a powers review is foolproof. Like any constitutional argument, it is prone to manipulation. I am not suggesting that a powers review is a mechanical principle that, once applied, will always lead to the same result. Rather, my point is that such a review frames the constitutional question in a more transparent light. For if manipulation of this review is to occur, it will hinge on whether the law's actual purpose is based on a constitutionally inadmissible rationale. Certainly, a justice that seeks to impose his or her own ideological preference in striking down a law can argue that the actual purpose is indeed inadmissible. Consider that the Court will have an opportunity to review the constitutionality of affirmative action in 2013. Although a justice may invalidate such remedial policies, this is highly unlikely under a powers review. Again, a powers review does not ask the Court to decide whether affirmative action is based on a pressing or compelling purpose.

The tiers-of-scrutiny framework, however, requires that individual justices decide exactly this. Those who favor such policies will no doubt say they are indeed important. Those who do not favor such policies will say that they are not that important. The scrutiny framework provides an "easy way out" for justices to strike down such remedial legislation. They need only hide behind the language of scrutiny to argue that the purpose is not compelling enough. There is no argumentative hurdle or burden imposed on doing so. This is because the language of "compelling" and "narrowly tailored" can be defined in ways that achieve an ideologically infused result.

A powers review, on the other hand, makes the constitutional decision more straightforward and hence more transparent by closing off this "easy way out" argumentative option. The issue under this approach is only whether affirmative action laws are based on a constitutionally inadmissible rationale like animus. If a justice seeks to invalidate this kind of law, believing that it is bad policy, he or she must reason that it is indeed based on animus. This is a steeper argumentative burden than simply saying that racial diversity is not a good enough reason. That is, it will be harder for a justice to proclaim that racial animus is afoot in affirmative action than to argue that racial diversity is simply not a compelling purpose. After all, just because racial diversity is not a compelling purpose does not automatically mean that it is a constitutionally inadmissible one. Under a powers review, a justice must proclaim that animus against whites actually underlies such legislation. This is a more extreme conclusion, one that unsurprisingly no dissenting justice in *Grutter* makes. This is telling. It means that a powers review poses an uphill argumentative battle for any justice who seeks to strike down affirmative action laws.

The argument of this book suggests that as a constitutional matter there is more agreement about what equal protection means than the suspect class framework would imply. The constitutional language of identity and scrutiny invites disagreements – disagreements about immutability, about whether one is born gay, about the meaning of "compelling" or "narrowly tailored," or about which groups are constitutionally special. Constantly working within that framework to invalidate laws and policies only stands to exacerbate such disagreement. A powers review reveals that there is more agreement on the kinds of reasons that are constitutionally inadmissible. This constitutional logic, in turn, is a less problematic way of understanding legal equality.

REFERENCES

Abbey, Ruth. 2007. "Back toward a Comprehensive Liberalism? Justice as Fairness, Gender, and Families," *Political Theory* 35(5): 5–28.

Ackerman, Bruce. 1993. *We the People: Foundations* (Vol. 1). Cambridge: Belknap Press.

Ackerman, Bruce. 1985. *Beyond Carolene Products*, 98 Harvard Law Review 713.

Ackerman, Bruce. 1980. *Social Justice and the Liberal State.* New Haven: Yale University Press.

Adarand Constructors, Inc. v. Peña, 515 U.S. 200 (1995).

Alexander, Lawrence A. 2002. "Equal Protection and the Irrelevance of 'Groups'" *Issues in Legal Scholarship*, The Origins and Fate of Antisubordination Theory: Article 1. http://www.bepress.com/ils/iss2/art1.

Allan, T. R. S. 1999. "The Rule of Law as the Rule of Reason: Consent and Constitutionalism," 115 *Law Quarterly Review* 221.

Amar, Akhil Reed. 1996. "Attainder and Amendment 2: Romer's Rightness," 95 *Michigan Law Review* 203.

American Sugar Refining Company v. Louisiana, 179 U.S. 89 (1900).

Appiah, Kwame Anthony. 2005. *The Ethics of Identity.* Princeton: Princeton University Press.

Appiah, Kwame Anthony. 1994. "Identity, Authenticity, Survival: Multicultural Societies and Social Reproductions," in *Multiculturalism: Examining the Politics of Recognition*, ed. Amy Gutmann. Princeton: Princeton University Press.

Appleton, Susan Frelich. 2005. "Same-Sex Couples: Defining Marriage in the Twenty-First Century: Missing in Action? Searching for Gender Talk in the Same-Sex Marriage Debate," 16 *Stanford Law and Policy Review* 97.

Araiza, William D. 2007. "Irrationality and Animus in Class-of-One Equal Protection Cases," 34 *Ecology Law Quarterly* 493.

Avins, Alfred. 1966. "Anti-Miscegenation Laws and the Fourteenth Amendment: The Original Intent," 52 *Virginia Law Review* 1224.

Ayres, Ian. 1996. "Narrow Tailoring," 43 *UCLA Law Review* 1781.

Ayres, Ian, and Sydney Foster. 2007. "Don't Tell, Don't Ask: Narrow Tailoring After *Grutter* and *Gratz*," 85 *Texas Law Review* 517.

Babst, Gordon. 2002. *Liberal Constitutionalism, Marriage, and Sexual Orientation: A Contemporary Case for Dis-establishment*. New York: Peter Lang.

Baehr v. Lewin, 74 Haw. 645 (Haw. 1993).

Baker v. Nelson, 409 U.S. 810 (1972).

Baker v. Vermont, 744 A.2d 864 (Vt. 1999).

Balkin, Jack M. 2011. *Living Originalism*. Cambridge: Belknap Press.

Balkin, Jack M. 2005. *What Roe v. Wade Should Have Said: The Nation's Top Legal Experts Rewrite America's Most Controversial Decision*, ed. Jack M. Balkin. New York: New York Press: 31–62.

Balkin, Jack M., and Reva Siegel. 2003. "The American Civil Rights Tradition: Anticlassification or Antisubordination?" 58 *University of Miami Law Review* 9.

Ball, Carlos A. 2003. *The Morality of Gay Rights: An Exploration in Political Philosophy*. New York: Routledge Press.

Barnett, Randy. 2008. "Scrutiny Land," 106 *Michigan Law Review* 1479.

Barry, Brian. 2001. *Culture and Equality*. Cambridge: Harvard University Press.

Bartels, Brandon L. 2009. "The Constraining Capacity of Legal Doctrine on the U.S. Supreme Court," *American Political Science Review* 103(3): 474–95.

Beauvoir, Simone de. 2009 [1949]. *The Second Sex*, trans. Constance Borde and Sheila Malovany-Chevallier. New York: Knopf Press.

Bedi, Sonu. 2013. "Collapsing Suspect Class with Suspect Classification: Why Strict Scrutiny Is Too Strict and Maybe Not Strict Enough," 47 *University of Georgia Law Review* 301.

Bedi, Sonu. 2009. *Rejecting Rights*. Cambridge: Cambridge University Press.

Bedi, Sonu. 2007. "Debate: What Is So Special About Religion? The Dilemma of the Religious Exemption,'" *The Journal of Political Philosophy* 15(2): 235–49.

Bedi, Sonu. 2005. "Repudiating Morals Legislation: Rendering the Constitutional Right to Privacy Obsolete," 53 *Cleveland State Law Review* 447.

Benhabib, Seyla. 2002. *The Claims of Culture: Equality and Diversity in the Global Era*. Princeton: Princeton University Press.

Benhabib, Seyla. 1986. *Critique, Norm, and Utopia: A Study of the Foundations of Critical Theory*. New York: Columbia University Press.

Bertrand, Marianne, and Sendhil Mullainathan. 2004. "Are Emily and Greg More Employable than Lakisha and Jamal? A Field Experiment on Labor Market Discrimination," *The American Economic Review* 94(4): 991–1013.

Bickel, Alexander. 1962. *The Least Dangerous Branch: The Supreme Court at the Bar of Politics*, 2nd ed. New Haven: Yale University Press.

Blankenhorn, David. 2007. *The Future of Marriage*. Jackson, TN: Encounter Books.

Bolling v. Sharpe 347 U.S. 497 (1954).

Boonin, David. 2011. *Should Race Matter? Unusual Answers to the Usual Questions*. New York: Cambridge University,

Borooah, Vani K. 2001. "Racial Bias in Police Stops and Searches: An Economic Analysis," *European Journal of Political Economy* 17: 17–37.

Bork, Robert H. 1990. *The Tempting of America: The Political Seduction of the Law*. New York: Touchstone.

Bowers v. Hardwick, 478 U.S. 186 (1986).

Brake, Elizabeth. 2012. *Minimizing Marriage: Marriage, Morality, and the Law*. New York: Oxford University Press.

Brake, Elizabeth. 2004. "Rawls and Feminism: What Should Feminists Make of Liberal Neutrality?" *Journal of Moral Philosophy* 1(3): 293–309.

Bressman, Lisa Schulz. 2003. "Beyond Accountability: Arbitrariness and Legitimacy in the Administrative State," 78 *New York University Law Review* 461.

Brest, Paul. 1976. "Foreword: In Defense of the Antidiscrimination Principle," 90 *Harvard Law Review* 1.

Brest, Paul, Sanford Levinson, Jack M. Balkin, Akhil Reed Amar, and Reva B. Siegel, eds. 2006. *Processes of Constitutional Decision Making: Cases and Materials*. 5th ed. New York: Aspen Publishers.

Brettschneider, Corey. 2012. *When the State Speaks, What Should It Say? How Democracies Can Protect Expression and Promote Equality*. Princeton: Princeton University Press.

Breyer, Stephen. 2005. *Active Liberty: Interpreting our Democratic Constitution*. New York: Knopf Press.

Brown v. Board of Education of Topeka (Brown II), 349 U.S. 294 (1955).

Brown v. Board of Education of Topeka, 347 U.S. 483 (1954).

Brown v. City of Oneonta, 221 F. 3d 329 (2nd Cir. 2000).

Brown, Wendy. 2002. "Suffering the Paradoxes of Rights," in Left *Legalism/Left Critique*, eds. Wendy Brown and Janet Halley. Durham: Duke University Press: 420–34.

Brown, Wendy. 1995. *States of Injury: Power and Freedom in Late Modernity*. Princeton: Princeton University Press.

Butler, Judith. 1990. *Gender Trouble: Feminism and the Subversion of Identity*. New York: Routledge Press.

Bybee, Keith J., and Cyril Ghosh. 2009. "Legalizing Public Reason: The American Dream, Same-Sex Marriage, and the Management of Radical Disputes," *Studies in Law, Politics and Society* 49: 125–56.

Cahill, Sean. 2004. *Same Sex Marriage in the United States: Focus on the Facts: Post 2004 Election Edition*. Lanham, MD: Lexington Books.

Califano v. Goldfarb, 430 U.S. 199 (1977).

Califano v. Webster, 430 U.S. 313 (1977).

Card, Claudia. 1996. "Against Marriage and Motherhood," *Hypatia* 11(3): 1–23.

Case, Mary Anne. 1995. "Disaggregating Gender from Sex and Sexual Orientation: The Effeminate Man in the Law and Feminist Jurisprudence," 105 *Yale Law Journal* 1.

Chemerinsky, Erwin. 2011. *Constitutional Law*, 4th ed. New York: Aspen Publishers.

Chin, Gabriel J. 1996. "The Plessy Myth: Justice Harlan and the Chinese Cases," 82 *Iowa Law Review* 156.

City of Cleburne v. Cleburne, 473 U.S. 432, 441 (1985).

City of Richmond v. J.A. Croson Co., 488 U.S. 469 (1989).

Clayton, Matthew. 2006. *Justice and Legitimacy in Upbringing*. New York: Oxford University Press.

Clear, Todd R. 2002. "The Problem with 'Addition by Subtraction': The Prison-Crime Relationship in Low-Income Communities," in *Invisible Punishment: The Collateral Consequences of Mass Imprisonment*, eds. Marc Mauer and Meda Chesney-Lind. New York: The New Press.

Cohen, David S. 2011. "The Stubborn *Persistence of Sex Segregation*," 20 *Columbia Journal of Gender and Law* 51.

Cohen, David S. 2010. "Keeping Men 'Men' and Women Down: Sex Segregation, Anti-Essentialism, and Masculinity," 33 *Harvard Journal of Law and Gender* 509.

Cole, David. 1999. *No Equal Justice: Race and Class in the American Criminal Justice System*. New York: New York University Press.

Colker, Ruth. 1986. "Anti-Subordination above All: Sex, Race, and Equal Protection." 61 *New York University Law Review* 1003.

Cooke, Jacob E., ed. 1961. *The Federalist*. Middletown, CT: Wesleyan University Press.

Craig v. Boren, 429 U.S. 190 (1976).

Crenshaw, Kimberle. 1989. "Demarginalizing the Intersection of Race and Sex: A Black Feminist Critique of Antidiscrimination Doctrine, Feminist Theory, and Antiracist Politics," 1989 *University of Chicago Legal Forum* 139.

Crittenden, Ann. 2001. *The Price of Motherhood: Why the Most Important Job in the World Is Still the Least Valued*. New York: Henry Holt and Company.

Cruz, David. 2010. "Equality's Centrality: Proposition 8 and the California Constitution," 19 *Southern California Review of Law and Social Justice* 45.

Dahl, Robert. 1957. "Decision-Making in a Democracy: The Supreme Court as a National Policy-Maker," *The Journal of Public Law* 6: 279–95.

Dane, Perry. 2009. "A Holy Secular Institution," 58 *Emory Law Journal* 1123.

Delgado, Richard. 2003. *Justice at War: Civil Liberties and Civil Rights during Time of Crisis*. New York: New York University Press.

Den Otter, Ronald C. 2009. "Is There Really Any Good Argument Against Plural Marriage?" ExpressO. http://works.bepress.com/ronald_den_otter/1.

Den Otter, Ronald. 2009. *Judicial Review in an Age of Moral Pluralism*. New York: Cambridge University Press.

DePaulo, Bella. 2006. *Singled Out: How Singles Are Stereotyped, Stigmatized, and Ignored, and Still Live Happily Ever After*. St. Martin's Griffin: New York.

"Developments in the Law: Race and the Criminal Process," 1998. 101 *Harvard Law Review* 1427.

Dudas, Jeffrey R. 2008. *The Cultivation of Resentment: Treaty Rights and the New Right*. Palo Alto, CA: Stanford University Press.

Dudas, Jeffrey R. 2005. "In the Name of Equal Rights: "Special" Rights and the Politics of Resentment in Post–Civil Rights America," *Law & Society Review* 39(4): 723–58.

Dworkin, Ronald. 1986. *Law's Empire*. Cambridge: Harvard University Press.

Eberle, Christopher J. 2002. *Religious Conviction in Liberal Politics*. Cambridge: Cambridge University Press.

Eisenberg, Melvin A. (2002). "Symposium: A Tribute to Professor Joseph M. Perillo, The Duty to Rescue in Contract Law," 71 *Fordham Law Review* 647.

Ellison, Christopher G., Jason D. Boardman, David R. Williams, and James S. Jackson, 2001. "Religious Involvement, Stress, and Mental Health: Findings from the 1995 Detroit Area Study," *Social Forces* 80(1): 215–49.

Elshtain, Jean Bethke. 1993. *Democracy on Trial. CBC Massey Lecture Series.* Toronto, ON: House of Anansi Press Ltd.

Ely, John. 1980. *Democracy and Distrust: A Theory of Judicial Review.* Cambridge: Harvard University Press.

Epperson v. Arkansas, 393 U.S. 97 (1968).

Epstein, Cynthia Fuchs. 1993 [1981]. *Women in Law*, 2nd ed. Champaign: Illinois University Press.

Epstein, Lee, and Jack Knight. 1998. *The Choices Justices Make.* Washington, DC: CQ Press.

Epstein, Lee and Thomas G. Walker. 2013, 2012. *Constitutional Law for a Changing America: Institutional Powers and Constraints and Rights, Liberties, and Justice*, 8th Edition (Vols. 1 and 2).

Epstein, Richard, ed. 2009. *Economics of Constitutional Law.* Northampton: Edward Elgar Publishing.

Epstein, Richard A. 1995. *Cases and Materials on Torts*, 6th ed. New York: Aspen Publishers.

Eskridge, William N., Jr. 2000. "Comparative Law and the Same-Sex Marriage Debate: A Step-by-Step Approach Toward State Recognition," 31 *McGeorge Law Review* 641.

Eskridge, William N., Jr. 1999. *Gaylaw: Challenging the Apartheid of the Closet.* Cambridge: Harvard University Press.

Eskridge, William N., Jr. 1996. *The Case for Same-Sex Marriage: From Sexual Liberty to Civilized Commitment.* New York: The Free Press.

Eskridge, William N. Jr. 1993. "A History of Same-Sex Marriage," 79 *Virginia Law Review* 1419.

Estlund, David. 1997. "Shaping and Sex: Commentary on Parts I and II," in *Sex, Preference, and Family: Essays on Law and Nature*, eds. David M. Estlund and Martha C. Nussbaum. New York: Oxford University Press: 148–70.

Estlund, David. 1996. "Debate: The Survival of Egalitarian Justice in John Rawls's *Political Liberalism*," *The Journal of Political Philosophy* 4(1): 68–78.

Everson v. Board of Education, 330 U.S. 1 (1947).

Farber, Daniel, and Suzanne Sherry. 1996. "The Pariah Principle," 13 *Constitutional* Commentary 257.

Fallon, Richard. 2007. "Strict Judicial Scrutiny," 54 *University of California at Los Angeles Law Review* 1267.

Farrell, Robert C. 2011. "The Two Versions of Rational-Basis Review and Same-Sex Relationships," 86 *Washington Law Review* 281.

Farrell, Robert C. 2009. "The Equal Protection Class-of-One Claim: *Olech, Engquist,* and the Supreme Court's Misadventure," 61 *South Carolina Law Review* 1.

Farrell, Sandi. 2004. "Reconsidering the Gender-Equality Perspective for Understanding LGBT Rights," 13 *Law and Sexuality* 605.

Feldblum, Chai R. 1996. "Sexual Orientation, Morality, and the Law: Devlin Revisited," 57 *University of Pittsburg Law Review* 237.

Fineman, M. A. 1995. *The Neutered Mother, the Sexual Family and Other Twentieth Century Tragedies.* New York: Routledge.

Finnis, John. 1993. "Law, Morality, and Sexual Orientation," 69 *Notre Dame Law Review* 1049.

Fisher v. University of Texas at Austin, 631 F.3d 213 (5th Cir. 2011), *certiorari granted* 132 S.Ct. 1536 (Feb. 21, 2012).

Fiss, Owen M. 1976. "Groups and the Equal Protection Clause," *Philosophy and Public Affairs* 5(2): 107–77.

Foley, Edward B. 1992. "Political Liberalism and Establishment Clause Jurisprudence," 43 *Case Western Reserve Law Review* 963.

Ford, Richard T. 2002. "'Beyond 'Difference': A Reluctant Critique of Legal Identity Politics," in *Left Legalism/Left Critique,* eds. Wendy Brown and Janet Halley. Durham: Duke University Press: 38–79.

Forde-Mazrui, K. 2011. "Tradition as Justification: The Case of Opposite Sex Marriage," 78 *University of Chicago of Law Review* 281.

Forst, Rainer. 2002. *Contexts of Justice: Political Philosophy beyond Liberalism and Communitarianism.* Berkeley: University of California Press.

Frank, John P., and Robert F. Munro. 1950. "The Original Understanding of "Equal Protection of the Laws," 50 *Columbia Law Review* 131.

Fraser, Nancy. 1997. *Justice Interruptus: Critical Reflections on the "Postsocialist" Condition.* New York: Routledge.

Frontiero v. Richardson, 411 U.S. 677 (1973).

Fullilove v. Klutznick, 448 U.S. 448 (1980).

Galston, William A. 1991. *Liberal Purposes: Goods, Virtues, and Diversity in the Liberal State.* Cambridge: Cambridge University Press.

Gaus, Gerald F. 1996. *Justificatory Liberalism*. Oxford: Oxford University Press.

Geduldig v. Aiello, 417 U.S. 484 (1974).

George, Robert. 2004. "What's Sex Got to Do with It? Marriage, Morality, and Rationality," 49 *American Journal of Jurisprudence* 63.

George, Robert. 1999. "Same-Sex Marriage and Moral Neutrality," in *Homosexuality and American Public Life*, ed. Christopher Wolfe. Dallas, TX: Spence Publishing, pp. 141–53.

George, Robert P. 1993. *Making Men Moral: Civil Liberties and Public Morality*. New York: Oxford University Press.

Gerstmann, Evan. 2008. *Same-Sex Marriage and the Constitution*, 2nd ed. New York: Cambridge University Press.

Gerstmann, Evan. 1999. *The Constitutional Underclass: Gays, Lesbians, and the Failure of Class-Based Equal Protection*. Chicago: University of Chicago Press.

Gilligan, Carol. 1982. *In a Different Voice: Psychological Theory and Women's Development*. Cambridge: Harvard University Press.

Gillman, Howard, Mark Graber, and Keith Whittington, eds. 2013. *American Constitutionalism: Structures of Government* (Vol. I); *Rights and Liberties* (Vol. II). New York: Oxford University Press.

Gilroy, Paul. 1993. *The Black Atlantic: Modernity and Double Consciousness*. Cambridge: Harvard University Press.

Goldberg, Suzanne B. 2004a. "Equality without Tiers," 77 *Southern California Law Review* 481.

Goldberg, Suzanne B. 2004b. "Morals-Based Justifications for Lawmaking: Before and After Lawrence v. Texas," 88 *Minnesota Law Review* 1233.

Goldberg, Suzanne B. 1995. "Civil rights, 'Special rights,' and Our Rights," in *Eyes Right! Challenging the Right Wing Backlash*, ed. Chip Berlet. Boston: South End Press, pp. 109–12.

Goldberg-Hiller, Jonathan. 1998. "'Entitled to be Hostile': Narrating the Political Economy of Civil Rights," *Social and Legal Studies* 7(4): 517–38.

Goldberg-Hiller, Jonathan, and Neal Milner. 2003. "Rights as Excess: Understanding the Politics of Special Rights," *Law and Social Inquiry* 28(4): 1075–118.

Gonzales v. Carhart, 550 U.S. 124 (2007).

Goodell, Maia. 2010. "Physical-Strength Rationales for De Jure Exclusion of Women from Military Combat Positions," 34 *Seattle University Law Review* 17.

Goodridge v. Dept. of Public Health, 440 Mass. 309 (Mass. 2003).

Gotanda, Neil. 1991 *A Critique of "Our Constitution Is Color-Blind,"* 44 *Stanford Law Review* 1.

Graber, Mark. (2002). "Constitutional Politics and Constitutional Theory: A Misunderstood and Neglected Relationship," *Law & Social Inquiry* 27(2): 309–38.

Graham v. Richardson, 403 U.S. 365 (1971).

Gratz v. Bollinger, 539 U.S. 244 (2003).

Greenawalt, Kent. 1995. *Private Consciences and Public Reasons.* New York. Oxford University Press.

Griswold v. Connecticut, 381 U.S. 479 (1965).

Grossberg, Michael. 1988. *Governing the Hearth: Law and the Family in Nineteenth-Century America.* Chapel Hill: University of North Carolina Press

Grutter v. Bollinger, 539 U.S. 306 (2003).

Gunther, Gerald. 1972. "Foreword: In Search of Evolving Doctrine on a Changing Court: A Model for a Newer Equal Protection," 86 *Harvard Law Review* 1.

Gutmann, Amy. 2003. *Identity in Democracy.* Princeton: Princeton University Press.

Gutmann, Amy. 1993. "The Challenge of Multiculturalism in Political Ethics," *Philosophy and Public Affairs* 22(3): 171–206.

Gutmann, Amy, and Dennis Thompson. 1996. *Democracy and Disagreement.* Cambridge: Harvard University Press.

Habermas, Jürgen. 2001. "Remarks on Legitimation through Human Rights," in *The Postnational Constellation: Political Essays,* ed. and trans. Max Pensky. Cambridge: Polity Press.

Habermas, Jürgen. 1996. *Between Facts and Norms: Contributions to a Discourse Theory of Law and Democracy,* trans. William Rehg. Cambridge: MIT Press.

Habermas, Jürgen. 1990. *Moral Consciousness and Communicative Action,* trans. C. Lenhardt and S. W. Nicholsen. Cambridge: MIT Press.

Hackstaff, Karla B. 1999. *Marriage in a Culture of Divorce.* Philadelphia: Temple University Press.

Hall, Stuart. 1992. "New Ethnicities," in *'Race', Culture and Difference,* eds. J. Donald and A. Rattansi. London: Sage, p. 258.

Halley, Janet. 2010. "Behind the Law of Marriage (I): From Status/ Contract to the Marriage System," 6 *Unbound: Harvard Journal of the Legal Left* 1.

Halley, Janet. 1994. "Sexual Orientation and the Politics of Biology: A Critique of the Argument from Immutability," 46 *Stanford Law Review* 503.

Harcourt, Bernard E. 2007. *Against Prediction: Profiling, Policing, and Punishing in an Actuarial Age*. Chicago: University of Chicago Press.

Harris, David. 2002. *Profiles in Injustice: Why Police Profiling Cannot Work*. New York: The New Press.

Harris v. McRae, 448 U.S. 297 (1980).

Hartley, Christie, and Lori Watson. 2010. "Is a Feminist Political Liberalism Possible?" *Journal of Ethics and Social Philosophy* 5 (1).

Hartley, Christie, and Lori Watson, 2009. "Feminism, Religion, and Shared Reasons: A Defense of Exclusive Public Reason," *Law and Philosophy* 28(5): 493–536.

Hasday, Jill Elaine. 2008. "Fighting Women: The Military, Sex, and Extrajudicial Constitutional Change," 93 *Minnesota Law Review* 96.

Helfand, Michael A. 2009. "The Usual Suspect Classifications: Criminals, Aliens and the Future of Same-Sex Marriage," 12 *University of Pennsylvania Journal of Constitutional Law* 1.

Hellman, Deborah. 2008. *When Is Discrimination Wrong*. Cambridge: Harvard University Press.

Heymann, Jody. 2000. *The Widening Gap: Why America's Working Families are in Jeopardy and What Can Be Done about it*. New York: Basic Books.

In re Marriage, 43 Cal. 4th 757 (Cal. 2008).

Irons, Peter. 1993. *Justice at War: The Story of the Japanese-American Internment Cases*. University of California Press.

Jagose, Annamarie. 1997. *Queer Theory: An Introduction*. New York: New York University Press.

Jenkins, David. 2003. "From Unwritten to Written: Transformation in the British Common-Law Constitution," 36 *Vanderbilt Journal of Transnational Law* 863.

Jones, Nicole, Bernadette Pelissier, and Jody Klein-Saffran. 2006. "Predicting Sex Offender Treatment among Individual Convicted of Sexual Offense Crimes," *Sexual Abuse: A Journal of Research and Treatment* 18(1): 83–98.

Jordan-Zachery, Julia S. 2007. "Am I a Black Woman or a Woman Who Is Black? A Few Thoughts on the Meaning of Intersectionality," *Politics and Gender* 3(2): 254–63.

Joslin, Courtney G. 2011. "Searching for Harm: Same-Sex Marriage and the Well-Being of Children," 46 *Harvard Civil Rights-Civil Liberties Law Review* 81.

Kahn v. Shevin, 416 U.S. 351 (1974).

Kalscheur, Gregory A. 2006. "Moral Limits on Morals Legislation: Lessons for U.S. Constitutional Law from the Declaration on Religious Freedom," 16 *Southern California Interdisciplinary Law Journal* 1.

Katz, Sanford N. 2003. *Family Law in America*. New York: Oxford University Press.

Keck, Thomas. 2009. "Beyond Backlash: Assessing the Impact of Judicial Decisions on LGBT Rights," *Law and Society Review* 43(1): 151–86.

Kennedy, Randall. 1997. *Race, Crime and the Law*. New York: Pantheon Books.

Khalsa, Ruth K. 2005. Note. "Polygamy as a Red Herring in the Same-Sex Marriage Debate," 54 *Duke Law Journal* 1664.

Klarman, Michael J. 2005. "*Brown* and *Lawrence* (and *Goodridge*)," 104 *University of Michigan Law Review* 431.

Klarman, Michael J. 1994a. "*Brown*, Racial Change, and the Civil Rights Movement," 80 *Virginia Law Review* 7.

Klarman, Michael J. 1994b. "How *Brown* Changed Race Relations: The Backlash Thesis," *The Journal of American History* 81(1): 81–118.

Knowles, John, Nicola Persico, and Petra Todd. 2001. "Racial Bias in Motor Vehicle Searches: Theory and Evidence," *Journal of Political Economy* 109: 203–29.

Koppelman, Andrew. 2004. "The Fluidity of Neutrality," *The Review of Politics* 66(4): 633–48.

Koppelman, Andrew. 2002. *The Gay Rights Question in Contemporary American Law*. Chicago: University of Chicago Press.

Koppelman, Andrew. 1994. "Why Discrimination against Lesbians and Gay Men Is Sex Discrimination," 69 *New York University Law Review* 197.

Koppelman, Andrew. 1990. "Forced Labor: A Thirteenth Amendment Defense of Abortion," 84 *Northwestern University Law Review* 480.

Korematsu v. United States, 323 U.S. 214 (1944).

Kukathas, Chandran. 2003. *The Liberal Archipelago: A Theory of Diversity and Freedom*. Oxford: Oxford University Press.

Kutz, Christopher. 2003. "Groups, Equality, and the Promise of Democratic Politics," *Issues in Legal Scholarship*, The Origins and Fate of

Antisubordination Theory: Article 13. http://www.bepress.com/ils/iss2/
art13.

Kymlicka, Will. 1995. *Multicultural Citizenship.* Oxford: Clarendon Press.

Kymlicka, Will. 1989. *Liberalism, Community, and Culture.* Oxford:
Oxford University Press.

Larmore, Charles E. 1987. *Patterns of Moral Complexity.* Cambridge:
Cambridge University Press.

Lawrence v. Texas, 539 U.S. 558 (2003).

Law, Sylvia. 1988. "Homosexuality and the Social Meaning of Gender,"
1988 *Wisconsin Law Review* 187.

Law, Sylvia A. 1984. "Rethinking Sex and the Constitution," 132 *University of Pennsylvania Law Review* 955.

Lax, Jeffrey R. and Justin Phillips. 2009. "Gay Rights in the States: Public
Opinion and Policy Responsiveness," *American Political Science Review*
103(3): 367–86.

Lecce, Steven. 2008. *Against Perfectionism: Defending Liberal Neutrality.*
Toronto: Toronto University Press.

Lee v. Weisman, 505 U.S. 577 (1992).

Leeb, Claudia. 2008. "Toward a Theoretical Outline of the Subject: The
Centrality of Adorno and Lacan for Feminist Political Theorizing,"
Political Theory 36(3): 351–76.

Lemieux, Scott. 2007. "Scalia and Thomas: Originalist Sinners,"
American Prospect. June. http://prospect.org/article/scalia-and-thomas-
originalist-sinners.

Lemieux, Scott E., and David J. Watkins. 2009. "Beyond the 'Countermajoritarian Difficulty': Lessons from Contemporary Democratic
Theory," *Polity* 41(1): 30–62.

Lemon v. Kurtzman, 403 U.S. 602 (1971).

Levin, Ronald M. 1997. "The Anatomy of *Chevron*: Step Two Reconsidered," 72 *Chicago Kent Law Review* 1253.

Levinson, Sanford. 1995. "How Many Times Has the United States Constitution Been Amended? (A)<26; (B) 26; (C) 27; (D) >27: Accounting for Constitutional Change," in *Responding to Imperfection: The Theory and Practice of Constitutional Amendment,* ed. Sanford Levinson.
Princeton: Princeton University Press: 13–36.

Littleton, Christine A. 1987. *Reconstructing Sexual Equality,* 75 *California
Law Review* Cal. L. 1279.

Liu, Frederick, and Stephen Macedo. 2005. "The Federal Marriage
Amendment and the Strange Evolution of the Conservative Case against
Gay Marriage," *PS: Political Science & Politics* 38: 211–15.

Loving v. Virginia, 388 U.S. 1 (1967).

Luker, Kristin. 1984. *Abortion and the Politics of Motherhood*. Berkeley: University of California Press.

Lynch v. Donnelly, 465 U.S. 668 (1984).

Lyng v. Castillo, 477 U.S. 635 (1986).

MacIntyre, Alasdair. 1988. *Whose Justice? Which Rationality?* Notre Dame: University of Notre Dame Press.

Mac Donald, Heather. 2001. "The Myth of Racial Profiling," *City Journal* 11(2): 15–27.

Macedo, Stephen. 1997. "Sexuality and Liberty: Making Room for Nature and Tradition," in *Sex, Preference, and Family: Essays on Law and Nature*, eds. David M. Estlund and Martha C. Nussbaum. New York: Oxford University Press.

Macedo, Stephen. 1995a. "Homosexuality and the Conservative Mind," 84 *Georgetown Law Review* 261.

Macedo, Stephen. 1995b. "Reply to Critics," 84 *Georgetown Law Review* 329.

MacIntyre, Alasdair. 1984. *After Virtue: A Study in Moral Theory*, 2nd ed. Notre Dame: University of Notre Dame Press.

MacKinnon, Catharine A. 1989. *Toward a Feminist Theory of the State*. Cambridge: Harvard University Press.

MacKinnon, Catharine A. 1987. "Difference and Dominance: On Sex Discrimination," in *Feminism Unmodified: Discourses on Life and Law*. Cambridge: Harvard University Press: 32–45.

March, Andrew. 2011. "Is There a Right to Polygamy? Marriage, Equality, and Subsidizing Families in Liberal Public Justification," *Journal of Moral Philosophy* 8: 246–72.

March, Andrew. 2010. "What Lies beyond Same-Sex Marriage? Marriage, Reproductive Freedom and Future Persons in Liberal Public Justification," *Journal of Applied Philosophy* 27(1): 39–58.

Markell, Patchen. 2003. *Bound by Recognition*. Princeton: Princeton University Press.

Mason, Rebecca. 2010. "Reorienting Deliberation: Identity Politics in Multicultural Societies," *Studies in Social Justice* 4(1): 7–23.

Massachusetts v. U.S. Dept. of Health and Human Services, 682 F.3d 1 (1st Circuit 2012).

Mathews, Jud, and Alec Stone Sweet. 2011. "All the Things in Proportion? American Rights Review and the Problem of Balancing," 60 *Emory Law Journal* 797.

Maynard v. Hill, 125 U.S. 190 (1888).

McConnell, Michael W. 1997. "The Importance of Humility in Judicial Review: A Comment on Ronald Dworkin's "Moral Reading" of the Constitution," 65 *Fordham Law Review* 1269.

McConnell, Michael W. 1996. "Segregation and the Original Understanding: A Reply to Professor Maltz," 13 *Constitutional Commentary* 233.

McConnell, Michael W. 1995. "Originalism and the Desegregation Decisions," 81 *Virginia Law Review* 947.

McConnell, Michael W. 1991. "The Selective Funding Problem: Abortions and Religious Schools," 104 *Harvard Law Review* 989.

McCreary County v. ACLU of Kentucky, 545 U.S. 844 (2005).

McCulloch v. Maryland, 17 U.S. 316 (1819).

McLaughlin v. State of Florida, 379 U.S. 184 (1964).

McNulty, Thomas L. 2001. "Assessing the Race-Violence Relationship at the Macro Level: the Assumption of Racial Invariance and the Problem of Restricted Distributions," *Criminology* 39(2): 467–90.

Meloy, Michelle L. 2005. "The Sex Offender Next Door: An Analysis of Recidivism, Risk Factors, and Deterrence of Sex Offenders on Probation," *Criminal Justice Policy Review* 16(2): 211–36.

Metro Broadcasting, Inc. v. FCC, 497 U.S. 547 (1990).

Metz, Tamara. 2010. *Untying the Knot: Marriage, the State, and the Case for Their Divorce*. Princeton: Princeton University Press.

Metz, Tamara. 2007. "The Liberal Case for Disestablishing Marriage," *Contemporary Political Theory* 6: 196–217.

Michael M. vs. Superior Court of Sonoma County, 450 U.S. 464 (1981).

Mississippi University for Women v. Hogan, 458 U.S. 718 (1982).

Morrison, Matthew M. 2009. Comment, "Class Dismissed: Equal Protection, the 'Class-of-One,' and Employment Discrimination after *Engquist v. Oregon Department of Agriculture*," 80 *University of Colorado Law Review* 839.

Nagel, Thomas. 1973. "Equal Treatment and Compensatory Discrimination," *Philosophy & Public Affairs* 2: 348–63.

Nickel, James W. 2007. *Making Sense of Human Rights*, 2nd ed. New York: Wiley-Blackwell.

Nussbaum, Martha. 2010. *From Disgust to Humanity: Sexual Orientation and the Law*. New York: Oxford University Press.

Nussbaum, Martha. 2009. Reply. 54 *Villa Nova Law Review* 677.

Nussbaum, Martha. 2004. *Hiding from Humanity: Disgust, Shame, and the Law*. Princeton: Princeton University Press.

Nussbaum, Martha. 1999. *Sex and Social Justice*. New York: Oxford University Press.

Okin, Susan Moller. 2005. "'Forty Acres and a Mule' for Women: Rawls and Feminism," *Politics, Philosophy & Economics* 4(2): 233–48.

Okin, Susan Moller. 2004. "Justice and Gender: An Unfinished Debate," 72 *Fordham Law Review* 1537.

Okin, Susan Moller. 2002. "'Mistresses of Their Own Destiny': Group Rights, Gender, and Realistic Rights of Exit," *Ethics* 112(2): 205–30.

Okin, Susan Moller. 1999. *Is Multiculturalism Bad for Women?* Princeton: Princeton University Press.

Okin, Susan Moller. 1994. "Political Liberalism, Justice, and Gender," *Ethics* 105(1): 23–43.

Okin, Susan Moller. 1989. *Justice, Gender, and the Family*. New York: Basic Books.

Oyama v. California, 332 U.S. 633 (1948).

Palmore v. Sidoti, 466 U.S. 429 (1984).

Parekh, Bhikhu C. 2000. *Rethinking Multiculturalism: Cultural Diversity and Political Theory*. Basingstoke: Macmillan.

Parents Involved in Community Schools v. Seattle School District No. 1, 551 U.S. 701 (2007).

Parker, Frank R. 1996. "Damaging Consequences of the Rehnquist Court's Commitment to Color-Blindness versus Racial Justice," 45 *American University Law Review* 763.

Perry, Michael. 2009. "Religion as a basis of law-making? Herein of the non-establishment of religion," *Philosophy Social Criticism* 35(1–2): 105–26.

Perry, Michael J. 2003. *Under God? Religious Faith and Liberal Democracy*. Cambridge: Cambridge University Press.

Perry v. Brown, 671 F.3d 1052 (9th Cir. 2012).

Perry v. Schwarzenegger, 704 F.Supp.2d 921 (N.D.Cal. 2010).

Persico, Nicola. 2002. "Racial Profiling, Fairness, and Effectiveness of Policing," *American Economic Review* 92(5): 1472–97.

Personnel Administrator of Mass. v. Feeney, 442 U.S. 256, 279 (1979).

Peterson, Ruth D., and Lauren J. Krivo. 2005. "Macrostructural Analyses of Race, Ethnicity, and Violent Crime: Recent Lessons and Directions for Research," *Annual Review of Sociology* 31: 331–56.

Pettinga, Gayle Lynn. 1987. "Rational Basis with Bite: Intermediate Scrutiny by Any Other Name," 62 *Indiana Law Journal* 779.

Pettit, Philip. 1997. *Republicanism: A Theory of Freedom and Government.* New York: Oxford University Press.

Pinello, Daniel R. 2003. *Gay Rights and American Law.* New York: Cambridge University Press.

Planned Parenthood of Southeastern Pennsylvania v. Casey, 505 U.S. 833 (1992).

Plessy v. Ferguson, 163 U.S. 537 (1896).

Plyler v. Doe, 457 U.S. 202 (1982).

Polikoff, Nancy D. 2008. *Beyond (Straight and Gay) Marriage: Valuing All Families Under the Law.* Boston: Beacon Press.

Posner, Richard. 2010. *Economic Analysis of Law,* 8th ed. New York: Aspen Publishers.

Posner, Richard. 1992. *Sex and Reason.* Cambridge: Harvard University Press.

Powe, Jr., Lucas A. 2000. *The Warren Court and American Politics.* Cambridge, MA: Belknap Press.

Powell, Jefferson. 2011. "Reasoning about the Irrational: The Roberts Court and the Future of Constitutional Law," 86 *Washington Law Review* 217.

Pratt, Travis, and Frances Cullen. 2005. "Assessing Macro-Level Predictors and Theories of Crime: A Meta-Analysis," in *Crime and Justice: A Review of Research,* ed. M. Tonry. Vol. 32. Chicago: University of Chicago Press: 373–450.

Quong, Jonathan. 2011. *Liberalism without Perfection.* New York: Oxford University Press.

Quong, Jonathan. 2004. "The Scope of Public Reason," *Political Studies* 52(2): 233–50.

Quong, Jonathan. 2002. "Are Identity Claims Bad for Deliberative Democracy?" *Contemporary Political Theory* 1: 307–27.

Rauch, Jonathan. 1997. "Marrying Somebody," in *Same-Sex Marriage: Pro and Con, A Reader,* ed. Andrew Sullivan. New York: Vintage Books: 285–8.

Raven v. Deukmejian, 52 Cal.3d 336 (Cal. 2009).

Rawls, John. 1999 [1971]. *A Theory of Justice,* rev. ed. Cambridge: Harvard University Press.

Rawls, John. 1996 [1993]. *Political Liberalism.* New York: Columbia University Press.

Rawls, John. 1997. "The Ideal of Public Reason Revisited," 64 *University of Chicago Law Review* 765.

Raz, Joseph. 1986. *The Morality of Freedom*. Oxford: Oxford University Press.

Reed v. Reed, 404 U.S. 71 (1971).

Regan, Donald H. 1979. "Rewriting Roe v. Wade," 77 *Michigan Law Review* 1569.

Regents of the University of California v. Bakke, 438 U.S. 265 (1978).

Reynolds v. United States, 98 U.S. 145 (1878).

Richards, David A. J. 2005. *The Case for Gay Rights: From Bowers to Lawrence and Beyond*. Lawrence: Kansas University Press.

Richards, David A. J. 1999. *Identity and the Case for Gay Rights: Race, Gender, Religion as Analogies*. Chicago: University of Chicago Press.

Richter, Nicole. 2000. "A Standard for 'Class of One' Claims under the Equal Protection Clause of the Fourteenth Amendment: Protecting Victims of Non-Class Based Discrimination From Vindictive State Action," 35 *Valparaiso University Law Review* 197.

Risse, Mathias, and Richard Zeckhauser. 2004. "Racial Profiling," *Philosophy and Public Affairs* 32(2): 131–70.

Robinson, Greg, and Toni Robinson. 2005. "Korematsu and Beyond: Japanese Americans and the Origins of Strict Scrutiny," 68 *Law and Contemporary Problems* 29.

Roe v. Wade, 410 U.S. 113 (1973).

Romer v. Evans, 517 U.S. 620 (1996).

Roosevelt, Kermit, III. 2006. *The Myth of Judicial Activism*. New Haven: Yale University Press.

Rosenberg, Gerald. 2009. "Much Ado about Nothing? The Emptiness of Rights' Claims in the Twenty-First Century United States," *Studies in Law, Politics, and Society* 48: 1–41.

Rosenberg, Gerald. 2006. "Courting Disaster: Looking for Change in All the Wrong Places," 45 *Drake Law Review* 759.

Rosenberg, Gerald. 2004. "Substituting Symbol for Substance: What Did *Brown* Really Accomplish?" *PS: Political Science & Politics* 37(2): 205–9.

Rosenberg, Gerald. 1991. *The Hollow Hope: Can Courts Bring About Social Change?* Chicago: University of Chicago Press.

Rosenblum, Darren. 1994. "Queer Intersectionality and the Failure of Recent Lesbian and Gay "Victories," 4 *Law & Sexuality: Review Lesbian & Gay Legal Issues* 83.

Rosenfeld, Michael. 1991. *Affirmative Action and Justice: A Philosophical and Constitutional Inquiry*. New Haven: Yale University Press.

Rosky, Clifford J. 2011. "Perry v. Schwarzenegger and the Future of Same-Sex Marriage Law," 53 *Arizona Law Review* 913.

Rostker v. Goldberg, 453 U.S. 57 (1981).

Rubenfeld, Jed. 2005. *What Roe v. Wade Should Have Said: The Nation's Top Legal Experts Rewrite America's Most Controversial Decision*, ed. Jack M. Balkin. New York: New York Press: 109–20.

Rubenfeld, Jed. 1997. "Affirmative Action," 107 *Yale Law Journal* 427.

Sampson Robert J. 1987. "Urban Black Violence: The Effect of Male Joblessness and Family Disruption," *American Journal of Sociology* 93(2): 348–82.

Sampson, Robert J., and Lydia Bean, 2006. "Cultural Mechanisms and Killing Fields: A Revised Theory of Community-Level Racial Inequality," in *The Many Colors of Crime: Inequalities of Race, Ethnicity, and Crime in America*, eds. Ruth D. Peterson, Lauren J. Krivo, and John Hagan. New York: New York University Press: 8–38.

Sampson, Robert J., and William Julius Wilson. 1995. "Toward a Theory of Race, Crime, and Urban Inequality," in *Crime and Inequality*, eds. John Hagan and Ruth D. Peterson. Stanford: Stanford University Press: 37–54.

San Antonio v. Rodriguez, 411 U.S. 1, 28 (1973).

Sandel, Michael J. 2010. *Justice: What's the Right Thing to Do?* New York: Macmillan.

Sandel, Michael J. 1982. *Liberalism and the Limits of Justice*. Cambridge: Cambridge University Press.

Scalia, Antonin. 1997. *A Matter of Interpretation: Federal Courts and the Law*. Princeton: Princeton University Press.

Scanlon, T.M. 1998. *What We Owe to Each Other*. Cambridge: Harvard University Press.

Schacter, Jane. 1994. "The Gay Civil Rights Debate in the States: Decoding the Discourse of Equivalents," *Harvard Civil Rights-Civil Liberties Law Review* 29: 283–317.

Schauer, Frederick. 2003. *Profiles, Probabilities, and Stereotypes*. Cambridge: Harvard University Press.

Schlesinger, A. M. 1992. *The Disuniting of America*. New York: W. W. Norton.

Schlesinger v. Ballard, 419 U.S. 498 (1975).

Schwartz v. Brodsky, 265 F.Supp. 2d 130 (D. Mass. 2003).

Schwartzman, Micah. 2011. "The Sincerity of Public Reason," *The Journal of Political Philosophy* 19(4): 375–98.

Schweber, Howard. 2012. *Democracy and Authenticity: Toward a Theory of Public Justification*. New York: Cambridge University Press.

Segal, Jeffrey A., and Harold J. Spaeth. 1993. *The Supreme Court and the Attitudinal Model*. New York: Cambridge University Press.

Segal, Jeffrey A., and Harold J. Spaeth. 2002. *The Supreme Court and the Attitudinal Model Revisited*. Cambridge: Cambridge University Press.

Shachar, Ayelet. 2001. *Multicultural Jurisdictions: Cultural Difference and Women's Rights*. Cambridge: Cambridge University Press.

Shapiro, Ian. 1999. *Democratic Justice*. New Haven. Yale University Press.

Shapiro, Martin. 1966. *Freedom of Speech: The Supreme Court and Judicial Review*. Englewood Cliffs, NJ: Prentice-Hall.

Sher, George. 1997. *Beyond Neutrality: Perfectionism and Politics* New York: Cambridge University Press.

Sher, George. 1979. "Reverse Discrimination, the Future, and the Past," *Ethics* 90: 81–8.

Shihadeh, Edward S., and Wesley Shrum. 2004. "Serious Crime in Urban Neighborhoods: Is There a Race Effect?" *Sociology Spectrum* 24(4): 507–33.

Siegel, Reva B. 2005. *What Roe v. Wade Should Have Said: The Nation's Top Legal Experts Rewrite America's Most Controversial Decision*, ed. Jack M. Balkin. New York: New York Press: 63–85.

Siegel, Reva. 2000. Discrimination in the Eyes of the Law: How "*Color Blindness*" Discourse Disrupts and Rationalizes Social Stratification," 88 *California Law Review* 77.

Siegel, Reva B. 1992. "Reasoning from the Body: A Historical Perspective on Abortion Regulation and Questions of Equal Protection," 44 *Stanford Law Review* 261.

Siegel, Stephen A. 2006. "The Origin of the Compelling State Interest Test and Strict Scrutiny," 48 *American Journal of Legal History* 4.

Simon, Larry. 1978. "Racially Prejudiced Governmental Actions: A Motivation Theory of the Constitutional Ban against Racial Discrimination," 15 *San Diego Law Review* 1041.

Simon, Robert L. 1979. "Individual Rights and 'Benign' Discrimination," *Ethics* 90: 88–97.

Simon, William H. 1999. "Three Limitations of Deliberative Democracy: Identity Politics, Bad Faith, and Indeterminacy," *Deliberative Politics: Essays on Democracy and Disagreement*, ed. Stephen Macedo. New York: Oxford University Press: 49–57.

Simson, Gary J. 2012. "Religion by Any Other Name? Prohibitions on Same-Sex Marriage and the Limits of the Establishment Clause," 23 *Columbia Journal of Gender and the Law* 132.

Singer, Joseph William. 2005. "Same Sex Marriage, Full Faith and Credit, and the Evasion of Obligation," 1 *Stanford Journal of Civil Rights and Civil Liberties* 1.

Skinner v. Oklahoma, 316 U.S. 535 (1942).

Skinner, Quentin. 2008. "Freedom as the Absence of Arbitrary Power," in *Republicanism and Political Theory*, ed. Cécile Laborde and John Maynor. Blackwell: 83–101.

Solum, Lawrence B. 1993. "Constructing an Ideal of Public Reason," 30 *San Diego Law Review* 729.

Song, Sarah. 2007. *Justice, Gender, and the Politics of Multiculturalism.* Cambridge: Cambridge University Press.

Stanton v. Stanton, 421 U.S. 7 (1975).

Steiker, Carol. 1985. "The Constitutional Status of Sexual Orientation: Homosexuality as a Suspect Classification," 98 *Harvard Law Review* 1285.

Stein, Edward. 2001a. *The Mismeasure of Desire: The Science, Theory, and Ethics of Sexual Orientation.* Oxford: Oxford University Press.

Stein, Edward. 2001b. "Evaluating the Sex Discrimination Argument for Lesbian and Gay Rights," 49 *University of California, Los Angeles Law Review* 471.

Stewart, Monte Neil. 2008. "Marriage Facts," 31 *Harvard Journal of Law and Public Policy* 313.

Stewart, Monte Neil. 2006. "Genderless Marriage, Institutional Realities, and Judicial Elision," 1 *Duke Journal of Constitutional Law and Public Policy* 1.

Stone, Geoffrey R. 2009. "Same-Sex Marriage and the Establishment Clause," 54 *Villa Nova Law Review* 617.

Stone, Geoffrey R., Louis M. Seidman, Cass R. Sunstein, Mark V. Tushnet, Pamela S. Karlan. 2005. *Constitutional Law.* New York: Aspen Publishers.

Strauss v. Horton, 46 Cal.4th 364 (Cal. 2009).

Sullivan, Andrew. 2003. "The Conservative Case for Gay Marriage, *TIME*, June 30.

Sullivan, Andrew. 1997. "Three's a Crowd," in *Same-Sex Marriage: Pro and Con, A Reader*, ed. Andrew Sullivan. New York: Vintage Books.

Sullivan, Andrew. 1989. "Here Comes the Groom," *The New Republic,* August 28: 20–2.

Sullivan, Kathleen M., and Gerald Gunther, eds. 2001. *Constitutional Law,* 14th ed. New York: Foundation Press.

Sullivan, Nikki. 2003. *A Critical Introduction to Queer Theory.* New York: New York University Press.

Sunstein, Cass R. 2005. "The Right to Marry," 26 *Cardozo Law Review* 2081.

Sunstein, Cass R. 1994. "Homosexuality and the Constitution," 70 *Indiana Law Journal* 1.

Sunstein, Cass R. 1993. *The Partial Constitution.* Cambridge: Harvard University Press.

Sunstein, Cass R. 1988. "Sexual Orientation and the Constitution: A Note on the Relationship between Due Process and Equal Protection," 55 *University of Chicago Law Review* 1161.

Sunstein, Cass R. 1984. "Naked Preferences and the Constitution," 84 *Columbia Law Review* 1689.

Swaine, Lucas. 2008. *The Liberal Conscience: Politics and Principle in a World of Religious Pluralism.* New York: Columbia University Press.

Taylor, Charles. 1994. "The Politics of Recognition," in *Multiculturalism: Examining the Politics of Recognition,* ed. Amy Gutmann. Princeton: Princeton University Press: 25–74.

Tempelman, Sasja. 1999. "Constructions of Cultural Identity: Multiculturalism and Exclusion." *Political Studies* 47: 17–31.

Thomson, Judith Jarvis. 1973. "Preferential Hiring," *Philosophy & Public Affairs* 2: 364–84.

Thomson, Judith Jarvis. 1971. "A Defense of Abortion," *Philosophy and Public Affairs* 1(1): 47–66.

Tribe, Laurence. 2008. *The Invisible Constitution.* New York: Oxford University Press.

Turner v. Safley, 482 U.S. 78 (1987).

United States v. Carolene Products Company, 304 U.S. 144 (1938).

United States Railroad Retirement Board v. Fritz, 449 U.S. 166 (1980).

United States v. Avery, 137 F.3d 343 (6th Cir. 1997).

Village of Willowbrook, et al. v. Olech, 528 U.S. 562 (2000).

Valdes, Francisco. 1995. "Queers, Sissies, Dykes, and Tomboys: Deconstructing the Conflation of 'Sex,' 'Gender,' and 'Sexual Orientation' in Euro-American Law and Society," 83 *California Law Review* 1.

Varnum v. Brien, 763 N.W. 2d 862 (Iowa 2009).

Volokh, Eugene. 2003. "The Mechanisms of the Slippery Slope," 116 *Harvard Law Review* 1026.

Waldron, Jeremy. 2000. "Cultural Identity and Civic Responsibility," *Citizenship in Diverse Societies*, eds. Will Kymlicka and Wayne Norman. New York: Oxford University Press.

Walker, Adrian. 2000. "Give Partners the Right to Marry," *Boston Globe*, March 9. Section: Metro/Region: B1.

Wardle, Lynn D., ed. 2008. *What's the Harm? Does Legalizing Same-Sex Marriage Really Harm Individuals, Families or Society?* Lanham, MD: University Press of America.

Warner, Michael. 1999. *The Trouble with Normal: Sex, Politics, and the Ethics of Queer Life*. Cambridge: Harvard University Press.

Washington v. Davis, 426 U.S. 229 (1976).

Wasserstrom, Richard A. 1977. "Racism, Sexism, and Preferential Treatment: An Approach to the Topics," 24 *University of California, Los Angeles Law Review* 581.

Watkins v. U.S. Army, 875 F.2d. 699 (9th Cir. 1989).

Watkins v. U.S. Army, 837 F.2d 1428 (9th Cir. 1988).

Weinberger v. Wiesenfeld, 420 U.S. 636 (1975).

Weisburd, David, Stanton Wheeler, Elin Waring, and Nancy Bode. 1999. *Crimes of the Middle Classes: White-Collar Offenders in the Federal Courts*. New Haven: Yale University Press.

West, Robin. 2005. *What Roe v. Wade Should have Said: The Nation's Top Legal Experts Rewrite America's Most Controversial Decision*, ed. Jack M. Balkin. New York: New York Press.

West, Robin. 1988. "Jurisprudence and Gender," 55 *University of Chicago Law Review* 1.

West Virginia State Board of Education v. Barnette, 319 U.S. 624 (1943).

Widiss, Deborah A., Elizabeth L. Rosenblatt, and Douglas NeJaime. 2007. "Exposing Sex Stereotypes in Recent Same-Sex Marriage Jurisprudence," 30 *Harvard Journal of Law & Gender* 461.

Williams, Joan C. 1989. "Deconstructing Gender," 87 *Michigan Law Review* 797.

Williamson v. Lee Optical Co., 348 U.S. 483 (1955).

Wilson, James Q. 2003. *The Marriage Problem: How Our Culture Has Weakened Families*. New York: Harper Paperbacks.

Wilson, James Q. 1995. *The Moral Sense*. New York: The Free Press.

Windsor v. U.S. WL 4937310 (2nd Cir. 2012).

Winkler, Adam. 2006. "Fatal in Theory and Strict in Fact: An Empirical Analysis of Strict Scrutiny in the Federal Courts," 59 *Vanderbilt Law Review* 793.

Wolfson, Evan. 2004. *Why Marriage Matters? America, Equality, and Gay People's Right to Marry.* New York: Simon & Schuster.

Wolfson, Evan. 1994. "Crossing the Threshold: Equal Marriage Rights for Lesbians and Gay Men and the Intra-Community Critique," 21 *New York University Review of Law and Social Change* 568.

Wooldredge, John, and Amy Thistlethwaite. 2003 "Neighborhood Structure and Race-Specific Rates of Intimate Assault," *Criminology* 41(2): 393–422.

Yick Wo v. Hopkins, 118 U.S. 356 (1886).

Young, Iris Marion. 1990. *Justice and the Politics of Difference.* Princeton: Princeton University Press.

Yoshino, Kenji 1996, "The Literary Argument for Heightened Scrutiny for Gays," 96 *Columbia Law Review* 1753 (1996).

Zablocki v. Redhail, 434 U.S. 374 (1978).

Zerilli, Linda Marie-Gelsomina. 2005. *Feminism and the Abyss of Freedom.* Chicago: University of Chicago Press.

Zick, Timothy. 2001. "Angry White Males: The Equal Protection Clause and 'Classes of One,'" 89 *Kentucky Law Journal* 69.

Zivi, Karen. 2005. "Feminism and the Politics of Rights: A Qualified Defense of Identity-Based Rights Claiming," *Politics and Gender* 1: 377–97.

INDEX

CPSIA information can be obtained at www.ICGtesting.com
Printed in the USA
LVOW01*1719020314

375639LV00001B/1/P